REMAKING

New Zealand and Australian

ECONOMIC POLICY

REMAKING

New Zealand and Australian

ECONOMIC POLICY

*Ideas, Institutions and
Policy Communities*

Shaun Goldfinch

GEORGETOWN UNIVERSITY PRESS
Washington, D.C.

Georgetown University Press
Washington, D.C. 20007

1005837976

ISBN 0-87840-846-0

First published 2000

Library of Congress Cataloging-in-Publication Data

Goldfinch, Shaun, 1967-
    Remaking New Zealand and Australian economic policy / Shaun Goldfinch.
        p. cm.
    Includes index.
    ISBN 0-87840-846-0 (pbk. : alk. paper)
    1. New Zealand--Economic policy. 2. Australia--Economic policy. I. Title.

HC665 .G65 2000
338.993--dc21   00-047681

Printed by Publishing Press, Auckland

Contents

To John and Rosemary, and Sarita

Acknowledgments

Without the cooperation of the 180 people who agreed to be interviewed, this project could never have got off the ground, and they deserve special thanks. For a number of respondents, this help exceeded merely agreeing to be interviewed and included copying documents, sending me reading materials and even providing me with taxi chits. The New Zealand Treasury was particularly helpful in allowing me access to their files, which they then copied for me.

Special thanks should be given to Brian Galligan of the Centre for Public Policy at the University of Melbourne who supervised the PhD thesis from which this book is derived. Thanks also to Jonathon Boston, A. D. Brownlie, Colin Campbell, Keith Jackson, John Martin and Jack Vowles, all of whom made useful comments on various chapters and drafts of this book or on the earlier PhD thesis. Paul Dalziel and Philip Meguire from the Department of Economics at the University of Canterbury challenged some of my understandings of economics, while Paul Dalziel was kind enough to supply some statistics. My colleagues Miriam Laugesen, Tom Davis, Gabby Trifiletti and Penny Wilson at the University of Melbourne provided useful comments on draft chapters. The Hon. Brian Howe also provided important comments on a number of the Australian chapters.

A number of people have assisted me with accommodation and office support during my fieldwork during 1996–7. My friend Dr Niels Dugan provided me with accommodation and office support in Wellington; my brother Tim Goldfinch provided me with accommodation in Auckland and his firm Gosling Chapman provided office support; the Politics Program at ANU provided me with office support in Canberra; and my sister Annmarie Hay provided accommodation in Sydney. The Public Policy Program at Georgetown University in Washington DC provided a supportive environment in which to write up some of my earlier results. Thanks also to Fergus Barrowman, Rachel Lawson and Sue Brown at Victoria University Press for their support and assistance in publishing this study. Paul Bellamy assisted in the production of the index.

Some of my tentative results have been reported in different forms in three journal articles: Goldfinch, Shaun 1998. 'Remaking New Zealand's Economic Policy: Institutional Elites as Radical Innovators 1984–93.' *Governance* 11(2): 177–207. Goldfinch, Shaun 1999. 'Remaking Australia's Economic Policy: Economic Policy Decision-Makers During the Hawke and Keating Labor Governments.' *Australian Journal of Public Administration* 58(3): 3–20. Goldfinch, Shaun 2000. 'Paradigms, Economic Ideas and Institutions in Economic Policy Change: The Cae of New Zealand.' *Political Science* 52(1): 1–21.

The many people, including referees, who commented on drafts of these papers, also deserve my thanks. Any errors of fact and interpretation, remain, of course, my responsibility.

List of Abbreviations

Acct	Accounting
ACOSS	Association of Australian Social Services
ACTU	Australian Council of Trade Unions
ALAC	Australian Labour Advisory Council
ALP	Australian Labor Party
ANU	Australian National University
Ass	Associate
BCA	Business Council of Australia
Bus	Business
CBA	Commonwealth Bank of Australia
CE	Chief Executive
CIS	Centre for Independent Studies
Comm	Commission
Dep	Deputy
DOL	Department of Labour
DPMC	Department of Prime Minister and Cabinet
Econ	Economics
EET	Department of Employment, Education and Training
EPAC	Economic Policy Advisory Council until 1994, then Economic Policy Advisory Commission
ERC	Expenditure Review Committee
ET	Department of Education and Training
FAT	Foreign Affairs and Trade
Fed	Federation
Fin	Finance

FOL	Federation of Labour
GBE	Government Business Enterprise
GDP	Gross Domestic Product
Gov	Govenor
IAC	Industry Assistance Commission
IMF	International Monetary Fund
IR	Industrial Relations
JEFG	Joint Economic Forecasting Group
Lab	Labour
Min	Minister
MTIA	Metal Trade Industry Association
NDC	National Development Commission
NFF	National Farmers' Federation
NZBR	New Zealand Business Roundtable
NZCTU	New Zealand Council of Trade Unions
NZLP	New Zealand Labour Party
NZNP	New Zealand National Party
NZPC	New Zealand Planning Council
OECD	Organisation for Economic Cooperation and Development
PI	Primary Industry
PM	Prime Minister
PMO	Prime Minister's Office
RBA	Reserve Bank of Australia
RBNZ	Reserve Bank of New Zealand
Sec	Secretary
SOE	State Owned Enterprise
SRD	Statutory Reserve Deposits
SSC	State Services Commission or Commissioner
TO	Treasurer's Office

1
Introduction

Why do economic policies change? Why do the changes take the form they do? Economic imperatives will only ever provide part of the answer. Poor economic performance (or perceptions of such) and changes in the world or domestic economy may well explain why policy change is desired. What may not be explained is what this change will be, or how it will be introduced. Despite numerous claims of 'There is No Alternative', there is never one solution to policy problems, or one path to economic success. As such, in the face of questionable economic results, there are always a number of international examples and various schools of economics providing a diversity of policy alternatives and solutions. Policy change, then, will only be fully understood if the policy process itself is examined. This involves exploring the part played by ideas, how institutional factors impact on policy, and what role individuals and leaders have in this process. Central to this understanding is the investigation of how key economic policy decisions are actually made.

New Zealand and Australia provide a dramatic example of rapid and far-reaching economic liberalisation and a unique opportunity to study the processes of policy change. Both are comparatively wealthy countries with a long history of Westminster-style democracy and with developed systems of property rights and business law. Both have strong cultural similarities derived from their closely related British colonisation and settlement in the nineteenth century, and the structure of their economies share important characteristics. Importantly, both, initially under ostensibly social democratic Labour governments, comprehensively liberalised their economies in a process beginning in the early 1980s and continuing until the early 1990s. Changes included: the floating of the exchange rate; extensive liberalisation of financial, capital and other markets; lowering of trade protection; fiscal restraint and monetary deflation; changes to the machinery of government; corporatisation and then sale of some government assets; broadening of the tax base; and changes to industrial relations frameworks including the development of an incomes policy through the Accord (in Australia) and radical liberalisation of the labour-market (in New Zealand). Change in both economies was extensive. New Zealand moved from being what the *Economist* called one of the more 'hidebound' economies outside the former communist bloc, to amongst the most liberal in the Organisation for Economic Cooperation and Development (OECD). Both countries moved from having the highest manufacturing tariffs in the world in 1970 to amongst the lowest.[1]

This study draws on 180 interviews conducted with leading economic policy makers and policy influentials in Australia and New Zealand, as well as government files and reports, newspapers and published accounts. It examines the role of ideas, the institutions and processes of policy-making and analyses in depth the making of a number of key economic policy decisions. In New Zealand, in the context of a small unitary state with simple institutional structures and executive domination of parliament, economic policy-making was dominated by a rather closed policy community comprised of leading members of strategically located institutions, largely from the 'inner circle' of the Treasury, cabinet, the Reserve Bank (RBNZ), the Business Roundtable (NZBR) and later the Department of Prime Minister and Cabinet (DPMC). Members of this policy community often exerted influence over a number of decisions and over a considerable period of time, and promulgated policies based on neoclassical and related schools of economics, sometimes those associated with the New Right. In Australia's complex federal system, influence on economic policy decisions was more diffuse with a greater array of institutions and individuals being important. Theoretical influences on policy in Australia were also more varied than in New Zealand, with a greater diversity of influential economic ideas and of institutions and individuals contributing ideas to economic policy-making.

In New Zealand, a country that strongly values political participation and had traditionally made policy in a consultative manner, rapid economic policy changes were imposed, sometimes in the face of public opposition, often in secret and despite a number of explicit election promises to the contrary. In Australia, a more gradual process of change was introduced by a government that was skilful in building and maintaining support for the new policy directions, by cajoling and using the symbols and rhetoric of consensus and by incorporating key interest groups in policy formation. The 'crash through' approach to economic liberalisation in New Zealand led to the undermining of the legitimacy of the political system and contributed to electoral instability and radical constitutional change. In contrast, Australia's 'bargained consensus' managed to introduce far-reaching change while avoiding electoral instability and the breakdown in legitimacy experienced in New Zealand. Despite policy makers in New Zealand being able to achieve their policy aims to a remarkable extent and notwithstanding claims that New Zealand provides an exemplar of economic reform, the New Zealand economy has generally not performed well since 1984 as measured by commonly used economic indicators. Finally, it is argued that there are good reasons to believe that better policy can be made through compromise and negotiation. This introductory chapter will examine the economies of New Zealand and Australia before 1983, before analysing reasons for the policy changes.

The economic policy framework before 1983

The economic liberalisation of Australia and New Zealand was particularly dramatic because the two economies traditionally had relatively high levels of government involvement and regulation of the economy, and considerable state ownership of infrastructure and trading activities.[2] In these former colonies, strongly tied to the British economy for much of their history,[3] tariff protection of manufacturing was amongst the highest in the developed world. By 1970, it supported a manufacturing industry focused largely towards import substitution. Exports were dominated by highly productive primary industries; and the government played an important part in regulating the labour-market. After the Second World War both countries adopted variants of Keynesian demand management, with an explicit commitment to full employment.[4] Australia and New

Figure 1.1 Real GDP growth per capita 1950–99[1]

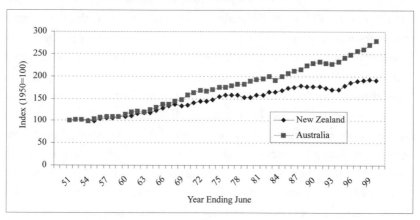

Notes
1. Source: Dalziel 1999b.

Zealand enjoyed high levels of prosperity throughout most of the twentieth century, vying with the United States to be the richest per capita countries in the world at the turn of the century, and still in the top five in the 1950s. Unemployment, especially in New Zealand, was at extremely low levels.[5] This period of prosperity seemed to be coming to an end by the 1970s, however, and, especially after the oil shock of 1973–4, both countries entered a period of relative economic decline. From 1971 to 1981 New Zealand had an average annual real Gross Domestic Product (GDP) per capita growth of 1.8 percent, while Australia's was 3.2 percent, marginally less than the OECD average of 3.4 percent (OECD 1999a, 227). Ranked in terms of GDP per capita within the OECD, New Zealand fell from tenth place in 1970 to nineteenth in 1980, while Australia slipped marginally to seventh (OECD 1999c).[6] Figure 1.1 shows the divergence of GDP growth per capita between Australia and New Zealand from 1950 to 1999. This divergence is less dramatic until the 1980s if measured by purchasing power parities, as in Appendix Three.

Tentative liberalisation

The seeming inability of existing policy frameworks to deal with the stagflation and other economic problems of the 1970s led the governments of New Zealand and Australia to look for new policy solutions. During the 1970s, there was some tentative liberalisation of the two economies, although this was applied inconsistently and sometimes reversed.

In Australia, the Liberal-National coalition under Prime Minister Malcolm Fraser (1975–83) rejected Keynesian demand management policies and adopted a neo-liberal programme of 'fighting inflation first'. This included adopting deflationary monetary policy targeted at monetary aggregates, using a wide range of regulatory measures, although with limited success in actually reducing inflation. There was some limited deregulation of the financial markets following the interim and final reports of the Campbell Inquiry into the Australian Financial System in 1980 and 1981. In other areas however, the neo-liberal rhetoric did not always lead to action. For example, while the previous Labor Government under Prime Minister Gough Whitlam (1972–5) had introduced a 25 percent across the board tariff cut, under Fraser the footwear and automobile industry received significant increases in protection (Garnaut 1994a). In 1982 the Government intervened directly in the labour-market by imposing a 'wage pause'.

While there was some initial success in restricting the fiscal deficit, which fell from 3.4 percent in 1977–8 to 0.3 percent in 1981–2, it increased again to 2.6 percent of GDP in 1982–3 with a move to fiscal stimulus in the face of a severe downturn (Mathews and Grewel 1997). By the time of the 1983 federal election Australia was in a severe recession facing unemployment at 9.9 percent, inflation at 11.5 percent, while

Figure 1.2 Australian terms of trade index 1959–97[1]

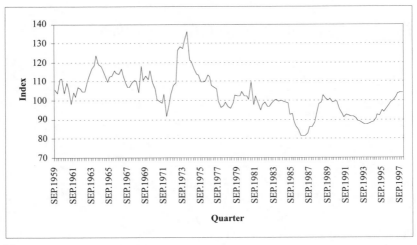

Notes

1. Quarterly. Source: ABS unpublished computer series. 1989–90 = 100.

GDP had fallen by 1.7 percent in 1982–3. Australia faced a downward trend in the terms of trade, as shown in Figure 1.2, and the current account deficit had moved out to 3.8 percent of GDP in 1982–3.

In New Zealand the National Government of Prime Minister Robert Muldoon (1975–84) took tentative steps to deregulate the economy in areas such as transport and meat processing, to allow tendering for import licenses and to liberalise some facets of the foreign exchange market. From 1976 to 1981 controls on interest rates were relaxed. There was also some movement towards the restructuring of farm subsidies and the removal of compulsory unionism (Nagel 1998). However, this trend towards liberalisation was reversed somewhat with a wage and price freeze introduced in 1982. An expensive universal superannuation scheme was introduced after an election promise made in the 1975 election. The National Government also engaged in a number of major investments in energy and capital-intensive industry (known as 'Think Big') most of which did not meet with commercial success (Easton 1989a; Wooding 1993). Macroeconomic policy continued in an eclectic Keynesian tradition with 'stop-go' policies and pre-election fiscal boosts (Bollard, Lattimore and Silverstone 1996). Monetary policy under Muldoon's National Government involved a variety of regulatory measures and had periods of tightness, although as the wage and price freeze took effect, policy was largely directed at lowering interest rates (RBNZ 1985a). Despite New Zealand's relatively poor performance during the 1970s, at the time of the 1984 election the New Zealand economy was exhibiting

Figure 1.3 New Zealand terms of trade index 1960–98[1]

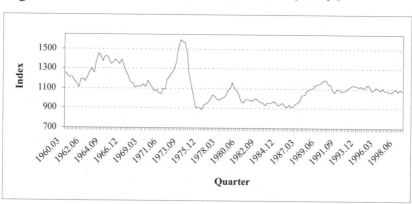

strength in some economic indicators. The wage and price freeze had had considerable impact in lowering the consumer price index to 3.5 percent by March 1984, the lowest since 1968 (RBNZ 1983; 1984a; 1984b). During the same period, expansionary fiscal policy coincided with an increase in employment, and economic growth reached 4 percent in the March 1984 year. However, the fiscal deficit reached record levels in 1984 at 6.5 percent,[7] up from 4.6 percent in 1982–3, and the current account deficit increased to 5.8 percent of GDP. Foreign debt increased and, as Figure 1.3 shows, New Zealand faced variability in its terms of trade, although on a downward trend.

Labo[u]r takes power

The Australian election of March 1983 and the New Zealand snap election of July 1984 saw Labo[u]r governments sweep to power in both countries, marking the beginning of a rapid and far-reaching programme of economic liberalisation.

In Australia the Labor Government came to power with well formulated economic policies. In the face of the severe recession of 1982–3, the 'National Recovery and Reconstruction' plan, released during the election campaign, outlined a programme of public capital works and investment in infrastructure, tax cuts for low and middle income earners, and borrowing opportunities for business, farmers and home-buyers (Langmore 1991, 75–6). As chapter seven outlines, a price and incomes policy was to be based around the Accord negotiated with the Australian Council of Trade Unions (ACTU) while Labor was still in opposition. Along with the Accord, firm monetary policy was to rein in any inflationary effects of the fiscal stimulus. An industry reconstruction policy was outlined and the Australian Labor Party (ALP) 1982 document 'New Directions for Australian Industry' seemed to provide some support for continued industry protection. Labor's economic policies were contrasted with the previous Government's; instead of 'fighting inflation first', inflation and unemployment would be fought simultaneously.

In accordance with the new Prime Minister Bob Hawke's (1984, 14) election rhetoric of 'national reconciliation, national recovery, [and] national reconstruction', a National Economic Summit was held only six weeks after the election of the Labor Government. The aim of the summit was, to a great extent, to co-opt business support for the Accord already negotiated with the ACTU, and broad support for the new policy measures was obtained. The unions agreed to wage restraint and an increase in business profit in exchange for the acceptance by business of centralised wage fixation, fiscal stimulus and increases in the 'social wage' (Walsh 1991). A number of election promises were abrogated after a fiscal blowout was 'discovered'.

Unlike the Labor Government in Australia, the New Zealand Labour Government under Prime Minister David Lange was thrust into power without settled economic policies. There had been debate in the years before the election between two sections within the (mainly parliamentary) Labour Party: one broadly supported economic liberalisation, the other a more corporatist model of economic management. These disagreements were not resolved by the time of the snap election in July 1984 and the two policy strands were 'patched up' in the party manifesto, albeit in such a way that little information was given to the prospective voter (NZ Labour Party 1984; Oliver 1989). As economic policy subsequently unfolded, it was clear that those promoting economic liberalisation had gained control of policy formation.

Like Labor in Australia, the electioneering rhetoric of consensus made by the incoming Labour Government in New Zealand gave rise to an economic summit. The summit included representation from unions, business groups and community groups and was held in September 1984, just a few months after the election. There was considerable disagreement amongst participants across a number of issues. Trade unions proposed greater state involvement and investment. Business groups wanted less state involvement in the economy with greater reliance on markets and a more liberal labour-market. Primary producers wanted a strategy of export-led growth, and community groups urged greater social spending and more attention to equity issues (Dalziel 1989). On one issue, that of unemployment, there was some agreement and it was noted as a particular problem in a communique unanimously approved by participants. At the same time, little support was given to macroeconomic disinflation, which was strongly rejected by trade unions. By the time the summit was held economic policy had largely been settled (Dalziel 1989) with the economic liberalisation programme supported by Finance Minister Roger Douglas winning out.[8]

Economic liberalisation

Once in power the two governments began a comprehensive programme of economic liberalisation. While there were a number of similarities in the economic policies introduced in the two countries, there were also differences. New Zealand's reforms were faster and more far-reaching. Australia made use of corporatist and labourist mechanisms such as industry plans and the incomes policy of the Accord, and was less rigorously tied to deflationary and non-discretionary monetary and fiscal policy. Change in both economies was extensive, with the reduction of manufacturing tariffs from amongst the highest in the world to lower than many of their trading partners. New Zealand moved from being one of the more regulated economies in the developed world to being amongst the most liberal, with the libertarian think-tank the Cato Institute placing New Zealand third behind Hong Kong and Singapore in its index of economic freedom (Economist 1996, 19–21).[9]

Economic policy, as it developed over the decade from 1983 to 1993 in the two countries, can be seen as having certain common characteristics. First, both countries floated their currency and deregulated their financial markets. Second, fiscal policy was largely aimed at reducing the fiscal deficit, although fiscal stimulus was used in Australia during the recessions of 1983 and 1992–3. New Zealand's commitment to fiscal disinflation was such that large pro-cyclical cuts to the fiscal deficit were made during the severe recession of 1991. Third, a broadening of the tax base was also carried out in both countries, with the introduction of a Goods and Services Tax in New Zealand. Fourth, both countries differed somewhat in the conduct of monetary policy. In New Zealand monetary policy was aimed at deflation, with the independence of the bank and the focus of monetary policy on inflation confirmed in the Reserve Bank Act 1989. In Australia monetary policy was initially targeted at monetary aggregates. From 1985 it was aimed at a check-list of indicators with a focus beyond just inflation. Inflation became the primary target of monetary policy in 1993. Fifth, there was some labour-market deregulation in both countries, although to a considerably differing extent. In Australia the Accord was a key component of economic policy and of wage control. Initially the Accord process worked through centralised wage indexation, but it later looked to increase productivity and moved to restructure awards and encourage enterprise bargaining. There were some tentative moves towards deregulation of labour-markets in New

Zealand with the Labour Relations Act 1987, and in 1991 the National Government introduced the Employment Contracts Act which radically deregulated the labour-market and adopted individual contracts in employment. Sixth, both countries undertook extensive programmes of microeconomic liberalisation with the intention of increasing efficiency in the economy. In Australia, in trade and industry policy, there was a movement away from the earlier intervention through industry plans towards the greater use of market mechanisms including large across-the-board tariff reduction and microeconomic reform. New Zealand introduced a wide range of deregulatory measures and made large cuts in trade protection. Seventh, both New Zealand and Australia corporatised and then sold a number of government assets.[10] Later chapters analyse a select number of economic policy decisions in detail.

Explaining the economic policy changes

Changing economic realities influence policy choices. As existing policy frameworks cease to produce good economic results, policy makers begin to question their value and seek out new solutions to policy problems. While changing economic conditions may explain the desire for change however, they do not always explain what policy responses will be. Economic crisis and globalisation are often advanced as explanations of the economic liberalisation carried out in Australia and New Zealand. This section will illustrate that both the extent of economic crisis and the demands of globalisation have been overstated. There is no one path to economic success and a variety of successful economic and social systems exist. The pressures that were apparent do not adequately explain why certain policy responses were adopted rather than others.

Economic change as a response to economic crisis

While the extent of economic crisis has sometimes been overstated, perceptions of crisis played an important part in facilitating the introduction of far-reaching and rapid change by encouraging the belief that such change was necessary and that it needed to be introduced quickly.

In New Zealand economic problems were indeed serious by the time of the 1984 election. Growth rates had been less than the OECD average since 1960, and there had been considerable variability in terms of trade during the 1970s, as Figure 1.3 shows.[11] Traditional British markets were threatened after the United Kingdom joined the EEC in 1972 (OECD 1993). As in many other countries, the oil shock of 1973–4 had a severe impact on the New Zealand economy, but, according to a number of critics, New Zealand seemed slower to adjust and recover. These critics argued that existing problems were compounded by several factors. First, rather than adjusting to new realities of shrinking demand and prices for agricultural goods, and seeking out new markets and developing new products, domestic agricultural prices were buoyed up by subsidies (Hawke 1992; Treasury 1984a). Second, the protection of domestic industries allocated resources away from the more efficient export sectors. Third, considerable overseas borrowing led to an increase in public sector debt from 11 percent of GDP in March 1974 to 95 percent in June 1984 (Evans et al 1996). This was often undertaken to fund large investments in 'Think Big' industries of questionable commercial value, or to maintain consumption at levels above that justified by production (Hawke 1992). Fourth, according to the Treasury and other critics, inconsistent macroeconomic policies and electoral budget cycles, labour-market rigidities, an overly large public sector and excessive government regulation during the Muldoon Government contributed to this relative decline and lack of adjustment to changing realities (Bollard 1994; Roper 1997; Treasury 1984a).[12] The feeling of crisis grew when there was a run on the dollar before and immediately after the 1984 election, in the expectation of a devaluation. This belief was compounded when the outgoing Prime Minister Robert Muldoon refused, for a time, to devalue the dollar on the advice of the incoming government, in direct contravention of constitutional conventions.

With the possible exception of the currency crisis, it may be that the degree of economic crisis has been overstated. Some economic indicators going into the election were positive. Despite claims to the contrary made by the Treasury and others, there was also some adjustment to the changing economic conditions: trade liberalisation under Muldoon after 1979; liberalisation of foreign exchange dealing; reduction in price controls; liberalisation of the transport laws; considerable diversification in exports and a broadening of export markets; and the negotiation of the free trade Closer Economic Relations (CER) treaty with Australia in 1983 (Easton 1997a; 1997b; Hazeledine 1993; 1998; OECD 1994).[13] As Dalziel (1999a) points out, between 1978 and 1984 New Zealand's real GDP grew at 2.9 percent a year; a rate that would have been seen as highly desirable at the depths of the recession of the late 1980s and early 1990s, and respectable even now. While change seemed desirable in many aspects of economic policy, the case for such extensive and rapid introduction was not overwhelming.[14]

In Australia there were also significant economic problems. Like New Zealand, Australia was facing considerable variability in its terms of trade, while manufacturing exports had declined as a percentage of exports (Ravenhill 1994). The policies of the Fraser Government did not seem to address problems facing the economy and, despite a mining boom in the early 1980s, Australia was in a severe recession when the Labor Government took power. The incoming Government was faced with a large fiscal deficit and a run on the currency. However, it is not clear that these economic problems constituted a crisis. Fraser's fiscal stimulus may have taken the economy out of recession, and some critics have doubted the severity of the fiscal deficit (Langmore 1988; 1991). Nor was there a pressing need for the incoming Labor Government to respond immediately to economic problems that had been apparent for some time. According to Professor Ross Garnaut, a former economic adviser in Prime Minister Bob Hawke's office:

> There was a sense in which the government was responding to a crisis, which became more severe with the collapse of the world system of agricultural trade in the 1980s. The crisis, however, was spread over time, and there was no inevitability that the problems would be addressed as they were, in the mid-1980s, rather than, say, the 1970s or the 1990s (Garnaut 1994a, 68).

Whether there was a genuine economic crisis in the two countries did not matter as much as the *perception* that there was a crisis, and the way that perception could be used by certain elites or individuals to marshal support for change. In New Zealand, there was a shared belief amongst political elites and many academic economists, often across the political and ideological spectrum, that things had gone 'off the rails' under Muldoon. According to Dalziel, 'there was near universal agreement in 1984 that things had to change, with the possible exception of Sir Robert himself' (Dalziel 1994, 51). The constitutional and currency crisis cemented this belief. Perhaps economic indicators do not support a belief in economic crisis, however, the perception at the time that a crisis did in fact exist may have produced a 'window of opportunity' for certain elites or 'advocacy coalitions' to convince others that the changes they were advocating needed to be made, and made quickly (Wallis 1997; Williamson 1994a; 1994b). As David Lange, the New Zealand Prime Minister from 1984 to 1989, said, in an interview with the author:[15]

> If we had been elected in the normal course of events in 1984, we would have had a victory session of Parliament, and come back in February. We would have been a reforming government, at a very slow pace, and we would have made no huge difference to New Zealand. But we came in, we hit the deck running, and it is a remarkable credit to our cohesion and ability to work together, and I suppose our basic intelligence and youth, that we went through a period of extraordinary crisis and persuaded the country.
>
> The [currency] crisis was absolutely critical to what we did. On the Saturday night [after the election result] I heard Muldoon say, 'Congratulations, but I've got bad news for them.' Sunday, when I heard the bad news, I actually considered calling in the World Bank because I didn't see how we could get away [with] doing the radical things that we would have to do, and still remain clean from charges of being politically duplicitous and having abandoned all our promises. Then Muldoon put on an absolutely virtuoso performance, destroying the economy that we inherited—scorched earth television performances—and the whole of New Zealand knew we were in crisis. He wanted a revolt against us so he could take control in three weeks, but all that happened was we took control of it. He convinced them there was a crisis, and we made a response.

Similarly, Hawke used the famous budget memo showing a budget blowout (delivered to him the day after the election) to justify abandoning a number of election promises.[16] There was a similar use of a 'fiscal crisis' in 1991 by the National Government in New Zealand as an excuse for abandoning some of its election promises and for making huge cuts to some welfare benefits. The Coalition Government in Australia also pointed to a 'fiscal crisis' during the 1996 budget to justify significant cuts to the fiscal deficit.

A crisis, or the perception of a crisis, may make change likely and give some urgency to that change. The crisis provides some constraints to that change, but it does not necessarily determine the direction or type of change that will be undertaken. As Garnaut (1994a, 68) says:

> The instinctive Australian response to macro-economic crisis, based

23

on historical precedents since the 1930s, was not to pursue internationally orientated or market-orientated reform, but rather to stimulate domestic demand (for recession) and to increase protection and exchange controls (for balance of payments weakness). Government used the crisis atmosphere of 1983 and 1986 to advance the reform effort, but there is no sense in which the shape of the reform program itself was determined by crisis.

Garnaut's comments would apply equally as well to New Zealand.

Globalisation

A vast literature has arisen outlining the constraints that growing globalisation of the world economy has placed on policy makers. The Australasian economies are small, tied into the world economy, relatively dependent on foreign trade and capital, with, as Figure 1.4 shows, a large part of their national incomes depending on exports. As such, it is claimed that their ability to make policy independently may be severely constrained.[17] While there is a considerable amount of truth to the globalisation thesis, some globalisation theorists have overstated both the degree of globalisation and the constraints it places on independent policy action. The globalisation that has occurred may well have encouraged some liberalisation of the Australian and New Zealand economies, but it would overstate the case to say that a particular response was inevitable from both governments.

Globalisation is seen by Bell (1997) to mean the increasing international interdependence of the international economy and the spread of capitalist economic relations. He describes three aspects. First, the 'increased interlinking of national economies, particularly in terms of macro-economic unification or interdependence'. Second, the 'increased interlinking of trade, investment, production, consumption and "globalisation" of corporate activity'. Third, the 'increasing global integration of financial markets' (Bell 1997, 346). Some theorists claim globalisation has limited the ability of governments to make independent social and economic policy. Some of the more extreme claims are summarised by Hirst and Thompson:

> National politics and political choices have been sidelined by the world market forces which are stronger than even the most powerful states. Capital is mobile and has no national attachments, it will locate wherever economic advantage dictates, but labour is both nationally static and relatively static, and it must adjust to

political expectations to meet the new pressures of the international competitiveness. Distinct national regimes of extensive labour rights and social protection are thus obsolete. So too are monetary and fiscal policies contrary to the expectations of the global markets and transnational companies. *The nation state has ceased to be an effective economic manager. It can only provide those social and public services international capital deems essential at the lowest possible overhead cost* (1996, 175–6, emphasis added).

It does seem true that the international economy is now markedly different to that dominant from the postwar years until the first oil crisis (Hirst and Thompson 1996). This has sometimes resulted in constraints on government action. Economic policy decisions (especially macroeconomic ones) that do not fit with the financial markets' preference for such neo-liberal policy targets as a focus on low inflation, balanced budgets and limited regulation, can be punished through capital flight (Bell 1997). The experience of Mexico in 1994 and the currency crisis in Sweden in 1992 provide examples,[18] while the Asian crisis of 1997–8 underlines the power the international financial markets can exert over national economies. However, while the globalisation thesis contains some convincing arguments, a number of critics have questioned its more extravagant claims. They point out a number of weaknesses. First, the present internationalisation of trade, capital flow and monetary systems is not an entirely new phenomenon and had previously existed between 1870 and 1914.[19] Second, there has *not* been a flight of capital from the advanced countries to the less developed

Figure 1.4 Exports of goods and services as percentage of GDP 1960–95: Australia, New Zealand and OECD[1]

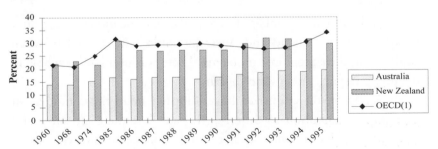

Notes
1. OECD small countries. Source: OECD 1997a.

ones with most cross border activity confined to the rich north. Third, there are few real transnational corporations. Most successful multi-nationals carry out the large part of their investment, production, management, and research and development in their national home bases (Bell 1997; Hirst and Thompson 1996). Fourth, there is no evidence that the overall tax burden for business has decreased in advanced democracies, and there appears to be 'no dramatic, irresistible pressure to radically retrench social spending and eliminate public goods provision' (Swank 1998, 691). Finally, in some cases the globalisation of financial markets has imposed *new* duties of market supervision on nation-states. This has possibly increased the effectiveness of the nation-state in certain areas (rather than always leading to an undermining of its effectiveness) (Lutz 1998).

Different paths to economic success

The neo-liberal convergence in economic policy in advanced nations has been greatly overstated by such writers as Henderson (1995) and Scobie and Lim (1992). There is a diversity of successful economic and social systems that currently exist. As Boix notes in his extensive study of capitalist economies:

> Even in a world of open and interdependent economies, it is still possible to detect widely divergent economic strategies . . . the accelerated technological change and the process of economic integration we are experiencing today are only sharpening the economic and political dilemmas confronted by advanced nations. Perhaps paradoxically for some, *they are intensifying the extent of divergence among the different economic strategies embraced by governments to respond to those dilemmas* (1998, xiii, emphasis added).

As such, there were a number of potential economic models that policy makers in New Zealand and Australia could have turned to when confronting their economic problems. There was nothing inevitable in the policy responses that were chosen.

Anglo-Saxon countries have adopted neo-liberal models of economic organisation to differing degrees, but there are successful alternatives including: the corporatist and social democratic economies of Western Europe (Casper and Vitols 1997; Schmitter and Gote 1998); the partly state-directed economies of the so-called Asian Tigers (Bell

1995; Wade 1990);[20] and the networked regional economies of the Third Italy, Baden-Wurttemburg and Japan (Goldfinch and Perry 1997; Perry and Goldfinch 1998). Nor has there been an abandonment of welfare systems, although these vary in type and comprehensiveness. For example, the United States has a minimal liberal welfare state, while more expansive welfare systems exist in the corporatist welfare state of Germany and the social democratic welfare state of the Netherlands (Goodin et al 1999).[21]

The Australasian economies also differ significantly from other national economies and from each other. New Zealand and Australia differed on the conduct of macroeconomic policy and strongly diverged on labour-market and industry policy. While the Accord in Australia shares characteristics with corporatist arrangements in a number of countries, according to Singleton (1990a; 1990b) it was a unique combination of circumstances, Australian institutions, individuals and a history of Australian labourism that allowed the Accord to proceed. Economic liberalisation happened more quickly and was more radical in Australia and New Zealand than in a number of countries. This was particularly the case in New Zealand where it was probably more extensive, carried out more quickly and showed a degree of theoretical purity that was unparalleled anywhere in the world until, arguably, the liberalisation of Eastern Europe.

Examining economic policy-making in New Zealand and Australia

The New Zealand and Australian economies underwent a period of rapid economic liberalisation beginning in the early 1980s. While changing economic conditions delimit and impact on economic policy choices, there is never one response to policy problems and hence no one path to economic success. To explain economic policy change in the Australasian economies only in terms of changing economic conditions will always be inadequate. To further understand why such a remarkable period of economic liberalisation occurred in this short period, a study of economic policy-making in both countries must be carried out. Important factors that need to be investigated include: the role of ideas; and the institutions, individuals and processes involved in the making of economic policy and economic policy decisions.

New Zealand's small population, unitary Westminster system of government, and institutional simplicity suggest it is likely that economic policy-making is dominated by a small number of individuals based in key institutions. Australia's considerably larger population, its complex federal system and two houses of Parliament, and its greater institutional complexity, suggest that influence in economic policy is likely to be more diffuse and policy-making considerably more complex. To examine whether this is indeed the case, and to ascertain the broad processes of economic policy-making, as well as the role of ideas, this study used a number of methods. First, it drew on published secondary sources, newspapers and primary government sources where available. Second, interviews were conducted with two sample selections. The first selection consisted of institutional elites in each country thought to be potentially influential in economic policy-making. These included former federal[22] treasurers, finance ministers and other cabinet ministers, past and present chief executives of government departments and other senior public servants (especially from the central agencies), ministerial staffers, business and union leaders, political party leaders, academic leaders and senior print journalists. The second selection comprised persons nominated by respondents as influential in a select number of key economic policy decisions in each country and in economic policy-making generally, who were not already in the initial selection (Figure 1.5). As well as establishing influence in economic policy-making, these audiotaped interviews provided details of the processes of economic policy-making, the influence and importance of ideas and the role and structures of important policy-making institutions. Eighty-seven interviews (including 17 self-completed questionnaires) were carried out in New Zealand and 93 in Australia (including 25 self-completed questionnaires). The methods used are explained in greater depth in Appendix One.

This investigation begins with a general study of the role of ideas and the broad processes of economic policy-making in Australia and New Zealand. Once this broad framework is established, there is an in-depth investigation of the making of a number of select economic policy decisions. The concluding chapter draws together the main themes and arguments contained in this study.

Chapter two illustrates the role of ideas and reports on the sources of ideas and those institutions and individuals important in contributing ideas to economic policy-making. It shows that in Australia neoclassical economic theory was important, but that it was departed from on certain occasions. In some situations, such as the early Accords, some industry policy, and the fiscal stimulus of 1983 and 1992, neoclassical economics does not seem to have been the only or major influence, with labourism and corporatism also important. In contrast, policies in New Zealand were heavily derivative of neoclassical and related schools of economics, including some schools of economics associated with the New Right. These schools include the Chicago School, New Classical economics, Public Choice and New Institutional Economics. Part of the reason for the comparatively greater diversity of ideas in Australia was the wider spread of those (including academics) contributing ideas to policy-making. While ideas provide the broad framework in which policy-making is carried out, to understand further how ideas are adopted and modified, the processes of policy-making and the roles of institutions and individuals must be investigated.

Chapters three to five illustrate the processes and institutions of economic policy-making in New Zealand, and investigate a select number of key economic policy decisions. Chapter three depicts the simple nature of New Zealand's unitary state and policy-making institutions and the structure and roles of the 'inner circle' in economic policy-making in New Zealand. This 'inner circle', consisting of the cabinet, the Treasury, the Reserve Bank and the Business Roundtable (and later the DPMC,

Figure 1.5 Australia and New Zealand respondents by occupation[1]

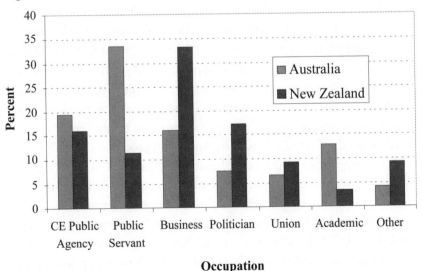

Notes
1. Australia = 93, New Zealand = 87.

although to a considerably lesser extent), dominated economic policy-making under the Labour (1984–90) and National governments (1990–1999). The 'first tier' organisations are those that would be expected to be influential in economic policy-making and while some did exert influence on certain issues and decisions, by-and-large they were excluded and economic policy-making was dominated by the 'inner circle'. Chapters four and five illustrate how a select number of key economic policy decisions were made and report on those individuals nominated as influential on each decision. Influence in New Zealand economic policy was found to be highly concentrated within a stable and relatively long-lived policy community, with central institutions and individuals exercising influence across a number of economic policy decisions and over a considerable period of time.

Chapters six to eight look at Australia. Chapter six demonstrates the federal nature of the Australian constitution and the institutions and processes of economic policy-making under the Labor governments. The 'inner circle', consisting of the cabinet, the ministerial offices, the central agencies, the ACTU and the Reserve Bank of Australia (RBA), are those institutions generally most important in economic policy-making. While the influence of the 'first' and 'second' tier institutions varied, at times they could also be extremely important in economic policy-making. Chapters seven and eight investigate a select number of key economic policy decisions made during the Labor governments of Bob Hawke and Paul Keating. Influence of institutions and individuals on economic policy decisions was relatively diffuse and varied according to the decision.

Chapter nine summarises and contrasts economic policy-making in the two countries. The simple unitary state and institutional simplicity of New Zealand is compared to the more complex federal structure of Australia. In Australia a more negotiated and gradual 'bargained consensus' approach to policy change was used, compared to the 'crash through' method used in New Zealand. The Australian process avoided the loss of political legitimacy and electoral instability suffered in New Zealand. While New Zealand policy makers have achieved their aims to a remarkable extent, despite many claims to the contrary, the New Zealand economy has not performed well since 1984, as compared to Australia and the OECD. Finally, it is argued there are good reasons to believe that a more negotiated and consensual approach to policy development may well deliver better policy advice.

2

The Influence of Economic Ideas in Economic Policy-making

Ideas provide the framework by which policy makers interpret reality, a set of concepts and language to describe and understand policy problems, and often a toolbox of solutions (Hall 1993; Sabatier 1998). As such, the role of ideas in economic policy change can be highly significant (Skogstad 1998). A number of commentators have claimed the economic liberalisation of Australia and New Zealand owes much to neoclassical and related schools of economic thought. For example, Pusey's (1991) much cited book *Economic Rationalism in Canberra* claims a doctrinaire form of 'economic rationalism' took hold in Australia amongst the younger bureaucrats in the central agencies. These bureaucrats, university educated in economics or business, largely influenced 'a nation building state to change its mind' and embrace economic policies influenced by this neo-liberal thought and neoclassical economics. Other commentators have cited the influence of corporatism or labourism on labour-market and industry policy in Australia (Capling and Galligan 1992; Singleton 1990a; 1990b). In New Zealand, a number of commentators have also seen neoclassical and related schools of economics as influential. For example, in a 1988 book edited by Alan Bollard, a number of authors argue that American schools of economics, including Chicago School, New Classical and Contestability theory, have been important (Bollard 1988; see also Bollard, Lattimore, and Silverstone 1996). Bertram (1997) sees arguments

Figure 2.1 Theoretical influences on policy decisions in New Zealand

Microeconomic policy

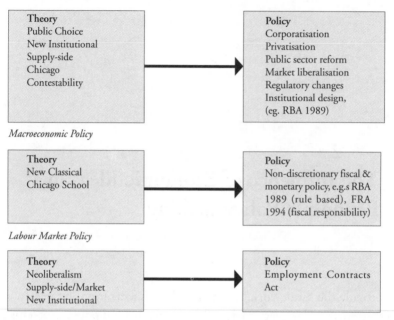

Theory	Policy
Public Choice	Corporatisation
New Institutional	Privatisation
Supply-side	Public sector reform
Chicago	Market liberalisation
Contestability	Regulatory changes
	Institutional design,
	(eg. RBA 1989)

Macroeconomic Policy

Theory	Policy
New Classical	Non-discretionary fiscal &
Chicago School	monetary policy, e.g.s RBA
	1989 (rule based), FRA
	1994 (fiscal responsibility)

Labour Market Policy

Theory	Policy
Neoliberalism	Employment Contracts
Supply-side/Market	Act
New Institutional	

Notes

RBA is the Reserve Bank Act which committed the Bank to combatting inflation only and contracted the Governor to achieve an inflation rate (originally 0-2%). FRA is the Fiscal Responsibility Act, which tied the government into a 'fiscally responsible' path. The Employment Contracts Act introduced individual contracting in the labour market.

regarding the role of the Supply-side in encouraging economic growth as influential. Patterson (1996) claims recent changes to New Zealand competition law were derived from Chicago School theories. Boston et al (1996) see the influence of Public Choice, Agency theory, and to a lesser extent, Transaction Cost analysis, on the public sector reforms. Others have also noted the influence of law and economics (Kelsey 1995).

Figures 2.1 and 2.2 summarise these theoretical influences as they seem to be reflected in actual policy decisions, while Appendix Two discusses the characteristics of some of these schools of economics. As Figure 2.1 shows, economic policy in New Zealand seems to be highly derivative of neoclassical and related schools of economics, including some schools associated with the New Right.[1] Together these different strands of economics have provided a more-or-less coherent policy paradigm. Monetary policy was used in a non-activist manner and targeted solely at the inflation rate, as would accord with neoclassical theory and particularly New Classical and Chicago School economics. This is the case even in the face of the recession of the late 1980s and early 1990s and immediately after the 1987 stock market crash. The inflation-only focus of monetary policy was confirmed in the Reserve Bank Act 1989. Fiscal policy focused on being non-activist and deflationary, including when such a stance might have been seen to be pro-cyclical, such as during the 1991 recession, and when large parts of the world (including Australia) were rediscovering fiscal stimulus. Financial liberalisation, trade policy, deregulation and corporatisation and privatisation seem to be heavily derivative of schools of neoclassical economics. The Employment Contracts Act 1991, which extensively deregulated the labour-markets and introduced individual contracting, was heavily influenced by neoclassical economics and New Right thought. Changes to public sector management were influenced by Public Choice and New Institutional economics, which also gave direction on institutional design to insulate policy instruments, such as monetary policy in the case of the Reserve Bank Act, from opportunistic politicians and rent-seeking interest groups.

Figure 2.2 Theoretical influences on economic policy in Australia

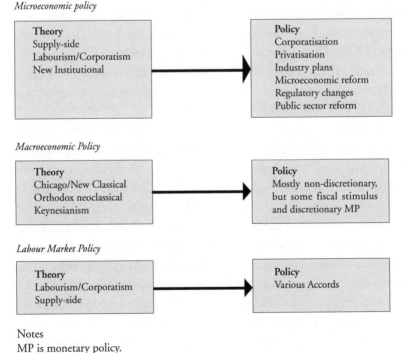

Microeconomic policy

Theory	Policy
Supply-side	Corporatisation
Labourism/Corporatism	Privatisation
New Institutional	Industry plans
	Microeconomic reform
	Regulatory changes
	Public sector reform

Macroeconomic Policy

Theory	Policy
Chicago/New Classical	Mostly non-discretionary,
Orthodox neoclassical	but some fiscal stimulus
Keynesianism	and discretionary MP

Labour Market Policy

Theory	Policy
Labourism/Corporatism	Various Accords
Supply-side	

Notes
MP is monetary policy.

As Figure 2.2 shows, economic policy does not seem to have been as highly derivative of neoclassical economics in Australia as it was in New Zealand, with its influence varying during the Labor Government. The Labor Government was elected on promises of fiscal stimulus and consensus, and did establish a number of apparently non-neoclassical economic policies, most notably the Accord, which drew on elements of labourism and corporatism. The first Labor budget was significantly expansionary, but considerably less than might have been expected if all election promises had been delivered. In monetary policy, the Labor Government, early in its life, abandoned the monetary aggregate rule-based policy that had been adopted under the Fraser Government, and adopted a checklist approach with a focus beyond just inflation. After 1993, it also confirmed the focus of monetary policy on inflation control. In Australia, fiscal discipline was largely maintained throughout the early to mid-1990s, especially from the 1985–6 budget on, but fiscal stimulus was rediscovered in 1992 in the 'One Nation' statement. The Accord moved from reinstating centralised wage indexation (a 'non-market' response) to progressively opening wage determination to enterprise bargaining (a 'more-market' response).[2] Like New Zealand, Australia liberalised its trade regime, but only after instigating a number of significant industry plans that used sectoral–corporatist type models to reorientate their focus towards international markets (Capling and Galligan 1992). The adoption of 'microeconomic reform', including some privatisation and trade liberalisation, showed the influence of neoclassical thought. Similarly, financial reform was justified mainly on neoclassical grounds (Kelly 1994, ch. 4).

While earlier studies are useful in highlighting the importance of ideas, most infer influence from the similarity between policy prescriptions of schools of economics and how these appear to be reflected in policy advice or policy decisions. In Pusey's case, strong conclusions were reached about the beliefs of public servants from often equivocal data (Bell 1993).[3] Studies have not asked actual policy makers and policy influentials *their* views on the sources of theoretical influence and the importance and role of theoretical ideas in policy-making. This chapter addresses that gap in the literature. It draws on interviews that asked respondents to: nominate the sources of ideas influential on economic policy-making; name those institutions and individuals important in contributing ideas to policy-making; discuss the importance of theoretical ideas in policy-making; and note influences on how they, as individuals, thought about policy issues.

In New Zealand economic policy changes were highly derivative of neoclassical and related schools of economics. The method of transmission into policy-making was often through domestically based policy makers, especially public servants from the Treasury and the Reserve Bank, and key ministers. These key figures, sometimes educated in graduate programmes in American economics departments in the late 1970s, were important in convincing their respective institutions and other policy makers to support the new policy directions. Often these theories had little empirical basis, were adopted quite self-consciously and were little modified in the to-and-fro of policy-making.

The situation was considerably more complex in Australia. While neoclassical economics was influential, it was challenged in the areas of labour-market and industry policy by corporatism and labourism.[4] Neoclassical economics in Australia drew on more empirical and less theoretical strains than found in New Zealand; it was applied in a less doctrinaire manner; and it faced greater modification in the policy process. Respondents nominated a greater variety of individuals and institutions as influential in contributing ideas to policy-making, including academic and international sources.

Thus while ideas are important, providing the broad canvas on which policy-making is carried out, they give only a partial understanding of why particular polices were adopted. Also important is the way ideas are adopted and modified in policy-making. Therefore, it is important to examine the role of institutions and key individuals and processes of economic policy-making, and to understand how key economic policy decisions are actually made.

Sources of economic ideas

New Zealand

Respondents nominated a variety of influences on economic policy in New Zealand, most of which can be seen as broadly neoclassical, or from related schools of economics (Table 2.1). Of key importance were those schools of economic analysis sometimes associated with the New Right such as Chicago School, New Classical and Public Choice, although respondents also saw general neoclassical ideas, New Institutional economics, Pragmatism and eclecticism as important. While a variety of schools were named as influential, a large majority of respondents saw some common basis to those ideas underpinning the reforms, and 60 percent characterised the level of influence as 'to a great extent'; possibly recognising their common derivation from a broadly neoclassical policy paradigm.[5] Key policy makers, such as the extremely influential former Treasury secretary Graham Scott and his co-authors, note the importance of Public Choice and Agency theory in influencing public sector and other changes. These other changes include the manager-contracted inflation targets in the Reserve Bank Act 1989 and the requirements of the Fiscal Responsibility Act 1994 (Scott and Gorringe 1989; Scott, Ball and Dale 1997). Another former Treasury secretary, Murray Horn (1995), notes the importance of Transaction Cost analysis on organisational design including that contained in the Reserve Bank Act and the Fiscal Responsibility Act constraining future actions of legislatures and administrators. Dr Roderick Deane, a former deputy governor of the Reserve Bank and State Services commissioner noted the influence of economist Edmund Phelps[6] and Chicago economist Milton Friedman on macroeconomic policy (Deane 1986; see also Evans et al 1996).

Theoretical ideas were often adopted self-consciously into economic policy-making. As Table 2.2 shows, 84 percent of respondents

Table 2.1 Nominated sources of economic ideas in New Zealand[1]

Description	Votes	Description	Votes
Chicago/Friedman	16	Public Choice	5
Free market	10	Thatcher/Reagan	5
Orthodox	10	Agency theory	4
Neoclassical[2]	8	Globalisation	4
New Right	7	Transaction Cost	4
Pragmatism	7	New Classical	3
US Economics[3]	6	Property Rights/L&E[5]	2
Neo-liberal[4]	6	Other	6
Eclecticism	5		

Notes
1. Respondents were asked, 'What were these ideas and where did they come from?' Multiple and unprompted responses.
2. Includes one 'Canterbury Department of Economics'.
3. Includes one 'overseas economics'.
4. Includes 'neo-liberal' plus 'Hayek', 'Austrian' and 'individualism'.
5. L&E is law and economics.

Table 2.2 Influence of theoretical economic ideas on views of individuals *by* Influence of theoretical ideas on economic policy in New Zealand[1]

Influence of ideas on individual	Influence of ideas on economic policy				Total[2]
	Very Important	Important	Some Importance	Little Importance	
Very Important	14	5	2	1	22 (27.5)
Important	10	9	3	-	22 (26.3)
Some Importance	14	9	1	2	26 (32.5)
Little Importance	3	3	3	1	10 (12.5)
No Importance	-	2	-	-	2 (1.3)
Total	41 (50)	28 (34.1)	9 (11)	4 (4.9)	82 (100%)

Notes
1. The questions asked were, 'How important are theoretical economic ideas in forming how *you* think about economic policy?' and 'How important do you think theoretical economic ideas were in influencing economic policy during 1984-93?' Missing cases: 5.
2. No respondents rated ideas as having 'no importance' on economic policy.

rated theoretical ideas as either 'very important' or 'important' in influencing economic policy, while a number of senior policy makers saw theory as having a highly significant role, even a dominant one, in driving change. One former departmental secretary and highly placed Treasury official interviewed by the author noted the theoretical nature of influential ideas and that 'contrary to what was going on in North America where empirical [work] was very strong, a lot of the debate in New Zealand [was] very unempirical.'[7] A former Treasury secretary noted that he saw policies as theories to be tested in the real world. For one departmental chief executive, economic policy change:

> was theory driven . . . it's been a theory driven revolution. Because, Contestability theory, for example, is hugely controversial, and still remains [so]. At the time we were depending on it in New Zealand there was very little empirical evidence. And that is still the case. It also had the logic of eighteenth century and seventeenth century political economists behind it as well. So we had a western tradition and notions of property that were critically important: Public Choice theory, Agency theory, Contestability theory, aspects of Transaction Cost analysis. Under that are the notions of ownership and voluntary transactions of ownership and property rights and the role of the state therein.[8]

Australia

In Australia, as Table 2.3 shows, respondents nominated a variety of sources of ideas as influential on economic policy. Neoclassical economics (or associated terms) were most often nominated, but the influence of Labourism–Corporatism and the Accord, Pragmatism and Keynesian economics were also noted. The sources of influence were more eclectic, less theoretically based, and derived from a broader range of economic schools than in New Zealand. Respondents recognised the greater diversity of sources with 47 percent seeing the reforms as underpinned 'to some extent' by a common basis of ideas, while 17 percent saw no common basis of ideas to the reforms. Michael Keating, a former secretary of Finance and of the Department of Prime Minister and Cabinet, rejects the belief that the policy agenda had been captured by 'neo-classical economic rationalists' (Keating 1994, 1). He does, however, see the influence on public policy of a number of propositions closely linked with economics, most of which could be seen as broadly neoclassical. These are 'the disposition in favour of competitive markets'; that 'government programs should focus on assisting consumers and beneficiaries, rather than suppliers'; the 'recognition of government failure . . . [which] has made us more cautious about fine tuning'; and the 'increasing attention [given] to the formation of expectations as part of the attempt to deal with inflation' (Keating 1994, 4–5). He also sees the economists' preference for transparency of information and decision making as having an influence on the machinery of policy-making.

Table 2.3 Nominated sources of economic ideas in Australia[1]

Description	Votes	Description	Votes
Neoclassical	19	Small Govt[2]	4
Accord/Labourism	9	Keynesian	2
Free market	8	Safety net	2
Chicago/Friedman	7	Swedish Economics	2
Orthodox	7	Supply-side	2
Globalisation	5	Soc Dem/collective	2
Pragmatism	5	Incremental	2
Economic rationalism	4	Other	6

Notes
1. Respondents were asked, 'What are these ideas and where do they come from?' Multiple responses.
2. Includes 'small government' plus 'Public Choice' and 'neo-liberal'.

Table 2.4 Influence of theoretical economic ideas on views of individuals *by* Influence of theoretical ideas on economic policy in Australia[1]

Influence of ideas on individual	Influence of ideas on economic policy				Total[2]
	Very Important	Important	Some Importance	Little Importance	
Very Important	16	7	1	1	25 (28.7)
Important	8	20	6	1	35 (40.2)
Some Importance	3	6	8	1	18 (20.7)
Little Importance	3	1	3	2	9 (10.3)
Total	30 (34.5)	34 (39.1)	18 (20.7)	5 (5.7)	87 (100%)

Notes

1. The questions asked were 'How important are theoretical economic ideas in forming how you think about economic policy?' and 'How important do you think theoretical economic ideas were in influencing economic policy during 1983–93? Missing cases: 6.
2. No respondents rated ideas as having 'no importance'.

Australian respondents rated theoretical ideas as important in influencing economic policy and in influencing their views of economic policy, with almost three quarters seeing theoretical economic ideas as either 'very important' or 'important' in influencing economic policy, and almost 70 percent rating theoretical ideas as 'very important' or 'important' in influencing how they individually thought about economic policy (Table 2.4). The Australian period of reform does however lack the self-conscious adoption of new theories found in New Zealand, and instead Australian policy makers saw themselves as drawing more heavily on empirically based economic research.[9] For example, former Treasury secretary, Tony Cole, saw pragmatic ideas and applied economic studies, especially those produced by the OECD and the World Bank, as most important in influencing policy—rather than '"high falutin" theory'. As well as the broadly neoclassical paradigm that dominated, there was the competing one of corporatism that influenced the Accord and the industry plans. It drew on models in operation in other countries, as well as tapping into the Australian history of labourism. According to Barry Hughes, a senior economics adviser in Treasurer Keating's office, there was an argument in the Labor Government that the Accord should look to European examples of corporatism:

> We ought to copy the successful consensus experience of particularly Austrian and some European countries. It was more than

controlling inflation—it was macroeconomic policy.

The economic summit copies absolutely the Austrian model. The Technical Committee was the English translation of the Austrian committee.

Contributing ideas to economic policy-making

Ideas do spontaneously appear in policy frameworks, but will often be developed and/or championed by individuals and institutions. In New Zealand, the source of theoretical influences in economic policy seems to be largely overseas, and especially US-based, schools of economics. However, their method of transmission into actual policy frameworks and decision making seems to be through domestically based policy makers and policy influentials (Tables 2.5 and 2.6). These include politicians, public servants, business people and business associations, with the New Zealand Treasury, the Reserve Bank and the Business Roundtable being particularly important. International organisations and thinkers are mentioned only on the margins. Key individuals, sometimes educated in graduate programmes in American economics departments in the 1970s, were sometimes important in introducing their respective institutions and other policy makers to the new ideas. These theories and ideas were then workshopped within those institutions. In Australia contributors of ideas were considerably more diverse in origin and included a large variety of politicians and public servants, but also union officials, academics and international organisations, as seen in Tables 2.7

Table 2.5 Institutions nominated as contributing ideas to economic policy-making in New Zealand[1]

Name	Votes
Treasury	29
NZBR	10
RBNZ	10
Federated Farmers	5
Cabinet	4
Employers Federation	2
Finance Sector	2

Notes
1. Respondents were asked, 'Who were the important individuals and institutions contributing ideas to economic policy during 1984–93?' Multiple and unprompted responses. Responses were split into one table each for institutions and individuals.

Table 2.6 Persons nominated as contributing ideas to economic policy-making in New Zealand

Name	Position	Votes	Name	Position	Votes
Douglas	Min Fin	36	Trotter	Business/NZBR	4
Scott	Sec Treas	24	Andrew[1]	Treas	3
Kerr	Treas/NZBR	22	Fancy	Treas/Comm	3
Deane	RBNZ/SSC/SOE	21	Holmes	NZPC	3
Prebble	Min SOEs/Ass Fin	12	Holt	Academic historian	3
Cameron	Treas/Business	9	de Cleene	Min Tax	2
Wilkinson	Treas/Business	9	Elworthy	Fed Farmers	2
Richardson	Min Fin	8	Fletcher	Business	2
Caygill	Min Fin	7	Friedman	Chicago economist	2
Gibbs	Business/NZBR	4	Galvin	Sec Treas	2
Lange	PM 1984–89	4	Grimes	RBA official	2
McKenzie	Treas/Sec DOL	4	Moore	PM 1990	2
Myers	Business/NZBR	4	Russell	Minister	2

Notes
1. Seconded to the opposition before the 1984 election.

and 2.8. This section will examine the role of the most important of these institutions and individuals in contributing ideas to policy-making.

Public servants

Public servants play an important role in the initiation, formulation and implementation of policy. They can also have a crucial role in fostering and promoting new ideas and new policy frameworks. In New Zealand, public servants, especially those in the Treasury and the Reserve Bank, were seen as key contributors of ideas to economic policy-making. Within these organisations, individuals such as Rob Cameron, Bryce Wilkinson, Graham Scott and Roger Kerr (in the Treasury at the time) and Roderick Deane (then in the Reserve Bank) were important in introducing their respective organisations to the new theories. As one former departmental chief described it:

> Scott, and Kerr and Cameron and Wilkinson in the Treasury were the main players, and there was [Deane] and one or two others in the Reserve Bank who were well disposed. We were the ones who wrote the papers that changed the ideas, who led the different groups. They were not the ideas of the heads of the government departments [at the time],[10] quite the contrary, they were not the ideas of the business community either.

By 1984, the Treasury had rejected the social democratic Keynes-ianism that had dominated in New Zealand for fifty years and were advocating a range of policies derived from neoclassical and related schools of economics (Goldfinch 1997). These new policy ideas were generated in three ways. First, the Treasury was making considerable efforts to recruit trained economists, so that by the early 1970s the organisation was largely dominated by them. Second, promising young bureaucrats were sent overseas, especially to the United States, for postgraduate training, where they picked up the fashionable ideas then being taught in some American economics and business departments (Choat 1993). For example, during the late 1970s New Zealand Treasury officials Rob Cameron and Bryce Wilkinson received Harkness Fellowships to study in the United States, and were seen by a number of respondents as important in introducing New Classical, Public Choice and New Institutional ideas into the Treasury. According to one former Treasury official:

> [Wilkinson] had been over at Massachusetts Institute of Technology (MIT) and did Dornbusch's courses and a lot of reading on monetary policy. Cameron had a Harkness scholarship and went to the Kennedy school, and he had done a lot of the microeconomic reading that I hadn't caught onto—Agency, Public Choice . . . intellectually that was a shot in the arm. We were reading heavily this microstuff.

Third, the ideas introduced by new graduates and especially the postgraduate trainees, were further developed and applied to the New Zealand situation within the Treasury itself. Other Treasury officials, encouraged by the new ideas, began to read up on these new theoretical directions. While the Treasury played a highly significant role in policy implementation, it was to some extent unhappy with the direction of economic policy as it developed under the Muldoon Government of 1975–84.[11] The poor performance of New Zealand's economy after 1974 and Muldoon's often erratic economic management gave further stimulus to longer term policy development. In 1977 two policy divisions, Economics I (internal) and Economics II (external), were set up. Originally Economics II looked mostly at trade protection and economic relations, particular interests of Secretary N.V. Lough at the time. Under the leadership of Roger Kerr (later of the Business Roundtable) and Graham Scott during the early 1980s, Economics II was pivotal in developing the policies that would be set down in the important 1984 post-election briefing to the Labour Government, *Economic Management*.[12] The Treasury was also extremely important in developing the rationale and structure of the public sector reforms, which built heavily on Public Choice and New Institutional economics (Goldfinch 1998).

In the Reserve Bank there was also some policy development and questioning of existing frameworks. According to a number of respondents, senior Reserve Bank official Roderick Deane was central in introducing pro-liberalisation ideas and New Classical and Chicago School economics into the Reserve Bank. The Bank also had a relatively independent publishing outlet, the *Reserve Bank Bulletin* and a greater focus on research than the Treasury. In a series of articles and books in the late 1970s and early 1980s, many authored or co-authored by Deane, the Reserve Bank questioned existing policy frameworks (see, for example Deane, Nicholl and Smith 1983). Although these criticisms were often muted (as they were criticisms of the government policies of the time), many of the policy proposals given reflected the influence of neoclassical and Chicago School and New Classical ideas.

In Australia, the Treasury gradually adopted neoclassical economics

Table 2.7 Institutions nominated as contributing ideas to economic policy-making in Australia[1]

Name	Votes	Name	Votes
Treasury	38	Cabinet	4
OECD	19	Campbell Inquiry	4
RBA	19	CIS	4
ACTU	18	EPAC	4
DPMC	15	Institute of Public Affairs	4
Industry Commission	16	MTIA	4
BCA	13	Evatt Foundation	3
Department of Finance	13	Financial markets	3
IMF	10	Media	3
Ministerial offices[2]	9	Think-tanks	3
Academic economists[3]	7	World Bank	3
ACOSS	4	Other govt depts	2

Notes
1. Respondents were asked, 'Who were the important institutions and individuals contributing ideas to economic policy-making in Australia during 1983–93?' Multiple and unprompted responses. Responses were split into one table each for institutions and individuals.
2. Includes three each of Treasurer's Office and Prime Minister's Office.
3. Includes two ANU economists.

under the strong leadership of Secretary John Stone as shown in Whitwell's (1986) much cited book *The Treasury Line*. In response to the questionable economic management of the Whitlam Government and the stagflation of the 1970s, and drawing on its research programme staffed by highly trained economists, the Treasury had largely rejected Keynesian economics by the second half of the 1970s and moved 'closer to a purely neoclassical stance' (234). While there were still marginal elements of Keynesian analysis, policy advice was largely based on the belief that 'governments were essentially impotent in their ability to reduce unemployment directly . . . [T]he emphasis throughout was on the economic rationality of the agent'. The Treasury also believed with 'certainty, that market forces operated always to move toward the equilibration of supply and demand in all markets and hence towards the full use of capital and labour' (235). The Treasury was split in 1976 into a Ministry of Finance and a Treasury, and this neoclassical view continued in the Ministry as well as the Treasury.

In the Reserve Bank of Australia there was also a gradual move towards the adoption of neoclassical economics and developing support for deregulation. At times this change led to acrimonious debate within the Bank. Partly due to the influence of the strongly pro-liberalisation official Austin Holmes and partly to the retirement of several 'regulators', by the late 1970s the Bank had become strongly in favour of market liberalisation. This view was cemented by the appointment of deregulation advocate Bob Johnston as Governor in 1982 by the Coalition Treasurer John Howard.

Politicians

Politicians, or more correctly, ministers, are constitutionally responsible for policy decisions and are identified as such by a voting public. Some may be policy activists wishing to make their mark on the direction of their country and so come into power with strong views on what policies should be introduced. Previous life and work experiences, education and/ or their reading, may give them certain agendas or core beliefs that underpin the way they view policy. These ideas and agendas often evolve and change once they gain power and have to operate within a government and discuss their ideas with others such as close advisers. According to a former New Zealand finance minister, for a politician entering a government:

There is a stock of intellectual capital you run down unless you rebuild it. But there is not a single source of ideas [with which this is done]—constituents lobby you, officials advise you, interest groups come up with ideas all the time.

Roger Douglas, Finance Minister from 1984 to 1988, had worked before the 1984 election to develop a policy programme, along similar lines to that outlined by the Treasury in *Economic Management* (Oliver 1989). In this, he received strong input from Treasury official Doug Andrew who was seconded to the opposition, and Labour Party researcher Geoff Swier. His policy agenda, despite its apparent difference to Labour policy traditions and the 1984 manifesto, was to dominate for the life of the Labour Government until it lost power in 1990.[13] Often seen as a key 'ideas man', Douglas developed ideas largely through discussion and his own experiences.[14] Douglas was not seen as a big reader by a number of respondents, although he was influenced by the management theorist Peter Drucker's writings and by some American think-tanks.[15]

In 1988, David Caygill succeeded Douglas as the Labour Government's Finance Minister. Caygill's training in economics was a key factor in his understanding of economic policy. Also important was

Table 2.8 Persons nominated as contributing ideas to economic policy-making in Australia

Name	Position	Votes	Name	Position	Votes
P. Keating	Treasurer/PM	22	Johnston	Gov RBA	4
Garnaut	PMO/Academic	14	M. Keating	Sec Fin/DPMC	4
Kelty	Sec ACTU	12	Porter	Australian economist	4
Hawke	PM	9	Smith	TO/Treasury	4
B. Fraser	Treas/Gov RBA	7	Willis	Min IR/Fin	5
Higgins	Sec Treas	7	Cole	TO/Treas	3
Walsh	Min Fin	7	Crean	Pres ACTU	3
D. Russell	TO/PMO	7	Holmes	RBA official	3
Gregory	ANU economist	6	Pitchford	ANU economist	3
Thatcher/ism	British PM 79–90	6	Preston		3
Button	Min Indus	5	Regan/ism	US Pres 1980–8	3
Corden	Australian economist	5	Chapman	ANU economist	2
Friedman	Chicago economist	5	Edwards	TO/PMO	2
Morgan	Treas official	5	Fitzgerald	Dep Sec Fin	2
Sedwick	Sec Fin	5	Hayek	Austrian economist	2
Stone	Sec Treas	5	K. Henry	Treas	2
Dawkins	Min Fin	4	Hilmer	Academic/Business	2
T. Evans	Sec Treas	4	Howe	Dep PM	2
Gruen	ANU economist	4	Sheehan	TO/Academic	2

his reading of the publications of the policy advice body, the New Zealand Planning Council, from late 1970s on, which 'no one could accuse of being radical [as they were] very orthodox and commonsense.' Caygill sees the policy of the Labour Government reflecting this economic orthodoxy of the time:

> You are hard pressed to find a single decision of any significance [made by my Government] that doesn't fit well within prevailing economic orthodoxy. The [previous] governments had tried one thing after another. Someone said the only thing the government hadn't tried was economic orthodoxy. What people are still surprised at is, you had a Government that stuck as rigorously to an orthodox line and moved as rapidly as we did. You had a Government that was interested in economic advice [and] wanted to behave coherently in economic policy terms, did so, and within three years we got through the Planning Council agenda and got beyond the Planning Council.

The way ideas develop can vary from politician to politician. According to Edwards (1996), the Australian Treasurer (1984–91) and Prime Minister (1991–6) Paul Keating developed some of his political ideas through his long talks with political figures and through his extensive time as a member of parliament. Not generally seen as a reader by a number of respondents, he was quick to learn from verbal briefings by his Treasury officials and key advisers in his office. This was to the extent that he eventually considered himself having a greater understanding of economic management than that held by his advisers. Later, he relied heavily on a smaller group of trusted advisers largely in his office, especially Don Russell, as well as his close relationship with ACTU Secretary Bill Kelty. Prime Minister Bob Hawke, a former research officer, advocate and president of the ACTU, had formative experiences as a member of the Reserve Bank Board and on the Committee of Inquiry into Australia's manufacturing industry which gave him 'a detailed understanding of both the weaknesses and opportunities for Australian manufacturing industry' (Hawke 1994, 82). A considerable reader of ministerial briefs, Hawke also relied on key advisers such as Ross Garnaut in his office, as well as business 'mates' such as transport magnate Sir Peter Abeles for information and ideas. Industry Minister John Button also saw talking to business people as an important source of information and ideas, and conducted a number of overseas trips to study industry.

Academe

The relationship of economic policy-making bureaucracies and politicians to the academic world will influence the way economic ideas are taken up and the way the beliefs of bureaucrats are challenged. A number of New Zealand academics attempted to make a contribution to public policy debate. These included economists Paul Dalziel, Brian Easton, Susan St John and Claudia Scott, and political scientist Jonathan Boston. Some were commissioned to investigate certain aspects of public policy, such as Professor Garry Hawke who wrote an influential report (1988) into the post-compulsory education system (Grace 1990). While a number of respondents saw some academics as important, for example Sir Frank Holmes, most took pains to note the limited role played by academics in the changes, or saw professional academics as 'unhelpful', presumably because they were not necessarily wholehearted supporters. A former Treasury secretary's comment is typical:

> The amazing thing in terms of this whole reform programme is the relatively weak contribution that academics have made. They weren't as actively involved in public policy comment and public policy as you get in other countries. They were pretty much a negative force if anything . . . apart from Canterbury [economics department], which would have been more positive.[16]

This lack of regard for academic commentators and for their influence in economic policy reflected a number of factors in New Zealand public policy. First, the high educational achievement of some top public servants bred, amongst a number of them, a certain level of self-pride. This led them to be quite confident in their own beliefs and dismissive of those who did not share them. Second, a number of public servants had become frustrated with dealing with the more erratic economic policy management of Robert Muldoon and welcomed the chance to follow new policy directions. This manifested itself after 1984 in an element of annoyance towards those who would oppose or question the new policy directions and the 'mission' of those promoting those directions—something approaching 'either you are for us, or you are against us'. Third, few academics obtained important advisory positions equivalent to Garnaut and Hughes in the Australian ministerial offices, although, as noted, there was involvement in inquiries. Fourth, and possibly most important, New Zealand is a country that does not value or respect theoretical and policy debate, or see a role for academics in that policy debate.

This lack of respect for theoretical debate and for academics manifested itself in a number of ways. When not ignored, academic critics in New Zealand were sometimes responded to with some harshness. There were personal attacks at an Association of Economics meeting after Zanetti and others' (1984) mild critique of the Treasury 1984 post-election briefing paper. In 1991, Finance Minister Ruth Richardson called the 15 members of the Auckland University economics department 'shallow and unscholarly' (amongst other less restrained comments) for pointing out in a letter to a national newspaper that the Government's pro-cyclical fiscally deflationary policies would in all likelihood intensify the 1991 recession (Richardson 1995, 116–7).[17]

In Australia, relations between the public bureaucracies and policy makers and the academic community have been considerably warmer. While a number of respondents were dismissive of the role of academics, others were more positive, naming some academics as contributors of ideas. Economics Society gatherings, regularly attended by many senior bureaucrats and academics in Canberra, facilitated the exchange of ideas, and certain academics (often Australian National University (ANU) economists) were seen as directly influential in education, labour relations and social policy issues (Armitage 1996; Chapman 1996). Several academics made contributions through their roles in ministerial offices. These included Ross Garnaut in the Prime Minister Hawke's office and Barry Hughes in the Treasurer Paul Keating's office, with Garnaut's influence continuing once he returned to the academe.

International organisations

Certain international organisations, such as the International Monetary Fund (IMF), the World Bank and the OECD, produce a variety of research publications, sometimes of an extremely high quality. Most of these publications are of a strongly pro-market liberalisation and neo-liberal stance. Consultations are carried out by the OECD and the IMF with the Reserve Bank and the Treasury during preparation of their respective country reports. Senior New Zealand bureaucrats, such as former secretary of the Department of Labour, Jas Mackenzie, and former deputy governor of the Reserve Bank, Roderick Deane, have held positions in such organisations as the IMF, the World Bank and the OECD, as well as attending meetings of these organisations (Choat 1993). Commentators, some of whom are former senior public servants, have seen these organisations as being influential in New Zealand (Evans et al 1996). A number of senior Australian officials have also held positions in these organisations. For example, Tony Cole, a former secretary to the Australian Treasury, spent two years as a senior World Bank official in the early 1980s. According to Cole, these years were crucial in developing his views on economic policy.

There was some ambivalence towards the OECD in the New Zealand Treasury during the early 1980s,[18] although later OECD reports have often lauded the New Zealand reforms, including those in the public sector (OECD 1996). While the IMF was important in the debates over GST in New Zealand and some mention was made of the role of the OECD as noted, Tables 2.6–2.8 show these international organisations received considerably more nominations as contributors to ideas in Australia than in New Zealand. In addition, a number of respondents in Australia noted the importance of IMF, OECD and World Bank writings on their perceptions and understanding of economic policy.

Information sharing between officials travelling to other countries to consult with other public servants and to study policy reforms can be an important source of ideas (Choat 1993). There was also some information sharing between New Zealand and Australia, with a former senior Treasury official noting that the Campbell Report, into the Australian financial system, had some influence on financial liberalisation in New Zealand, and with New Zealand Reserve Bank officials travelling to Australia to examine the Australian float of the dollar. Australian Treasury Secretary John Stone also visited New Zealand. It is possible that the close international ties that can develop between policy makers, through involvement and secondments in such organisations as the OECD and the IMF can produce a consensus—such as the so-called Washington Consensus—that may not always reflect the views of the wider academic community (see Appendix Two).

Interest and functional groups

Other sources of policy ideas are interest groups and think-tanks, although often they might act as transmitters of ideas rather than their generators.

Due to the elitist beliefs of policy makers and the influence of Public Choice theories, interest groups were at times excluded from policy-making in New Zealand after 1984, especially if they were not whole-hearted supporters of the new policy directions. A notable exception to this was the Business Roundtable, which provided a plethora of policy documents and submissions on myriad policy issues. Often quoted at length by a sometimes extremely compliant media, and with close ties to the economic policy bureaucracy and some politicians, the Roundtable submissions were extremely important in a number of issues including corporate takeover and industrial relations legislation. The radical individual contracting introduced by the Employment Contracts Act 1991 reflected the influence of the libertarian line pushed by the Business Roundtable in its many submissions and in the book *Freedom at Work* produced by Roundtable employee Penelope Brook (1990). The occasionally extreme market liberalisation agenda of the Business Roundtable also provided support for the deregulation efforts of the Labour and National governments as well as maintaining pressure for further liberalisation. After its own research programme Federated Farmers came to support liberalisation by the 1984 election, including the removal of agricultural subsidies, while the Employers' Federation also helped develop support for liberalisation.

In Australia a number of think-tanks and business groups also attempted to influence public policy and were nominated as important in contributing ideas. While some might have had less direct success than that experienced by the Business Roundtable in New Zealand, they did manage to have some indirect influence on policy formation and the language and agenda of policy debate, especially in industrial relations.

Key business people could also be important contributors of ideas through their close ties to politicians. For example, airline magnate Peter Abeles' close relationship to Hawke has already been noted, and businessman and Business Roundtable member Alan Gibbs also had a close relationship with Roger Douglas in New Zealand. These ties could also develop through appointments to such bodies as State Owned Enterprises (SOEs) and various taskforces and inquiries. New Zealand businessman and one-time Business Roundtable chairman, Sir Ron Trotter, played such a role in New Zealand (Deane 1994). Trade unions had surprisingly little influence over policy and policy debate in New Zealand, even under a Labour Government, but in Australia the ACTU and its General Secretary Bill Kelty were important contributors of ideas, both through the Accord process and through the personal relationships between the members of the Government and Kelty.[19] The media can also be a source of ideas for policy makers. Particular columnists were occasionally influential in an indirect way, although media often served more as an avenue for the selling of policies and as a method of tracking popular opinion for politicians, rather than as an original source of ideas (Gittins 1995).

The financial sector also had a role in contributing ideas to the economic policy process. Like the media this was not always in terms of agenda setting (although there may have been elements of this in financial liberalisation), but in terms of maintaining pressure for further liberalisation. Financial analysts were sometimes sought by the media for their views on policy, and market reactions were seen as indicators of the quality (or lack thereof) of policy decisions. In some cases, especially in New Zealand, important members of the financial sector had previously been public servants or Reserve Bank officials involved in earlier reforms and liberalisation.

How individuals form their views regarding economic policy issues

There are a variety of influences on how individuals form their views on economic policy, with just over half seeing experience as the most important factor (Figure 2.3).[20] At the same time, while 84 percent of New Zealand respondents noted theoretical ideas as 'important' or 'very important' in influencing economic policy, only 54 percent saw ideas as 'very important' or 'important' in determining the way they as individuals thought about economic policy issues (Table 2.2). Australian respondents (Table 2.4) saw little difference between the importance of ideas on economic policy (with almost 74 percent rating ideas as 'important' or 'very important'), and the importance of ideas on the way they thought about policy (with almost 70 percent rating ideas as 'important' or 'very important').

What conclusions can be drawn from these responses? First, there may be a reluctance amongst some respondents to say they are heavily influenced by theories. They may prefer to be seen (and see themselves) as pragmatic realists, responding to the situation at hand, rather than plucking some theory out of the air. (They are quite willing, of course, to see others as ideas driven.) Second, part of the answer may lie in the fact that personal experience does not give an understanding of the world apart from ideas. Ideas, or in this case economic theories, exist as part of a more-or-less coherent framework, or policy paradigm, which provides

Figure 2.3 Strongest influence on individual views on economic policy[1]

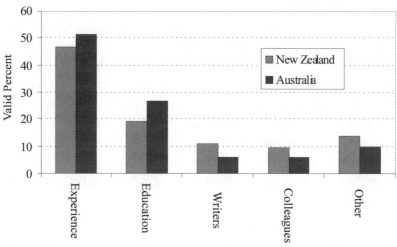

Notes
1. Respondents were asked, 'If I asked you what was the strongest influence on the way you think about economic policy issues, what would it be?' Missing cases: 14 NZ; 11 Australia.

concepts and language to describe, understand and give solutions to real life policy problems (Hall 1993; Hausman 1992). This policy paradigm gives structure and meaning to a complex and changing world and provides a way of understanding what personal experience actually means in policy terms. This view of how ideas function as a way of interpreting and understanding experience is given some credence by a number of comments by respondents. According to one former New Zealand Treasury secretary (who saw practical experience as the most important influence on his views on economic policy):

> What was important was having a consistent approach, a frame-work, a way of approaching policy, a set of questions you would ask, information and incentive type questions that drive you to certain answers. You read an enormous amount, you are interacting with people everyday, you are matching that against your own experience. Clearly there isn't one idea or one set of ideas.

For many policy makers and those attempting to influence policy, their education and their reading of economic and other literature is a crucial path by which ideas influence their view of policy and so enter the policy-making framework. In this study 30 percent of New Zealand respondents saw their education or reading as the most important influence. In Australia, 28 percent of respondents saw education as important, with a further 6 percent citing their reading of certain writers. Educational training, especially in such a strongly paradigmatically driven field as economics, may provide the crucial framework for understanding and dealing with reality and for providing policy solutions. The dominance of particular schools of economics in policy-making may be partly explained by the large number of trained economists in key policy-making positions and within other elite groups (Pusey 1991).[21] As Table 2.9 shows, 72 percent of Australian respondents had received an economics education. Of these 65 people, 41 were educated to post-graduate or doctorate level. An economics education may give a shared language and set of concepts amongst policy elites with which to describe and suggest solutions to policy problems, which may in turn facilitate the building of consensus on policy directions.

Individuals do not always form their views on policy in isolation. Instead they test their perceptions against the views of their colleagues, modify their views in discussion and may even be directed to think of certain issues in certain ways because of the views of influential colleagues or because of the literature these colleagues recommend. Almost 10 percent of New Zealand and 6 percent of Australian respondents saw the views of their colleagues as the most important influence on the way they thought about economic policy. Certain individuals, such as Deane in the Reserve Bank and Wilkinson, Cameron and Scott in the Treasury were highly influential within their respective organisations and on members of their organisation, as already noted. Roger Kerr, formally of the Treasury but appointed Executive Director of the Business Roundtable

Table 2.9 Highest level of education by degree/diploma major in Australia[1]

Highest level of Education	Major Econ	Bus/ Acct	Arts	Law	Science	Other	None	Total
High School	-	-	-	-	-	-	2	2 (2.2)
Undergrad deg/dip	24	4	3	4	3	-	-	38 (42.2)
Postgrad deg	13	1	4	1	-	1	-	20 (22.2)
PhD	28	-	1		1	-	-	30 (33.3)
Total	65 (72.2)	5 (5.6)	8 (8.9)	5 (5.6)	4 (4.4)	1 (1.1)	2 (2.2)	90 (100%)

Notes
1. Missing cases: 3. Unfortunately degree and degree major was not asked in New Zealand.

in 1986, exerted powerful influence on the direction of policy advocacy of the organisation and, by extension, to the views of the CEOs of private companies that were members. In Australia, Austin Holmes played a key role in introducing ideas in the Reserve Bank, while Chris Higgins was mentioned by respondents as playing a similar role in the Treasury.

Why are some ideas taken up and not others?

Despite claims that 'There is No Alternative' made at the time and since, it was not inevitable that the policy responses made during the 1980s would be derivative of certain schools of economics and (in Australia) aspects of corporatism and labourism. There is never one set of ideas and answers to policy questions and problems, and there are always competing paradigms, at least in the social sciences. In economics for example, while some broad variant of neoclassical economics is the current, although challenged, orthodoxy in economics, this and the major competing paradigms, Keynesianism and Marxism, include a host of competing and occasionally overlapping schools (for example, Cole, Cameron, and Edwards 1991). A wide variety of theoretical and research work, not strictly within any of these three paradigms, is carried out by institutional economists, economic geographers and political economists of various shades. Neither is there one 'neoliberal' consensus across the world that would adequately explain the adoption of economic restructuring, while the world exhibits a variety of successful economic and social systems. Even the much touted 'Washington consensus' is according to Hazledine (1998, 57) 'already crumbling, if it ever really existed'.

The questions remain. First, why did leading policy makers in both countries adopt elements of neoclassical economics? Second, why did their adoption differ in the two countries, both in terms of the relative success of competing paradigms in Australia and in the less doctrinaire way neoclassical economics was applied when it was successful in influencing policy? I will examine each of these in turn.

As New Zealand and Australia are English speaking, predominantly Anglo-Saxon countries, it was easier to look to the United States and the United Kingdom for sources of new ideas, through such avenues as educational, literary, cultural and institutional ties. The economics education received by many key policy makers reflected the dominance of the broadly neoclassical orthodoxy in the Anglo-Saxon world and especially in American universities, where many had received parts of their education. Some of the adoption of neoclassical ideas in leading policy institutions then, such as in the respective Treasuries, can be explained as reflecting the revitalisation of neoclassical economics within the wider economics community (see Whitwell 1986). The ties with international organisations, such as the IMF and World Bank, provided further support to this neoclassical consensus. The portrayal of American and British models as desirable by international (including internationally owned domestic media) and English speaking media, especially the *Economist*, may have also been a factor, and was noted as such by a number of respondents (see also Deane 1994).

Second, neoclassical ideas provided both a ready explanation for the apparent, relatively poor economic performance of the two countries since the mid-1970s, and a set of simple and ideologically attractive policy responses. As Painter (1995, 292) argues, old ideas:

> . . . become not so much 'wrong' or 'bad', but politically and organisationally inappropriate. The ascendancy of new ideas is due in part to their practical utility for discrediting failed ones— that is, for interpreting the meaning of failure—as well as for the relevance of their prescriptions for success.

These neoclassical policy responses in both countries were largely 'off the shelf', seemingly simple to operate. In New Zealand, they advocated a movement away from the social democratic Keynesianism of the past. In Australia, the movement was away from the questionable wisdom of some of Whitlam's policies and the, at times, inconsistent economic polices of the Fraser Government of 1975–83.

In New Zealand, there was an element of reaction to the policies of the previous National Government of Robert Muldoon (1975–84). While Muldoon's economic policies were generally in the broad New Zealand tradition of what might be called an eclectic social democratic Keynesianism with 'stop-go' policies and pre-election fiscal boosts, he also engaged in a number of policy innovations of questionable wisdom. For example, his Government undertook a number of capital intensive investments of doubtful commercial benefit known as 'Think Big'; he introduced an expensive universal superannuation scheme; and his regime was forever tarnished when, after losing the 1984 election, he refused for a time to devalue the New Zealand dollar in the face of an expensive run on the currency and despite the advice of the incoming Government.

There is an element of 'what would Muldoon do?—we will do the opposite' apparent in the adoption of neoclassical ideas. Muldoon had, in some policy elites' eyes at least, discredited government intervention in the economy as, according to one former Treasury secretary, when 'you have doubts about the effectiveness of government intervention, then you go back to market forms. Government intervention didn't work—it made things worse.' Economic theories seemed to explain not only why the New Zealand economy under Muldoon was not performing as well as hoped, and so helped to discredit his economic management (or lack thereof), but also gave simple and ideologically attractive new policy responses. For the Australian Treasury, as Whitwell (1986) shows, neoclassical ideas offered some explanation of Australia's relatively poor economic performance and helped to discredit the Whitlam Government's policies.

While certain policy makers and politicians adopted neoclassical ideas in both countries, the degree to which these ideas influenced actual policy decisions differed considerably. The New Zealand Treasury may only differ in degree in its adoption of neoclassical and related theories compared to the Australian Treasury and a number of other Treasuries in other Westminster systems, and other policy bodies in other economic systems (see, for example, Whitwell 1986). Other countries may also have powerful politicians that become enamoured of certain ideas and ideologies and/or the policy prescriptions of their ministries. What distinguishes the New Zealand case from the Australian one, and from many others, is not only that certain schools of economics influenced policy advice from key institutions, but that the peculiarities of New Zealand's policy-making and institutional structures allowed this policy advice to be reflected in actual policy decisions, with theories relatively unmodified in the policy process. This will be explored at greater length throughout this book.

Conclusion: The role of ideas in policy-making

Ideas do matter and can have an immense impact on policy decisions and even on how policy is made. The resurgent neoclassical and related schools of economics, taken up by key policy makers in the late 1970s and early 1980s, provided both an explanation of the apparent relative economic decline of Australia and New Zealand and a ready set of simple and ideologically attractive policy solutions. In New Zealand, Public Choice theories, along with the elitist beliefs of some leading policy makers and politicians, gave a rationale for excluding some groups from policy formation. New Institutional economics was influential in the reform of the public sector, at the same time providing direction on the design of institutions and policy instruments, so as to shield both instruments and institutions from opportunistic politicians and 'rent seeking' interest groups.

Australia and New Zealand were significantly different in which ideas were adopted in policy-making and the degree to which these ideas were modified in the to-and-fro of policy-making, however. New Zealand provides a dramatic example of a 'paradigm change' in policy-making. It shows how this policy paradigm can become immensely dominant in a wide variety of public policy areas, even after some of the theories contained in the paradigm have fallen somewhat from favour in the academic world. Before 1984 the 'policy paradigm' consisted of a broad and eclectic, social democratic Keynesianism. After 1984 there was a rapid and comprehensive adoption of a new paradigm, broadly based on neoclassical economics, and, once established, this became highly dominant in policy-making, gradually taking over more policy areas. Those seeking to extend its logic and coverage found much of the groundwork, such as developing terms and concepts, had already been laid. For example, the language and policy advice of the policy paradigm quickly took over the macro and microeconomic policy settings; then extended its reach to the management and ownership of the public sector, institutional design, and then to broadcasting and education policy. Eventually, after the National Government took power in 1990, the paradigm extended its reach to the hitherto relatively untouched areas of social policy and the labour-market.

In Australia, while neoclassical economics was extremely important, there was a less dramatic change from previous policy frameworks. The previous Coalition Government (1975–83) had also adopted elements of neo-liberal and neoclassical policies with the intention of 'fighting inflation first'. Neoclassical economics also faced successful challenges from corporatism and labourism in aspects of economic policy, such as industry policy and the labour-market. Where neoclassical economics was dominant in policy decisions, it often lacked the theoretical purity and doctrinaire application found in New Zealand. For example, while macroeconomic policy was mostly deflationary, this varied at times with Keynesian stimulus used in 1983 and 1991, and a less consistent use (at least until 1993) of monetary policy aimed solely at deflation. Social policy, at least under the Labor Government up to 1996, was better able to resist the spread of neoclassical ideas.

As well as ideas being important, institutions and interests matter too. The role of ideas in policy-making should not be considered separately from the institutional structures and culture of the country in which policy-making is being considered. The simpleness of policy structures and institutions, the way policy-making was conducted and the lack of an intellectual culture in New Zealand allowed ideas-driven policy makers, and the theories they were promoting, to dominate policy-making and achieve their policy aims to a remarkable degree. Those shown as influential in contributing ideas to economic policy-making in New Zealand in Tables 2.5 and 2.6, are often those nominated as having been directly influential on a number of select policy decisions analysed in later chapters of this book. In contrast, in Australia's complex federal system, with its greater institutional density, higher quality media, greater level of intellectual debate, and with a government more committed to consensus building, the dominant paradigm of neoclassical economics was successfully challenged in industry and labour-market policy by those pushing competing policy paradigms of corporatism and labourism. Influence was more diffuse on policy decisions; there were differences between those nominated as influential in contributing ideas and those nominated as directly influencing policy decisions. Similarly, theories faced greater modification in the more institutionally dense policy-making. Subsequent chapters of this book will demonstrate in detail how economic policy is made in New Zealand and Australia.

3
Economic Policy-making in New Zealand

In New Zealand's unitary state, economic policy-making structures can be simple and influence can be highly centralised and personalised. Under first-past-the-post, cabinet controlled the legislature, while the Treasury was by far the most powerful public sector policy body, and the Reserve Bank was in control of monetary policy after 1984. After 1990, the newly formed Department of Prime Minister and Cabinet assumed importance as the site in which a number of important committees and taskforces were located and serviced. At a time when most interest groups were excluded from policy development, the Business Roundtable, with ties to both the Labour and National governments and to the Treasury, and with the resources to produce a wide variety of policy submissions and reports on myriad policy issues, was able to wield important influence over some policy directions. Groups that would be expected to be influential during a Labour government, such as the trade union movement and the extra-parliamentary Labour Party, often found themselves excluded from economic policy-making.

Before 1984, New Zealand had a strong tradition of participation in policy-making where major interest groups were formally and informally incorporated into the process. Governments saw themselves as bound to follow party manifestos and election promises (Mulgan 1997b). This belief in consultation showed itself in a number of ways. Throughout the postwar period there were a number of formal mechanisms established to facilitate interest group participation in policy-making. For example, a 1940 Stablilization Conference led, in 1942, to the establishment of the Economic Stabilization Commission which was supported by a staff of government officials, chaired by the Secretary to the Treasury, and contained representation from the private sector and from unions (Moriarty 1945; 1956; Simkin 1948–9). The Commission was, however, mainly concerned with price and income control in a war economy, and its influence gradually diminished until its abolition in 1950. In 1953, the National Housing Conference, with representation from a variety of groups including those associated with the building industry, was held to address the shortage of houses arising from the war and set targets for the production of houses. These were subsequently met (Marshall 1983). In 1960 the Industrial Development Conference examined ways of encouraging industry. This was followed by the Export Development Conference in 1963, attended by representatives from a wide range of interest groups. These groups made a number of proposals adopted by later governments, such as tax exemptions on income from exports and on export development, and special depreciation allowances (Low 1970). Over 18 months during 1963–4, the Agricultural Development Conference investigated a number of agricultural issues, while over a number of months in 1968–9, and again in 1972, the National Development Conference (NDC) inquired into longer term prospects for the economy. Out of the NDC arose the National Development Council and 16 sector councils. The National Development Council was chaired by the deputy prime minister and included two departmental heads, as well as representatives from functional interest groups and a number of chosen individuals. It was served by a small group of officials and private individuals known as the Target Advisory Group (TAG); both TAG and the council were serviced by a secretariat based in Treasury (Galvin 1991). The council was abolished in 1973 and its planning responsibility moved to the Cabinet Committee on Policy and Priorities (which had taken over from the Cabinet Economic Committee).

In 1961, the independent Monetary and Economic Council was established to report on economic policy and to make public recommendations. This was abolished in 1977 and its functions were taken over by the New Zealand Planning Council, which had been established after the 1976 Task Force on Economic and Social Planning chaired by Sir Frank Holmes. The Planning Council was in operation from April 1977, although its enabling statute, the New Zealand Planning Act 1977, did not come into force until December 1977.[1] The council's functions and purpose, as redefined by the new New Zealand Planning Act 1982 became 'to monitor and report on trends, prospects and options in relation to the social, economic and cultural development of New Zealand.'[2] Successive chairs included Sir Frank Holmes, Ian Douglas and Professor Gary Hawke. Members included Ministers George Gair and Bill Birch, future Reserve Bank governor Don Brash, future commissioner for the environment Helen Hughes, a future State Services commissioner Mervyn Probine, Federation of Labour Vice-President Ted Thompson, future Human Rights commissioner Pamela Jefferies and others held to be broadly representative of the community.[3] The Secretary to the Treasury was an ex-officio member. The Planning Council was abolished in 1991, on the Treasury's recommendation.

Formal structures existed to facilitate consultation, and, because New Zealand is small, informal networks also developed that allowed access of individuals and interest groups to key policy makers and ministers. While this 'intimacy' thesis has been severely undermined by Harris' (1995) analysis and it is clearly not the case that all voters had equal access to the government, leaders of interest groups had substantial access to policy makers. This consultation continued under the National Government of Prime Minister Robert Muldoon (1975–84). While his regime has been described by Kelsey (1995, 26) as 'authoritarian' since he increasingly centralised power around himself, particularly in his final term, access of the main business associations, the Federation of Labour and professional groups to policy-making was still considerable. The most notable exception to this was the unilateral introduction by Muldoon, at the time both Prime Minister and Minister of Finance, of the wage and price freeze in 1982.[4] Muldoon also made a largely successful effort to keep election promises.

Economic policy-making after the election of the Labour Government

After 1984, the Labour Government, and to a lesser extent the National Government after 1990, moved away from consultative processes of policy-making. Shortly after the 1984 election, an economic summit was held with representation from the unions, business and social groups.

Even before the summit reported, however, the economic policy direction had been decided. Policy formation instead came to be personalised around a few key ministers, officials and business leaders, and was often made in secret, while party manifestos and party traditions were sometimes disregarded.

Formal structures in economic policy-making that did exist were often bypassed. For example, while the Labour Government had such structures as officials' co-ordination committees and the Cabinet Policy Committee, as well as cabinet committees in a variety of areas, to keep departments and others informed, key decisions were often made by the Minister of Finance, associate ministers and key (mostly Treasury) officials working outside official channels. The Reserve Bank was largely left the responsibility for monetary policy. There was a deliberate effort by Prime Minister Bolger to use formal processes after the election of the National Government in 1990, with a greater use of cabinet committees and revival of officials' committees to shadow these cabinet committees, as well as the establishment of some consultative mechanisms.

Personalisation of economic policy-making was facilitated as some leading policy makers formed close (and often relatively closed) trust and reciprocity policy communities in Wellington. Some of these

Table 3.1 Persons influential on economic policy 1984–93[1]

Name	Votes	Position	Name	Votes	Position
R. Douglas	58	Min Fin	Palmer	8	PM 1989–90
Scott	47	Sec Treas	Chetwin	6	Treas/Lab Dept
Deane	37	RBNZ/SSC/SOE	Galvin	6	Sec Treas
Prebble	36	Ass Min Fin	S. Rodger	6	Min Lab/SOE
Kerr	34	Treas/NZBR	Andrew	5	Treas official
Richardson	34	Min Fin	Gibbs	5	Bus leader/NZBR
Caygill	27	Min Fin	Horne	5	Treas official
Lange	21	PM 1984–9	Shipley	5	Min Soc Welfare
Trotter	18	Bus leader/NZBR	Upton	5	Ass Min Fin
Birch	15	Min Lab	Andersen	4	Union leader
Brash	14	Gov RBNZ	Duignan	4	Treas official
Wilkinson	12	Treas/consultant	Elworthy	4	Fed Farmers
Myers	10	Bus leader/NZBR	Jennings	4	Employers' Fed
Bolger	9	PM 1990–97	K. Douglas	3	Pres NZCTU
Cameron	8	Treas/Bus	Fletcher	3	Bus Leader
Fancy	8	Treas/Comm	Hunn	3	SSC 1986–97

Notes

1. Respondents were asked, 'Can you name a number of individuals you think were particularly influential in economic policy during 1984–93?' Down to three votes.

communities drew on relationships that had developed, at least in part, in the years before 1984. These communities and networks formed as key policy makers were educated together, as they worked together, and as they appointed each other to (sometimes high paying) senior positions within the bureaucracies and the private sector (Kelsey 1995; Wallis 1997). These personal networks allowed members to develop their policies and ideas over a number of years, often through discussion with each other. It also allowed them to resist criticism, as their beliefs would receive support from the network. As key members of this network obtained senior positions throughout the bureaucracy and private sector, they were able to dominate policy formation. A former departmental chief executive describes this process in an interview with the author:

> There was a cadre of us . . . a couple of dozen people and they exercised influence in a mighty way. We had been at university together, sometimes taught each other and were very compatible. Scott, Kerr, Cameron and Wilkinson in the Treasury, and [Deane] and one or two others in the Reserve Bank.
>
> It was only when Ron Trotter decided that the business community had to support the Government reforms that he got Roger Kerr to head the Roundtable and used him to persuade all the other [business people]. So people like Trotter who originally used to be a real rent seeker . . . gradually became a convert . . . and Ron was fantastic. Elworthy led the Federated Farmers. [Deane] asked Roger Douglas to ask Elworthy to come on the Reserve Bank board. Then we got Ron Trotter on the Reserve Bank Board.
>
> And then [Deane] knew people like Allan Gibbs and John Fernyhough . . . and persuaded them to give a hand in running these new corporations [SOEs] and persuaded the Government to appoint them as chairmen of these new corporations. So it was all a network of twenty people who had been talking about these ideas for a long time. In opposition was Ruth [Richardson]. So through that period people like Roger Kerr and [Deane] would interact with Simon Upton and Ruth [Richardson].

The rest of this chapter will examine in detail the operation of the economic policy-making after 1984, and the main institutions involved in this process. Table 3.1 shows those individuals nominated as most influential on economic policy, along with their institutional position, while Figure 3.1 shows those institutions nominated by respondents as most influential on economic policy. Summarising the broad structure

Figure 3.1 Institutions nominated as most influential on economic policy in New Zealand 1984–93[1]

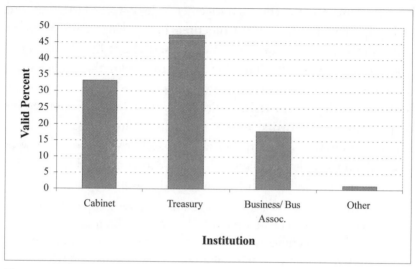

Notes

1. Respondents were asked, 'When you look at economic policy-making during 1983–93, which groups or institutions do you think were important in influencing economic policy? In order of importance.' Missing cases: 9. Business associations includes: 3 business leaders, 1 business association and 9 NZBR.

of economic policy-making in New Zealand during 1984–93, Figure 3.2 gives a model of economic policy influence. The most influential institutions, known as the 'inner core', are the cabinet, the Treasury, the Reserve Bank, the Business Roundtable and, after 1990, the Department of Prime Minister and Cabinet. Outside the inner core exist the 'first tier' organisations such as certain other government departments, business associations other than the Business Roundtable, political parties and the union movement.

The cabinet and economic policy-making

In New Zealand's Westminster system, the cabinet is responsible for policy decisions. Members of the cabinet, along with ministers outside cabinet, including deputy and associate ministers, parliamentary undersecretaries, and the parliamentary whips, can be as much as half of the ruling party in what was until recently a two party system. Along with strict party discipline, this gave the executive decisive power in determining policy directions and legislation, so much so that the New Zealand system has previously been described as an elective dictatorship (Mulgan 1992).[5] The convention of collective responsibility of cabinet also means that once a position is decided within cabinet, this position will be presented to the House. This could give a small clique of ministers (or even a single dominating personality) within cabinet immense power to set policy and drive through legislation.[6]

Ministers do not make decisions alone of course, but instead take advice from a variety of sources. These sources, such as ministerial advisers, public servants and interest groups, amongst others, can sometimes be as important as ministers in initiating, formulating, implementing and evaluating policies. This influence depends to some extent on the formal role given to certain institutions and the strategic location they hold in policy-making. In the New Zealand public service, for example, the Treasury has few if any rivals in economic policy,[7] with the Reserve Bank responsible for monetary policy.

The Treasury

Since before the Second World War, Treasury has been acknowledged as the most powerful department within New Zealand with influence over almost all aspects of public policy (Goldfinch 1997). This power derives from a number of sources. Most importantly, the Treasury's role as the

Figure 3.2 Institutional influences in economic policy-making in New Zealand 1983–93

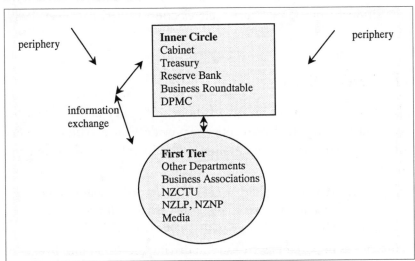

government's principal economic and financial adviser and controller of government finances gives it the function of overseeing general economic policy and the policy directions of the government. It reports to cabinet on all departmental submissions that have significant financial implications and has a key role in the budget process, including preparing forecasts and budget documents. The Treasury has been able to establish for itself a reputation for high quality advice, expertise and analytical strength, partly due to its comparatively large number of qualified policy and financial analysts (Boston and Cooper 1989, 126).[8] This, along with an effective socialisation and training process, gives Treasury analysts a confidence and ability to press the well-established Treasury view in policy-making, against competing perspectives (although on some economic policy issues there are no competing departmental views presented). The Treasury view also permeates through the public service and elsewhere by the appointment of Treasury officials to top posts in other departments, and to senior positions in the private sector (especially in the financial and consultancy sectors). The Treasury normally has strong backing in cabinet because of the high ranking of the finance minister in cabinet, as well as the support of the additional finance ministers (Boston 1989, 77). This support can be extremely important if there is a supportive minister of finance, which was the case during Douglas's and Richardson's tenures.[9] Treasury has also seconded officials to the leader of the opposition since 1975, with Treasury official Doug Andrew being an important influence on the formation of Roger Douglas's policy preferences before 1984, and with Iain Rennie being an important influence on the National opposition before (and after) their election in 1990 (Oliver 1989; Richardson 1995).[10]

The Reserve Bank

The Reserve Bank is in charge of monetary policy and oversees the operation of the financial sector, but also provides general economic policy advice, especially on macroeconomic policy. In 1997, the Reserve Bank saw its role as:

> operating monetary policy so as to maintain price stability; promoting the maintenance of a sound and efficient financial system; meeting the currency needs of the public (RBNZ 1997).[11]

While not as important as Treasury in driving the economic changes of the 1980s and early 1990s, in a number of areas such as financial liberalisation and the float of the dollar, as well as the broad focus of monetary policy aimed towards disinflation, the Bank provided key influential advice. At the same time, the Bank was recommending macroeconomic policies that were not significantly different to the Treasury line and providing broad support for the changes. As already noted, Rod Deane, one-time deputy governor of the Reserve Bank and then State Services commissioner, played a key role in influencing the direction and conduct of monetary policy and changes in the public sector.

After the change of government in 1984, the major purpose of monetary policy became inflationary control in the medium term and was largely left to the control of the Reserve Bank. Inflation was targeted initially through growth of monetary aggregates, but later in the decade through interest rates and the exchange rate, while a 'checklist approach' where multiple indicators were targeted was also used in the early 1990s, with the exchange rate remaining a key target (RBNZ 1990a). In the wake of the share market crash of 1987 and the severe recession that followed, the Reserve Bank recommended and maintained firm anti-inflationary policies including firm monetary policy (Bascand and Humphries 1988; Brash 1989). As outlined in chapter 5, the Reserve Bank Act 1989 gave the Bank greater independence in determining monetary policy with a 0–2 percent inflation target to be achieved within an agreed time-frame (originally December 1992, but actually reached before that).[12]

Ministerial offices

New Zealand has seen the growth of ministerial staffs during the 1980s so that by the 1990s, the average number of staffers had risen to about eight, and in some cases twelve (Boston 1990; McLeay 1995). Staffers have a variety of functions: the normal office duties of filing and administration; filtering the material for the minister; communicating and coordinating policy development with departments; setting priorities of policy development; and giving political advice. Since 1984, staffers have also become increasingly important in policy initiation, formation, and evaluation (McLeay 1995, 160). Examples of this include the abortive development of the flat tax package of mid-December 1987, which was developed in the office of the Minister of Finance rather than the Treasury (Boston 1990). According to McLeay, public servants must guard their neutrality and watch their public service careers.[13] Recruiting from outside the public service however, according to McQueen, a former member of Prime Minister Lange's office, 'blends activism and acumen. It means fresh blood. It means people have a commitment to ministerial decisions. It means things get done (McQueen 1991, 66).' Explicitly political appointments also give their loyalty primarily to the minister in question. At times, private offices have been extremely influential on policy; for example, the Finance Minister's private office played a key role in developing the economic policy initiatives introduced by the newly elected National Government in the 'Economic and Social Initiative' of 1990.

The Prime Minister's Office and the Department of Prime Minister and Cabinet

In 1998, the DPMC saw its mission as serving 'the Executive (the Prime Minister, the Governor-General, and the Cabinet) through the provision of high quality impartial advice and support services which facilitate government decision-making at both strategic and operational levels' (DPMC 1998). The DPMC has a number of largely independent operating units. These include: the Cabinet Office, which coordinates cabinet business; the Policy Advisory Group, which is responsible for providing advice directly to the prime minister and to other ministers, and for coordinating advice coming in from different government departments (DPMC 1998). It also serves as the base, and provides support, for a number of committees and taskforces whose members are drawn from the greater public service and from the private sector (including interest group members and employees). These have included the Employment Task Force, the Health Reforms Directorate, the National Interim Provider Board, the Change Team for Social Assistance and the Task Force on Positive Aging. While the DPMC has seen its role expand since its formation in 1990, it lacks a division devoted to economic policy, and its role in economic policy is considerably less than that of its Australian counterpart (although Mark Prebble, who was appointed Chief Executive in 1998, was formerly a senior Treasury official). The Department's importance in economic policy lies mainly as a base in which important taskforces and committees have been situated and serviced.

Before 1975, a Prime Minister's Department was administered by the Department of External Affairs (Henderson 1997). An independent Prime Minister's Department was then established under the Muldoon Government (1975–84), including an advisory group consisting of six to eight 'experts' drawn from the private and public sector. Under the Labour Government in 1987, the Prime Minister's Department was reorganised into a Cabinet Office and a Prime Minister's Office (PMO), with a distinction 'maintained between the policy related roles of the advisory group, and the political advisers, including press secretaries, speech writers and pollsters' (Henderson 1997, 77). After Geoffrey Palmer took over as Prime Minister (PM) in 1989, the currently existing Department of Prime Minister and Cabinet was formed, beginning operation in 1990 with an expanded role and resources. This followed a report recommending separate streams of advice to the prime minister. One was to be:

> a Government department to supply impartial, high quality advice and support to the Prime Minister and Cabinet, and another, a Prime Minister's Private Office, to provide personal support and media services, and advice of a party political nature (DPMC 1998).

The PMO's role includes office management and administration, advising the PM, liaising between the PM and others, and attending advisory committees. During the term of the National Government (1990–99) it became increasingly responsible:

> for the overall political strategy of the Government reflecting the heightened salience of political leadership in the age of television and . . . the exigencies of policy justification and presentation in an age of radical policy change (McLeay 1995, 159).

This distinction between the political advice of the PMO and the 'impartial' advice of the DPMC was not always apparent in practice, with a degree of policy integration between the PMO and DPMC. When the National Government came to power in 1990, the new PM expanded the DPMC, and the distinction between political and policy advice was blurred with the setting of a number of political initiatives and task forces within the aegis of the DPMC (McLeay 1995, 154–6).

The precursors of the DPMC during the Fourth Labour Government (1984–90), such as the Prime Minister's Office, had surprisingly little influence on economic policy decisions.[14] This lack of influence can be seen as proceeding from a number of factors. First, according to a leading member of the Prime Minister's Office during the Lange Government (interviewed by the author), the lack of influence was largely a result of the political failings of the Prime Minister, rather than a lack of resources, advice or policy expertise. While Lange was often briefed extensively on policy issues and had sometimes commissioned papers, such as in the case of the flat tax debate, he was often unable to win his case in cabinet debates. Rather than presenting detailed submissions, arguing his case at length or trying to muster prior support amongst caucus and cabinet colleagues, he would avoid confrontation and sometimes leave if he could not get immediate agreement on his preferred policy directions.[15] At the same time, the PMO obviously did not have as many trained economists as the Treasury; it lacked a head with economics training (although it contained other economists such as Diane Salter); it contained few figures with a high public profile; and it carried out much of its work behind the scenes, rather than publicly stating its policy preferences as did the Treasury in its briefing papers. This contrasts with the DPMC whose importance in economic policy during the years of the National Government was particularly in servicing the influential committees and taskforces mentioned above.

Cabinet committees and the budget process

Much of the work of the cabinet is carried out in the cabinet committees, at least formally, with the structure and use of committees changing considerably during the 1980s and 1990s. In 1984, the Labour Government abolished the existing coordinating committees including the key Cabinet Economic Committee and established five sectoral committees under the general financial oversight of the Cabinet Policy Committee (Roberts 1987; Boston 1990). Three special purpose committees were also established. The Cabinet Policy Committee was chaired by the prime minister (or his deputy) and considered the broad issues and policy 'clarity, coherence and integration, rather than the detailed implementation or formulation of policies' (Roberts 1987, 98). Ad hoc committees could be and were established as the need arose. Under the National Government, the Cabinet Strategy Committee (CSC) became the key coordinating committee. This existed to first, 'consider,

Figure 3.3 Making the budget under Douglas as Finance Minister

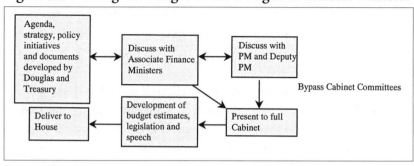

determine and bring together into a coherent framework, strategic policy directions and initiatives across the entire range of government activity'. Second, to monitor 'macroeconomic policy and [set] medium term Government objectives.' Third, to set 'the main goals and priorities for the budget' and monitor 'fiscal decisions' (Cabinet Office 1991). Along with the Cabinet Expenditure Control Committee (ECC), which replaced the Labour Government's Expenditure Review Committee, the Strategy Committee was the key committee in the budget process.[16] The budget was a key piece of legislation and was used by both Labour and National as a vehicle to introduce wide scale policy changes. As the budget process was traditionally a secret one, the time and opportunity available for debate (including with full cabinet) over policy directions was limited.

While there could be extensive use of the cabinet committee process, under the Labour Government key economic policy decisions were often made outside the formal process of cabinet and cabinet committees. Between 1985 and 1989, a committee outside the formal process existed to push certain items onto the cabinet agenda. Known as the Priorities Committee, it held weekly meetings and was serviced by an official from the Prime Minister's Office (Boston 1990). Roger Douglas, as Finance Minister, also tended to operate outside formal channels. He would often decide on a preferred policy in discussion with selected officials. He would then get his Associate Ministers David Caygill and Richard Prebble onside, before going to Deputy Prime Minister Geoffrey Palmer and Prime Minister David Lange. Issues that came up would be resolved before the package was presented to the whole cabinet. Prebble and Douglas would also occasionally table papers directly in cabinet to limit the time available for their discussion.[17] The way Douglas managed the budget process, often bypassing formal channels, is shown in Figure 3.3.[18] In 1989, under the prime ministership of Geoffrey Palmer, the Expenditure Review Committee was formed from an ad hoc committee to give greater formal structure to the budget process (McLeay 1995, 98).

The National Government that followed the 1990 election made considerable use of cabinet committees, especially during the budget process. Figure 3.4 shows the budget process when Ruth Richardson was finance minister. Richardson had to exert considerable efforts to convince some of her cabinet colleagues to support the economic policy direction. The large National Caucus, after the landslide victory of 1990, also ensured some check on the activities of the executive. Richardson involved her fellow ministers to a larger extent than the previous Labour administration in the preparation of budgets, although possibly after the broad agenda had been decided. At the same time, the National Cabinet during its first term did not exhibit the degree of factionalism seen in the previous Labour Government.[19] While there were occasional disputes, such as between Richardson and Wyatt Creech over tax issues (Richardson 1995, 106), these were mostly settled behind closed doors and did not spill into the public arena as occurred during the Labour Government. After

Figure 3.4 Making the budget under Richardson as Finance Minister[1]

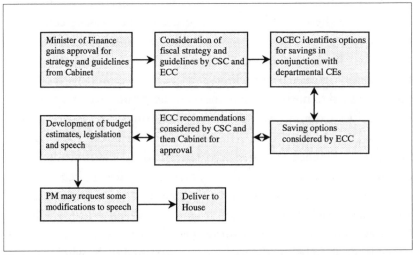

Notes
1. Sources: Richardson 1995; Shroff 1993. ECC is Cabinet Expenditure Control Committee, CSC is Cabinet Strategy Committee and OCEC is Officials Committee on Expenditure Control.

the close result in the 1993 election, Ruth Richardson, sometimes criticised for her abrasive style both within and outside cabinet, was removed from the finance portfolio and resigned from parliament. After the formation of the New Zealand First–National Coalition in 1996 there was some tension between ministers over policy directions, which contributed to the failure of the coalition in 1998.

Since the passing of the Fiscal Responsibility Act in 1994, there has been an improvement in the transparency of the budget process (Goldfinch 1998). The act, as its name suggests, requires the government to be 'fiscally responsible'.[20] This involves formulating and reporting its fiscal policy objectives to parliament. The government must report to parliament on how it is to comply with these fiscal principles, any departure from them must be justified, and an explanation must be given as to when they will be complied with in the future. The act also requires disclosure of the fiscal consequences of economic policy decisions. This includes publishing three-year forecasts every half year, and four to six weeks prior to a general election. Forecasts include the usual financial statements, as well as a statement of fiscal risks and contingent liabilities, which describes and (if possible) quantifies the fiscal risks associated with the forecasts. The minister of finance and the secretary to the Treasury sign statements of responsibility declaring that all policy decisions have been included in accordance with the act, and that the Treasury has used its best professional judgement in preparing the fiscal impacts of the policy decisions. The budget process as it stands following the Fiscal Responsibility Act is shown in Figure 3.5.

The introduction of Mixed Member Proportional (MMP) government has also changed the way budgets are prepared with more time being spent explaining and building agreement for policy directions from particular supporting parties and/or coalition partners. This has led to the development of the budget being described by a former National cabinet minister as 'a consensual process'. The dynamics of coalition government led to the division of the position of minister of finance into a treasurer and a minister of finance, a division that was maintained following the collapse of the National–New Zealand First Coalition. While the minister of finance played an important part in the budget process, the treasurer was the senior minister responsible.[21]

Government departments

Departments can be expected to wield important influence in their particular areas of expertise and sometimes do. The Department of Labour, for example, was central to the development of the Labour Relations Act 1987, although its role in the Employment Contracts Act 1991 was largely limited to implementing an agenda already set elsewhere. In general, however, government departments, with the exception of the Treasury and the DPMC, did not have a great influence on economic policy during 1984–93, although this influence marginally increased during the National Government of 1990–99. Treasury dominance has always been a factor of policy-making in New Zealand.[22] However, before 1984, this dominance was not absolute, as the Officials' Committee on Economic Policy also included permanent heads of Industries and Commerce, Statistics, External Affairs, as well as ad hoc members according to subject matter, such as the Reserve Bank, Customs, Agriculture and Labour (Moriarty 1956, 227; RBNZ 1960). This led to the officials' committee submitting reports and recommendations to the Cabinet Economic Committee that were generally agreed between departments, although there were occasional minority reports (Galvin 1991).[23] The presence of the Prime Minister's Department at the Cabinet Economic Committee after 1975 also balanced Treasury's power to some extent, although there was a close relationship between the permanent head of the department from 1975 to 1981, Bernie Galvin, and the Treasury, with Galvin taking over as the Secretary to the Treasury in 1981.

After 1984, departments were often excluded from economic policy development. This was for a number of reasons. As much of the reform was driven by the Government and the Treasury, there was a view that other departments should be kept out of policy development in case they tried to 'stymie' the reforms. For example, despite the State Services Commission (SSC) being the central employer for the public sector at the time, the public sector management reforms were largely driven from the Treasury and imposed on the public sector (Goldfinch 1998).[24] Rod Deane was appointed as the State Services Commissioner in 1986 largely to bring about a change in culture in the Commission and to encourage support for the changes. (A symptom of the avoidance of coordination and consultation with other departments was that committees that shadowed the cabinet committees fell into disuse, with policy being made

Figure 3.5 Making the budget after the Fiscal Responsibility Act 1994[1]

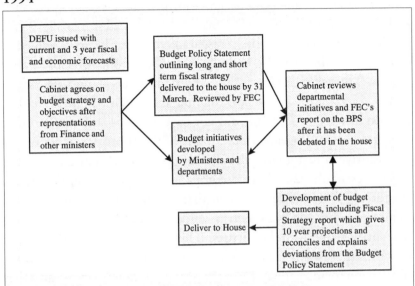

Notes
1. Sources: Treasury 1996. DEFU is December Economic and Fiscal forecast, FEC is the parliamentary Finance and Expenditure Committee.

by a small clique of officials and ministers.)[25] Several of the public sector changes removed possible threats to Treasury influence, such as in the case of the Ministry of Works and Development (Boston 1991a).

Attempts to improve coordination were, however, made in the late 1980s and 1990s. Departments were required to consult more widely, interdepartmental committees were formed to parallel cabinet committees[26] and to oversee the formulation and implementation of policies across departments, and the Department of Prime Minister and Cabinet was revived (Boston 1990; Boston et al 1996, 134). The *Cabinet Office Manual* strengthened the consultation requirements of departments before submission of documents to cabinet. Ministers were required to certify:

> whether consultation with other departments and ministers has taken place and whether there has been (or should be in the future) consultation with the Government caucus, opposition parties and other interested groups (Boston et al 1996, 134).

Business associations

During the Labour and National governments, interest groups were often excluded from economic policy-making, influenced in part by Public Choice theory that saw them as vested interests that had contributed to economic decline, and by elitist beliefs of key politicians and policy makers. The key exception to this was the Business Roundtable which exercised important influence during the late 1980s and early 1990s.[27] Formed in 1980, the NZBR did not have a formal structure or office until 1986 when Roger Kerr, previously of the Treasury, was appointed as executive director. Membership is open, by invitation, to chief executives of the 200 largest companies by market capitalisation. Resources of the NZBR are such that it can and has commissioned numerous reports from a variety of academics and putative experts on a diversity of public policy issues. These, by and large, present an unwavering New Right line on policy issues and the NZBR is a strong supporter of market and non-governmental solutions to nearly all policy problems and strongly supports reducing welfare provision.

The influence of the NZBR proceeds from a number of factors. First, it represents a large part of business in New Zealand, which makes it difficult to ignore in policy development.[28] Second, it presents itself as an organisation 'in pursuit of the national interest but is concerned to be, and be seen to be, strictly, apolitical' (Cullinane 1995, 2). This, along with the ability to present occasionally well-argued research with a 'public interest' element, has been a large factor in the NZBR's success. Third, also important is the fact that the NZBR has worked in a similar theoretical framework to that employed by the government and its advisers. This has facilitated the movement of ideas to and from both groups and allowed both groups to speak in a similar language. This has enabled the NZBR to argue for policies that are similar in logic to those that have gone before, or to argue for the extension of existing ones. For example, while on some issues (such as privatisation) the NZBR were not initiators, their pressure gave support to the process and encouragement for it to continue, as shown in chapter five. Fourth, the policy-making sector in New Zealand is small and gaps in policy advice provision can emerge. The NZBR has been able to fill some of these. For example, the NZBR has been able to supply well-funded research on such issues as takeover policy (along with similar Treasury advice) that managed to overwhelm less well-organised and well-funded opponents (Vowles and Roper 1997). During the lead up to the 1990 election, the NZBR (along with the Employers' Federation) was able to put a large effort into developing labour-market policy for the incoming National Government. Finally, and possibly most important, the influence of the NZBR has been increased by the ties between it and members of the public sector bureaucracy and with members of the government. As already noted, Kerr is a former Treasury official and there has been movement of officials between the public sector and the NZBR. Active members of the NZBR, such as Alan Gibbs and Sir Ron Trotter, have been appointed to important taskforces, committees and are on SOEs and other boards. The NZBR also has close ties to the Centre of Independent Studies of Australia and New Zealand and with Australian think-tanks such as the Tasman Institute.[29] Other business organisations, such as the Employers' Federation and Federated Farmers, also provided broad support for a move towards economic liberalisation, while the Manufacturers' Federation, highly influential in the 1960s and 1970s, saw its importance fade as it resisted the trade liberalisation of the Labour Government.[30]

Trade unions

Despite the affiliate ties of the union movement to the Labour Party, unions had surprisingly little influence on economic policy during the Labour Government, particularly if compared to Australia. Indeed, the relationship between the Labour Government and the trade unions was at times extremely strained. At the time of the election of the Labour Government, there was some expectation amongst unionists that they would have a role in the new Government. Apart from the affiliate ties to the Labour Party, there were other links between the Labour opposition and the unions. Stan Rodger, the Minister for Labour, had been a past president of the public sector union the Public Service Association, and a number of unionists had been involved socially with the Labour shadow cabinet. These ties were considerably less close than those found in Australia, however, where Prime Minister Hawke and a number of Labor ministers had held high positions within the Australian Council of Trade Unions, and where personal ties were maintained between senior members of the Government (including Hawke) and senior ACTU officials such as Bill Kelty. In the New Zealand Labour Cabinet there was some scepticism regarding the expertise of the then leadership of the peak union organisation, the Federation of Labour. The Federation and its successor, the New Zealand Council of Trade Unions (NZCTU), also lacked the policy depth and expertise found in the Australian Council of Trade Unions.

Some trade union respondents claimed there was an understanding between the unions and the parliamentary Labour Party before the 1984 election. According to a senior union official, this was not an agreement in the strict sense but an 'understanding that there would be a process of negotiation. The concept of tripartism was thrown up as the central vehicle . . . [but it] . . . stopped very early after the Economic Summit conference.'[31] Although compulsory unionism was reintroduced, once the flood of changes began, the unions found themselves on the back foot and, with the exception of the Labour Relations Act 1987, were largely excluded from consultation and policy formation. For example, in the development of the State Sector Act 1988, overseen by Stan Rodger, the public sector unions were largely presented with a *fait accompli*. According to former prime minister David Lange:

> The state sector unions who were, by and large, more privileged, less overburdened with work, and more articulate . . . caused great difficulty. They declared Stan Rodger, a life member of the organisation, to be *persona non grata* within the organisation. We did not enjoy the best of relations with the private sector trade union movement [but] we enjoyed very poor relations with the public sector trade union movement.

The unions largely attempted to influence the direction of policy and ameliorate its effects through their caucus ties in the parliamentary party and through the usual channels open to interest groups.

It is notable that despite the example of Australia, the Labour Government did not introduce an Accord-type model, possibly because it did not fit with the economic liberalisation direction sponsored by Douglas and his supporters. It is also possible that the New Zealand union movement did not have the level of discipline that would have been needed to deliver an agreement similar to the Accord. A former Labour president stated, 'Mike Moore . . . and Stan Rodger . . . stopped an Accord with the unions before 1984. I remember this very clearly because I was there at the policy council.' Mike Moore must have changed his mind regarding a move towards an Accord-type structure because he was a member the Compact Working Party on Consultative Mechanisms, which published a report on 18 September 1989 (Compact Working Party 1989). The working party, which included representation from the NZCTU and the Government, examined a number of consultative mechanisms that could be set up between the Government, the NZCTU and business, but its recommendations were not taken on board by the Government. The Government released a revised consultation model in March 1990, with a ten member council, split between the Government and unions and chaired by the Prime Minister (Sheppard 1999). The concept was revived when Mike Moore took over as Prime Minister in the last weeks of the Labour Government. He describes the Compact process thus:

> I was working on a thing called a compact with the unions; we got the paper up. Cabinet turned me down, they wouldn't even give me the money to do it. I paid for the piss out of my own pockets for the unions, they stayed at my house, and we negotiated what I thought was a deal. We didn't get anywhere with that. Then when I became Prime Minister I just dug up my old papers and did it myself. There was resistance from some of the Cabinet. I ignored them.

The Compact, or the Agreement for Growth as it was now called, traded real wage restraint for consultation of the unions on economic and social policy. However, the Labour Government lost the election a few weeks after it was launched and the new National Government was not inclined to continue the process. The National Government's rapid introduction of the anti-union Employment Contracts Act 1991, largely without taking union concerns on board (except possibly in the case of retaining the Employment Court), meant relations soured quickly between the union movement and the new Government.[32] The National Government did, however, include Ken Douglas, the NZCTU President, in the Taskforce on Employment and as the only union representative on the Enterprise Council.

The media

The media in New Zealand was generally not an initiator of policy, but often provided support for the new policy directions. Perhaps because of the small size of New Zealand and the high concentration of media ownership, the quality and diversity of the media in New Zealand is not high. Local television news and current affairs programmes are generally of tabloid-like quality, despite two publicly owned stations, while local print media are what might be called 'middle-brow'.[33] A senior print journalist in one of the major dailies describes the reason for this:

> Newspapers have to be pitched at the mid-market because it is a small market, it is not quite lowest common denominator because it is not tabloid, but we don't have the extremes of the tabloid and the high quality press, [like] say . . . Britain. The dailies are in the middle, so that means they are not very challenging. Not having very high standards in the media, maybe [this is from] concentrated ownership . . . that extends through television as well.

New policy directions of both the Labour and National governments were often treated uncritically, or even in some cases with unqualified support, especially in the business sections of the dailies and in the *National Business Review*.[34] At the same time critics of the policy changes would often be ignored or even ridiculed. According to another journalist:

> some opponents . . . became painted as dangerously extreme in their views and outside the mainstream. Whereas a Martian would have thought there was an alternative policy that could have been advocated, they came to be considered extreme. 'There Is No Alternative' became the catchcry, TINA became a very popular policy.

What influence the media had on policy formation is difficult to determine. It is possible that the media were important in reassuring policy makers and politicians of the wisdom of the new policy directions, if not always a doubtful public.

Other influences in policy formation

A number of other institutions have played some role in economic policy development, although this role was at times small. The New Zealand Planning Council undertook a number of studies of economic policy in New Zealand which recommended some liberalisation and these have been cited as influential by Finance Minister (1988–90) David Caygill (see, for example, EMG 1979; 1981; 1982; NZPC 1989). Other potential sources of advice were the royal commissions. While these were sometimes influential on public policy prior to 1984, the Royal Commission on Social Policy that reported early in April 1988 (in four volumes totalling over 4000 pages) was virtually snubbed and then largely ignored by policy makers (Easton 1994). The extra-parliamentary Labour Party, while ostensibly having a role in the formation of policy advice, was also largely ignored by the Labour Government. One exception was the Goods and Services Tax (GST) debate, where, after a series of debates, the party was convinced to support the new tax.[35] Relations were particularly strained during the privatisation debate and the divisions forced over Rogernomics were a significant factor in the split of the party and the formation of the New Labour Party in 1989 (later part of the Alliance). The National Government managed to maintain better relations with its extra-parliamentary party, but even it saw its membership drop after reneging on a 1990 election promise to remove the superannuation surtax.

The parliament, parliamentary committees and those who make submissions on bills before the House can also be sources of influence, although this is normally after an agenda has been set by the government. A variety of interest groups may also attempt to influence policy through submissions to government, rallying of electoral support, media releases, and attempts to create a climate supportive of the ideas or policies that they are promoting. However, as already noted, in a climate influenced by Public Choice theories and by the elitist beliefs of politicians and policy makers that saw interest groups as vested interests, they did not have as great an input as they might have had prior to 1984. A number of policy makers were also reacting to the experience of the 1970s and early 1980s, believing it to have been a time when interest groups exerted too much power in policy-making, leading to 'policy sclerosis' (see Appendix Two).

Consultants

Since the passing of the State Sector Act 1988 and the Public Finance Act 1989, departments have made increasing use of private consultants as sources of policy advice (Boston et al 1996). This became so widespread that in 1998–9 half of the Treasury's entire yearly expenditure was being spent on various consultancies (Brockett 1999).[36] Some of these consultants have been former government officials rehired by their former employers and have often provided valuable support for the policy directions of the government. For example, a number of Treasury officials, important in developing the new policy direction found in the Treasury economic briefing papers, later left to join the private sector, where they provided consultancy services and media comment, and contributed to a climate of support conducive to the continuing restructuring of the economy.[37] The outsourcing of advice has also encouraged the growth of domestic consultancy firms such as Strategos, while other merchant banks, stockbroking and accountancy firms, both domestic and international, have also become involved in the, at times, extremely lucrative business of providing advice. Most of these consultants consistently present a neo-liberal view on policy issues (McLeay 1995, 144). Various reports have been influential on issues including: departmental restructuring; the funding of training and education; housing mortgages; and the corporatisation and sale of various SOEs.

The Enterprise Council

After 1990, the new National Government introduced a number of consultative mechanisms. One of the more important was the Enterprise Council, announced in June 1991 and set up in November of the same year. The council was serviced by the DPMC, chaired by the prime minister and included representation from top business management, as well as one trade unionist. At its inception, there were high hopes it would provide a challenge to Treasury dominance, and, according to Prime Minister Jim Bolger, would 'give a view from those who have hands-on experience' (Kilroy 1991, 2). The Council originally 'assisted with the formulation of policy proposals as well as making its own suggestions' and looked at such things as education and training, tax, research and development, export strategy and business management (McLeay 1995, 157). It was able to commission its own reports, such as the New Zealand Institute of Economic Research's 1994 report into the New Zealand economy. While the council was ostensibly independent, according to McLeay, its role was largely to voice support for the government's economic policies rather than challenge them. For example, calls for economic incentives by members of the council were ignored by the government. The role of the council diminished over time and under Bolger's successor, Jenny Shipley, it became largely a council of 'wise heads' for the prime minister. It would meet three to five times a year and discuss issues only at the instigation of the prime minister, with the advice remaining secret.[38]

Conclusion

New Zealand is characterised by its smallness and simplicity of policy-making and institutional structures. Influence in policy-making can be highly centralised around a few key institutions and individuals. This chapter has illustrated the structures and roles of the most influential institutions in economic policy-making in New Zealand during the 1980s and 1990s. The cabinet is responsible for policy decisions, with cabinet committees playing an important part in policy development. Ministers do not make policy decisions alone however, and take advice from a select number of institutions and individuals in policy formation, the most important during 1984–93 being the 'inner circle' consisting of the Treasury, the Reserve Bank and the Business Roundtable, and after 1990, the DPMC. The Treasury in particular plays a central role in economic policy-making, with no significant rivals in the provision of economic policy advice. Before 1984, New Zealand had largely followed a consultative process of policy-making with key interest groups formally and informally incorporated into policy development. However, after 1984, partly influenced by Public Choice theory and the elitist beliefs of politicians and leading policy makers, interest groups were largely excluded from policy-making, formal channels were sometimes bypassed and economic policy-making became highly centralised around a few key individuals and institutions. For example, while Roger Douglas was finance minister, the budget, often comprising a large number of policy innovations, was sometimes made by a select group of ministers and officials working outside official channels. During the National Government of 1990–99, there were some small attempts to revive consultation between departments and outside the government with the formation of such institutions as the Enterprise Council, while the budget process made greater use of cabinet committees. The Fiscal Responsibility Act 1994 has increased the transparency of the budget process, with the government required to signal its fiscal policy objectives. The next two chapters examine the making of a number of key economic policy decisions under the Labour and National governments.

4

Economic Policy Decision Making in New Zealand from Financial Liberalisation to the Labour Relations Act 1987

Examining key economic policy decisions is central to understanding the processes of policy change and the ideas, institutions and individuals important in that process. In the decisions studied in this chapter, financial liberalisation was dominated by select ministers and officials from the Reserve Bank and the Treasury. The 1984 budget was largely drawn up by Roger Douglas, his associate finance ministers and Treasury officials. The Labour Relations Act 1987 was largely unique in this period in that it was introduced after a considerable period of consultation. It saw the influence of a range of groups including ministers, union officials, business association officials and members of the extra-parliamentary Labour Party, with the Department of Labour being particularly important. Influence in economic policy decision making in New Zealand was often concentrated amongst a small select group of key individuals from strategically located institutions such as the Treasury, the cabinet, the Reserve Bank and the Business Roundtable. This relatively stable 'policy community' and the individuals in this community, such as Treasury Secretary Graham Scott, Business Roundtable Chief Executive Roger Kerr, Roderick Deane and a small number of ministers (usually finance), often exercised influence over a number of decisions and over a number of years.

The focus on decisions gives a number of interesting results. In some cases, officials were seen as having more influence on key decisions (such as the 1984 budget) than even the prime ministers and their deputies. Thus, although the voting public may identify prime ministers with particular policy directions and decisions, in fact, given the way the cabinet and policy system operates and is managed by ministers within that cabinet, there may be policy decisions where this expected influence is not evident. The study of particular decisions also shows how particular economic theories and ideas can impact directly on policy. The Reserve Bank Act, for example, was strongly influenced by Chicago and New Classical economics, as well as drawing on general changes in the public sector that were themselves derivative of New Institutional economics and Public Choice. The Employment Contracts Act drew on neoclassical economics and neo-liberal streams of thought promulgated by the Business Roundtable, amongst others.

Why study decision making?

Focusing on the decision-making level is important for a number of reasons. First, it is less likely to give an overly general picture of economic policy-making and highlights political, institutional, ideological and personal factors involved in making that particular decision. Second, it also lessens the danger of imputing too much influence to certain institutions and individuals. While on a general level they may have a great deal of power, there may be certain decisions or issues where this power is not evident. Third, focusing on the decision-making level engages with the burgeoning literature on policy networks and policy communities and underlines the importance of subsectoral levels of analysis in understanding broader issues of policy-making and policy change. Often examining the 'meso-level' and 'micro-level' of policy-making, the network approach often sees public policy formation fragmented and specialised into policy areas with their own characteristics, both within a country and between countries. This means that an eclecticism of approaches is needed to describe and/or theorise these different policy areas.[1] Within these policy areas, webs of different public and private individuals, groups and institutions are involved in policy formation (and sometimes implementation), tied to each other through often informal or non-official links based on norms of reciprocity, resource dependence and repeated interaction (Atkinson and Coleman 1992). Network studies have often discovered different groupings influential in different policy areas and decisions.

This study adds to the understanding of policy networks in the following ways. It studies the role of individuals and institutions and the relationship between them. This means that personal relationships and their role in policy-making can be examined. These personal relationships form, at least in part, through the personal contact and trust built up during the making of policy decisions and can be important across the policy area. Micro-level linkages are important in understanding broader issues and the role that social networks and institutional ties play in this process. This study of decision making also illustrates the degree to which influence across decisions differed, as is the case to some extent in Australia, or how it was concentrated amongst a stable policy community across decisions, as in the case of New Zealand.

Once it is decided to study decision making, the question then

Table 4.1 Financial liberalisation in New Zealand[1]

1984
- Run on the dollar leads to foreign exchange market closure
- Devaluation—20%
- Removal of interest rate controls
- Private overseas borrowing regulations relaxed
- Credit growth guidelines abolished[2]
- Abolition of exchange controls

1985
- Reserve Asset Ratios (RAR) and other ratio requirements abolished[3]
- Float of dollar
- Limits on foreign ownership of financial institutions removed

1986
- Reserve Bank given power to register financial institutions as banks (previously this had required legislation in each instance). Bank's power of prudential supervision extended

1987
- Restrictions on operations of building societies removed and they are allowed to register as companies

1988
- Trustee Banks required to become companies and remaining restrictions on their operations removed
- Postbank sold

1990
- Reserve Bank Act 1989 revises and extends approach to prudential supervision of financial system

Notes
1. Sources: Spencer and Carey 1989; New Zealand Economic Chronology 1985–93 in Reserve Bank Bulletin.
2. Credit growth guidelines allowed financial institutions to increase credit creation by one percent per month (seasonally adjusted).
3. Ratio requirements obliged financial institutions to place a proportion of their funds in government securities (RAR applied to Trading Banks only).

arises which decisions to study. As Polsby (1980, 95–6) notes, when studying decision making one can look at whether decisions are 'representative' of decisions made or 'important' decisions that affect large numbers of people and resources. He concludes that studying 'important' decisions is more useful. This study seeks to understand which individuals and institutions were influential in economic policy-making during a period of economic policy change; so the selection needs to be 'representative' of economic policy and 'important' in terms of the direction of economic policy.[2] For New Zealand, the seven decisions selected were the key economic policy changes: financial liberalisation;[3] the 1984 Budget; the Labour Relations Act 1987; privatisation of state assets; the Reserve Bank Act 1989; the Employment Contracts Act 1991; and the 1991 Budget. These contributed the main components of 'Rogernomics' and made the most important changes to the existing policy framework.[4] This chapter will analyse the first three: financial liberalisation; the 1984 Budget; and the Labour Relations Act 1987. The next chapter will examine privatisation of state assets, the Reserve Bank Act 1989, the Employment Contracts Act 1991, and the 1991 Budget.

Financial liberalisation

Immediately upon taking office in 1984, the Labour Government was faced with a run on the currency and a constitutional crisis that resulted in a 20 percent devaluation of the New Zealand dollar (Lissington 1987; Russell 1996).[5] Immediately after the devaluation some interest rate controls were lifted. A flood of changes was then introduced, including the abolition of exchange controls, credit guidelines and ratio requirements, the float of the dollar, and the removal of restrictions on foreign ownership of banks (Table 4.1). Table 4.2 shows those individuals nominated by respondents as influential in financial liberalisation, along with their institutional position. These include Deputy Governor of the Reserve Bank, Roderick Deane, Ministers Roger Douglas and Richard Prebble and Treasury officials Scott, Kerr and Galvin. Drawing on this table, as well as interviews with respondents and other sources, this section will show that financial liberalisation was initiated and developed by officials of the Reserve Bank and the Treasury, with the Cabinet largely following their advice.

While the speed and the extent of financial deregulation was nothing short of remarkable, the Reserve Bank had been arguing for financial deregulation for some twenty years through its research agenda and various publications. A joint Treasury–Reserve Bank committee known as the Knight Committee (chaired by Reserve Bank official Frank Knight and with the Treasury team led by Graham Scott) had examined financial market deregulation during the early 1980s. It made a number of recommendations including liberalising the foreign exchange market, amending the reserve asset ratios systems, and making a number of regulatory changes to interest rate and monetary policy settings (O'Shaughnessy 1997). These recommendations were rejected by the Muldoon administration in 1983. At the same time, the Reserve Bank was influenced by resurgent neoclassical economic thinking such as the Chicago School and New Classical economic ideas introduced by such people as Deputy Governor Roderick Deane, as well as international developments in financial markets, including those in Australia. It also had the experience of operating the financial system after the removal of interest rate controls in 1976–7, a policy that was reversed in 1981 when controls were reimposed. In addition, the difficulties the Reserve Bank experienced in administering the financial system as it stood, influenced it to become solidly in favour of extensive deregulation. Before the 1984 election of the new Labour Government, the Reserve Bank had already developed a comprehensive list of changes it wished to see (Deane et al 1983; RBNZ 1984c). The Treasury, through its own research and consultations with the Reserve Bank, had also developed a programme of financial liberalisation and this was outlined in the Treasury post-election briefing notes, *Economic Management* (Treasury 1984a).

By their effective handling of the currency crisis, Reserve Bank and Treasury officials had proved themselves in the eyes of the new Cabinet who, in opposition, had been vaguely suspicious of the New Zealand public service. A sense of urgency had also been instilled in the new Government by the currency crisis itself. Cabinet was ready to take the advice of the officials and roll out the already developed programme, although there was initial resistance from some members of the Cabinet over removing interest rate controls. According to one respondent, 'within days [of the election] we were moving on a range of things'. While the financial sector was generally supportive of the programme and had lobbied to relax the registration requirements for trading banks (which then required legislation in each case), bank leaders did not see themselves

Table 4.2 Persons nominated as influential on financial liberalisation[1]

Name	Votes	Position	Name	Votes	Position
Deane	52	Dep Gov RBNZ	Palmer	6	Dep PM
Douglas	44	Min Fin	Knight	5	RBNZ official
Scott	32	Dep Sec Treas	Myers	4	Bus leader/NZBR[3]
Prebble	19	Ass Min Fin	Andrew	4	Treas official[4]
Kerr	17	Treas official	Cameron	4	Treas official
Galvin	14	Sec Treas	Sherwin	3	RBNZ official
Caygill	13	Ass Min Fin	Zohrab	3	Treas official
Lange	13	PM	Duignan	2	Treas official
Russell	13	Gov RBNZ	de Cleene	2	Min Tax
Trotter	7	Bus leader/NZBR[2]	Fancy	2	Treas official
Wilkinson	8	Treas official	Muldoon	2	Previous PM

Notes
1. Respondents were asked 'Can you name about five or six individuals you think were particularly influential in formulating this policy?' They were then prompted further by being asked if there was anyone else they thought was influential. This question was repeated for all decisions studied in this and the following chapter.
2. Chair of the Business Roundtable from 1985 to 1988.
3. Chief Executive of Lion Nathan, became Chair of the Business Roundtable (NZBR) in 1990.
4. Seconded to the Labour opposition before the 1984 election.

as important in influencing the programme. This was especially so in the first few months following the devaluation when the speed of change surprised even some of them.[6]

Floating the dollar

The floating of the dollar had been advocated in Treasury's post-election briefing papers for a variety of reasons, and the Reserve Bank post-election briefing notes discuss some move to a more flexible exchange rate.[7] The difficulties encountered controlling the exchange rate under Muldoon, and the experience of the financial crisis, including the losses sustained by the taxpayer,[8] were important in developing the feeling that a float was appropriate. Officials had also argued that under a floating exchange regime, the exchange rate:

> will vary in a highly visible way with fluctuations in demand and supply conditions, and the information generated will enhance the ability of the price mechanism to indicate changing market opportunities and thus ensure responsiveness to changing circumstances (Treasury 1984a, 166).

Some officials also believed that monetary policy would be more effective under a floating regime, although this view was held more strongly by the Reserve Bank. As a Treasury official noted, the Reserve Bank wanted to float the dollar because:

> given the structural changes in the economy and the financial markets internationally, and given the deregulation that had taken place, they would be unsuccessful in money policy. They needed to float the dollar to gain control over monetary growth.

The Treasury was particularly sceptical that a government could successfully operate a pegged regime, given informational limitations and its previous experience. As the same official noted:

> The Treasury's approach was more . . . that there is no reason for believing that the government is more efficient at setting the exchange rate. I suspect one of the reasons Treasury took this line is that it didn't want to be implicated or otherwise in the running of monetary policy.

The view that a float was appropriate was shared, or came quickly to be shared, by the new Cabinet.[9] According to Easton (1989), Douglas had wanted to float during his first days in office, but was dissuaded by officials because the supporting institutions and policies were not in place. This is disputed by the then prime minister David Lange in an interview with the author. Lange claims:

> It wasn't Roger Douglas. I wanted it to be done before [him]. It seemed to me that I never wanted to be at risk again of doing what we had to put up with post-Muldoon, assuring everyone that the dollar was perfect. [It had] cost us a vast amount of money.

What is clear is that while there was general support for floating at least from within the economic policy bureaucracy, the Reserve Bank was more keen on an immediate float than was Treasury, although as a deputy governor of the Reserve Bank notes, 'people changed their minds at least four times' during the barrage of memos and papers on the issue. A former Treasury secretary describes the reason for Treasury's caution:

> We started off in December 1984 announcing the liberalisation of the capital account and it was fairly clear from that point that it was going to be very hard to hold onto a pegged exchange regime. With liberalised domestic financial markets and an open capital account, it was fairly clear that we would have to move from a [pegged] regime.
>
> There was a delay of three months—a period of market

thickening [and] capability in financial institutions and physical market infrastructure needed to operate the floating regime.

As Easton documents, by February of 1985, there was agreement that the Government should move towards a float, although the type of float (whether it was to be a constrained or 'clean' or 'dirty' float) was still undecided. However, a new, although less dramatic, run on the currency began and on 2 March an officials' memorandum recommended an immediate clean float on the following Monday (it was then Saturday). As a senior official of the Bank said:

> after a long discussion with officials and Ministers . . . Prebble [the Associate Minister of Finance] finally said; 'look, we are never going to know what is going to happen until we do it . . . why don't we do it' and the decision was made to move.[10]

Prime Minister David Lange was overseas at the time and Dr Roderick Deane, then deputy governor of the Reserve Bank, was sent to inform him. According to Lange:

> I was in London. When I was asked to meet Rod Deane . . . he walked in and I said, 'You've come to tell me you're going to float the dollar.' And he looked very surprised. He said, 'Yes,' and I said. 'Well go back and do it. Because you should have done it before.' [It hadn't been done before] . . . because there was concern on the part of the Minister of Finance that we weren't up to speed on how to handle it. [The float] was an inevitability.[11]

The 1984 Budget

The Labour Government's first Budget in 1984 was a marked departure from what had been the orthodoxy in New Zealand for almost fifty years. It was delivered on 8 November 1984, not quite four months after the Labour Government was elected. Changes introduced or prefigured included a value added tax (called the Goods and Services Tax), a fringe benefit tax, and a surcharge on national superannuation (the universal pension then operating). As well, an income support programme for low income families was introduced, personal tax exemptions for contributions to superannuation and life assurance and first home mortgages were removed, trade liberalisation was extended and various agricultural subsidies and export incentives were abandoned, and cost recovery for state supplied electricity and coal was begun (Douglas 1984). In his

Table 4.3 Persons nominated as influential on Budget 1984

Name	Votes	Position	Name	Votes	Position
Douglas	50	Min Fin	Fancy	4	Treas official
Scott	33	Dep Sec Treas	Trotter	4	Bus leader/NZBR
Prebble	28	Ass Min Fin	Zohrab	4	Treas official
Caygill	22	Ass Min Fin	Myers	3	Bus leader/NZBR
Kerr	18	Treas official	McKenzie	3	Treas official
Deane	16	Dep Gov RBNZ	Swier	3	Labour researcher
Galvin	12	Sec Treas	de Cleene	2	Min Tax
Wilkinson	11	Treas official	Dickson	2	Treas official
Cameron	9	Treas official	Gibbs	2	Bus leader
Andrew[1]	7	Treas official	Moore	2	Min Trade
Lange	6	PM	Moyle	2	Min Agric
Chetwin	4	Treas official			

Notes
1. Seconded to the Labour opposition before the 1984 election.

Budget speech Finance Minister Roger Douglas talked of the lowering of fiscal deficits and the tight anti-inflationary monetary policy that were to be concerns of his tenure as Finance Minister:

> We are committed to maintaining firm monetary control; to reducing the fiscal deficit substantially during the next three years and to maintaining a realistic exchange rate.
>
> A policy which maintains firm control of increases in the monetary and credit aggregates, in a manner that does not accommodate higher inflation, will be a critical part of our economic strategy (Douglas 1984, 2–3).

Table 4.3 shows those persons nominated by respondents as influential on the budget including Ministers Roger Douglas, Richard Prebble and David Caygill, Treasury official Graham Scott and the Deputy Governor of the Reserve Bank, Roderick Deane. As the table and personal interviews illustrated below show, the 1984 Budget was initiated and developed by a group of ministers and (mainly Treasury) officials.

The radical[12] nature of the new Budget and its departure from what had been Labour Party, and indeed New Zealand, orthodoxy for almost fifty years, has led some to look for the source of these ideas. One possible candidate was the Economic Summit conference held in September 1984, with representation from unions, business groups and community groups.[13] However, while people such as David Caygill saw the Economic Summit as giving a mandate for the changes to follow—and while there was a degree of support for some liberalisation, as noted in chapter one, there was also considerable disagreement amongst participants on the direction policy should take—by the time the Summit was held economic policy had largely been settled with the economic liberalisation programme supported by Finance Minister Roger Douglas winning out.

There are a number of other possible sources for the new policy directions contained in the 1984 Budget. Various reports of the Economic Monitoring Group of the New Zealand Planning Council had been advocating some degree of deregulation (Economic Monitoring Group 1979; 1981; 1982). The move to flatter tax systems had been advocated over a number of years, notably in a 1982 Taskforce on Tax Reform (the McCaw Committee), which had recommended shifting more of the tax take to consumption, adopting a less progressive marginal tax scale and removing a number of tax exemptions. The business association Federated Farmers, had pressed for extensive deregulation, as had some other business associations. Possibly of more importance was the Treasury (1984a) post-election briefing paper *Economic Management,* which prefigures much of the 1984 Budget (and what was to follow), and it would be understandable to draw the conclusion that the 1984 Budget was a Treasury one. Certainly it was the view of many respondents that Treasury was particularly important in the 1984 Budget. As a one-time senior Treasury official says; '*Economic Management* was in large part adopted. It is key to understanding the period to 1987.'

However, as Oliver (1989) documents, Douglas and a wing within the Labour opposition (with strong support from Doug Andrew, a Treasury official seconded to the opposition, and from Geoff Swier, a Labour Party researcher) had been developing a programme of economic liberalisation. This was along similar lines to the policy advice being developed in the Treasury.[14] This meant Douglas himself had strong ideas coming into the budget process, and the budget's development may be better seen as a 'partnership between [mostly Treasury] advisers and ministers' as one departmental chief executive, at the time a senior Treasury official, describes it. While there was generally a concurrence of views 'there wasn't complete coincidence, [but] the argument wouldn't be over the objectives or strategies so much as over the best means of achieving them. The means would be debated.' One issue where Treasury did encourage Douglas to change his mind was over the introduction of GST. Douglas had been in favour of a retail sales tax but was convinced to change his mind through a series of reports and personal appeals, and, according to a former Treasury secretary, representation from an official from the IMF to the Cabinet (Treasury 1984b; 1984c).[15]

Douglas himself describes the budget process as follows. He had written a letter to Treasury in 1984. This letter gave rise to a number of reports, which he and Treasury discussed, often generating new ideas in the process (sometimes from seemingly unrelated areas) and so generating a new round of reports. These reports were worked on to make the Budget. The Associate Ministers were closely involved early in the Budget process, especially Caygill on monetary policy. However, the agenda would usually be settled by Treasury and Douglas, and Douglas would then get his Associate Ministers Caygill and Prebble onside, before going to Deputy Prime Minister Palmer and Prime Minister Lange. Issues that came up would be resolved before the package was presented to the whole Cabinet.

While the budget process was essentially a secret one, Douglas would often bounce ideas off his friends from the business world, such as Alan Gibbs. There was little consultation with other government departments however, as one departmental chief executive explained:

> It was a closed book in those days. Treasury played it extremely close to their chest because they were worried that the rest of the public service—including us—were going to stymie the reforms altogether. So their whole approach was very much one of working behind closed doors.

The Budget was prepared with some urgency. The election had been called during the time when a budget would normally be delivered and Douglas saw himself as having only a few months to prepare his Budget. According to Mike Moore, a one-time associate finance minister and prime minister:

> This completely suited the crisis management mentality of Douglas. He thought it was good. And he went like a madman. It was a normal budget process, except that here you had a very radical person, with an historic opportunity—a window of opportunity—so away they went.

This sense of crisis and this 'window of opportunity' sat well with Douglas's preference for large 'packages' of policy changes. He believed one could do more and do it more quickly through such a large package, and as the package contained a number of policies, if someone lost on one, they might gain on another. Douglas saw this as likely to achieve greater consensual support. The sheer size of the packages also meant a large volume of changes could be 'crashed through' before opposition could organise itself (Douglas 1993).

In summary, the 1984 Budget was a document largely prepared by Douglas, a few senior ministers, and Treasury officials. The budget process was at that time secret and the 1984 Budget's development reflected the belief of its key initiators and developers that change could be introduced most rapidly and successfully by avoiding consultation and discussion.

The Labour Relations Act 1987

The Labour Relations Act 1987 tried (largely unsuccessfully) to encourage enterprise bargaining by allowing employers to be 'cited out' of an industry collective agreement (called an award) where unions wished to negotiate separate agreements on an enterprise basis. Compulsory unionism was retained with the proviso that a ballot for its retention be held every three award rounds. The Act also encouraged the amalgamation of smaller unions into larger units by setting the minimum size of unions at one thousand. The distinction between arbitration and mediation was removed and the Arbitration Court divided into the Arbitration Commission (for disputes of interest) and Labour Court (for legal matters) (Brook 1989; Walsh 1989). Other measures to encourage union development were also introduced, such as leave for union officials and encouragement in the formation of the Council of Trade Unions. In contrast to the other economic policy decisions considered here, the Labour Relations Act 1987 was passed only after a comprehensive process of consultation. The range of groups and individuals that were important are reflected in Table 4.4, which shows a variety of individuals nominated as influential. These include union leaders such as Ken Douglas, members of employer groups such as Jones from the Employers' Federation, Cabinet Ministers Rodger and Douglas, Labour Party back-bencher Helen Clark and Department of Labour official Doug Martin. While some liberalisation of the labour-market was carried out, this was not as extensive as the Treasury and Douglas would have liked, and the consultative process led to one of the few important defeats of the Treasury and the right of the Labour Government on economic policy. This underlines the importance of process in limiting Treasury power and suggests that the Treasury was not powerful in other policy decisions simply because their ideas were 'better'—but also because they were able to dominate the policy-making process.

As Walsh (1989) documents, the incoming Government was presented with a report from the Long-Term Reform Committee, formed in 1982 to look at labour-market reform. The recommendations of this report were largely introduced in an amendment to the Industrial Relations Act in 1984, which reintroduced compulsory unionism, and instituted a Tripartite Wage Conference. This conference had responsibilities to look at the economic conditions in which the wage round would take place and what the wage settlement should be, to look at low paid workers, and to introduce more flexibility to wage negotiation. Voluntary arbitration was also introduced (Walsh 1989).

The amendments to the Industrial Relations Act were followed by a comprehensive process of consultation for the new Labour Relations Act. This consultation lasted eighteen months. On one hand, there were a number of groups pushing for extensive liberalisation of the labour-market. Treasury, for example, had outlined support for a move to more flexibility in *Economic Management*, and this general support for deregulation was given a more concrete form in a number of submissions and papers. The newly emergent Business Roundtable also called for labour-market deregulation, as did the Employers' Federation, influenced

Table 4.4 Persons nominated as influential on the Labour Relations Act 1987

Name	Votes	Position	Name	Votes	Position
S. Rodger	26	Min Lab	Lange	3	PM
K. Douglas	13	Union leader[1]	S. Marshall	3	Employers' Fed
R. Douglas	13	Min Fin	Scott	3	Sec Treas
Clark	7	Lab back-bencher[2]	Stockdill	3	Dept Lab official
Martin	6	Dept Lab official	Butterworth	2	Employers' Fed
Prebble	6	Ass Min Fin	Campbell	2	Union leader
Jones	5	Employers' Fed	Duignan	2	Treas official
McKenzie	6	Sec DOL	Harris	2	Union leader
Caygill	4	Ass Min Fin	Kerr[3]	2	NZBR
Palmer	4	Dep PM	Wilson	2	Pres Lab Party
Foulkes	3	Union leader			

Notes

1. President of the Federation of Labour, the peak private sector union body. When the FOL amalgamated with the public sector unions to become the New Zealand Council of Trade Unions, he took over as president of this new body.
2. Minister after 1987.
3. Left Treasury and was appointed Executive Director of the Business Roundtable in 1986.

in part by the direction the Business Roundtable was taking. The right of the Labour Government, such as Douglas and Prebble, were also keen to move in the direction of extensive deregulation. On the other side, some unions were pushing for some re-regulation of the labour-market by contributing to the debate through submissions on the Labour Relations Act, and through their ties within the Labour Party Caucus (as opposed to the Cabinet) and to extra-parliamentary party figures such as industrial law academic and Labour Party President Margaret Wilson. Margaret Wilson was an important figure in the development of the Act, helping to keep the consultative process going and countering the arguments of the right.[16] The Department of Labour also supported some deregulatory moves but was wedded to the existing system to some extent, with a commitment to collective bargaining and to encouraging stronger and more democratically accountable unions (Walsh 1989).

The actual policy process was largely steered by Stan Rodger, Minister of Labour and a past president of the main public sector union, the Public Service Association. Rodger was keen to oversee a major review of industrial relations law. A Green Paper called *Industrial Relations: A Framework for Review* was announced in August 1984 and released in December 1985, and was largely prepared by officials from the Department of Labour.[17] This was a major work; the first volume was a 47 page document setting out the existing framework and outlining points for discussion; while the second was an extensive 368 page survey of labour relations in New Zealand (NZ Government 1985a; 1985b). Submissions on these green papers were called for, and a document summarising these submissions was released (NZ Government 1986a). The Committee on Industrial Relations Reform was formed to consider the issues. It was chaired by Stan Rodger and run from his office and included in its membership a selection of participants such as: Richard Prebble; Geoffrey Palmer; Labour Members of Parliament, including Fran Wilde and Fred Gerbic who were seen to have expertise in the labour relations area; and Margaret Wilson, the Labour Party President. The committee was serviced by officials from the Department of Labour.

A 'Key Issues' paper, not released to the public, was prepared, drawing from the submissions. According to Stan Rodger, he then convened a meeting in Auckland, where two and a half days were spent going through issues raised in this paper with the Deputy Prime Minister Geoffrey Palmer, Richard Prebble, Fred Gerbic, Eddie Isbey, Fran Wilde,

Margaret Wilson, and officials from the Department of Labour, the Treasury, the Prime Minister's Office, and the State Services Commission. Another meeting was held in Vogel House in Wellington. According to Stan Rodger, there were about 20–25 people at these meetings who went through 'issue-by-issue' until broad conclusions were reached.[18] A paper outlining broad principles was prepared and presented to Cabinet for approval, a White Paper entitled *Government Policy Statement on Labour Relations* (NZ Government 1986b) was produced and a draft bill prepared. The draft bill underwent some fine tuning in the select committee headed by Fred Gerbic.

In such a consultative milieu, it is natural that influence on policy will be shared. It was notable that respondents' views of who was most important in influencing the Labour Relations Act seemed to differ largely in terms of their institutional ties. Members of the Cabinet, for example, largely saw the final form of the Act as Rodger's initiative. According to David Lange:

> There were very few ministers you can actually credit with having made policy reforms that were their specific intellectual baby. But the Labour [Relations Act] one was Stan's—no doubt about that. Stan nursed that one through. The unions were reasonably on board. They wanted to keep onside with us and they weren't going to go to war, and Stan nursed them through it.

A number of participants in the process saw Rodger more as a referee than a driver of policy; he was often referred to as 'Sideline Stan'. According to a former senior Federation of Labour official, Rodger refused to outline the Government position and 'tried to sit there as a neutral observer [leaving it to the unions and employers to reach an agreement] ... which then allowed the Employers' Federation to frustrate the process'. It was only when other Labour Members of Parliament became involved, that this union official saw progress as being made.

Some of those involved in employers groups saw the Act as largely a union victory.[19] As an Employers' Federation official noted:

> the union movement gave them a formula . . . which moved towards decentralisation whilst leaving all the power with the institutions. We had some influence, but the fact of the matter was, our input was basically ignored. That is one of the reasons the new legislation didn't work, because it was structured still around existing institutions and power bases. We weren't so much shut out, we were just ignored.

According to one respondent, union officials met for a couple of hours a fortnight with Stan Rodger and made a large number of submissions. They also exerted influence through their ties to certain members of the Labour Caucus and extra-parliamentary Party, possibly to a greater extent than through their direct involvement in the policy process. However, to see the Act merely as a union victory would be to overstate the case. At the time, a number of unions were ambivalent about being too closely involved in the actual process and, to some extent, were divided amongst themselves about what they actually wanted. A number of unions were also ambivalent about the final Labour Relations Act itself, although, in retrospect, many are now more supportive of what the Act was trying to achieve. Stan Rodger did not see the unions as important, describing them as 'not really . . . players'.

Rather than seeing the Act as a union victory, Walsh (1989) sees the role of the Department of Labour as key in understanding its final form. According to Walsh (1989, 162–3) the Department shaped 'the agenda and control[led] the process and pace of debate and policy-making'. This included preparing the initial Green Paper, servicing the committee on Industrial Relations Reform, and preparing the summary of submissions on the Green Paper and the Key Issues Paper. They were able to present a closely reasoned defence of collective bargaining. By defining the agenda, according to Walsh, the Department of Labour was able to exclude those wanting to push for more radical deregulation, while still allowing for significant liberalisation. These competing forces led to the final Act being what one respondent called a 'stand off', and a situation where influence on the final form of the Act was widely shared.

Conclusion

This chapter has examined three key economic policy decisions made during Rogernomics: financial liberalisation, the 1984 Budget and the Labour Relations Act 1987. The simple institutional structure of New Zealand interacted with ideas and ideology, and economic and political factors, as well as personalities, in the making of economic policy decisions. In the first two decisions, influence was concentrated around a select group of individuals from the Cabinet, the Reserve Bank, the Treasury and business. Financial liberalisation reflected the advice of the Reserve Bank and the Treasury, and was largely adopted by a supportive new

Government, partly in the face of the feeling of crisis induced by the run on the dollar. The 1984 Budget reflected the combined influence of the policy programme developed by Roger Douglas and a few key officials prior to the election, and similar thinking developed within the Treasury and promulgated in the post-election briefing paper *Economic Management*. The Budget was developed in secret—with little consultation outside a group consisting of Douglas, key minsters and officials—and contained a wide range of policy innovations. Influence was more widely shared during the making of the Labor Relations Act 1987, with trade unions, the Labour Party and the Employers' Federation also being important. This reflected the wide consultative process undertaken during the policy development of the Act, something unusual for this period.

Studying particular decisions and social networks, in this and the following chapter, gives a number of insights into policy networks and communities. First, trust relationships and social ties between leading officials, and between officials, politicians and others, such as those built up during the currency crisis and by Treasury officials seconded to the opposition before the 1984 and 1990 elections, can have important effects on policy decisions and how decisions are made. This underlines the importance of micro-level and social ties in understanding broad policy issues. Second, influence in New Zealand can be highly concentrated amongst a relatively stable and long-lived 'policy community' across a number of policy decisions, in a very broad policy area (in this case economic policy) and over a considerable period of time. This highlights the importance of context when making claims about how policy networks and policy-making operates. Third, public officials may wield greater influence than even prime ministers over key policy directions. These influential officials were not always highly placed secretaries or departmental chief executives, with a number of less well-placed officials noted as important. The next chapter examines four further key decisions; the privatisation of state assets; the Reserve Bank Act 1989, the 1991 Budget and the Employment Contracts Act 1991. It will show that in these decisions too, influence was highly concentrated around a select group of elites, largely from the cabinet, Treasury, the Reserve Bank and the Business Roundtable.

5
Economic Policy Decision Making in New Zealand from Privatisation to the Employment Contracts Act 1991

While the election of 1990 saw the end of the Fourth Labour Government, the National Government that followed accepted the new policy direction and extended it to areas which had been largely untouched: those of social policy and industrial relations. This chapter examines four key decisions: two made during the Labour Government and two made after the 1990 election when National took power. The Reserve Bank Act 1989 cemented into legislation the 'inflation-only' focus of monetary policy and gave the Reserve Bank independence in its conduct. Privatisation was carried out largely after 1987. It differed from privatisation in Australia because of the rapid way assets were sold, often despite election promises to the contrary, and, in some cases, at prices that were possibly lower than they should have (Jesson 1999). While the Australian Labor Government managed the privatisation process with considerable skill, in New Zealand it generated opposition and electoral damage. The Labour Government seemed unwilling to compromise or to persuade the electorate (and even its own extra-parliamentary party) of the wisdom of the new policy directions. The new National Government after 1990 accepted the new policy directions of the previous Labour Government, continued privatisation and extended liberalisation to areas comparatively untouched; that of social welfare and health (addressed in the 1991 Budget) and the labour-market (addressed in the

101

Employment Contracts Act). The 1991 Budget included massive cuts to welfare benefits, while the Employment Contracts Act introduced a radical system of individual contracting into the labour-market.

As found in the previous chapter, influence in decision making was largely concentrated amongst the key institutions of the cabinet, the Treasury, the Reserve Bank and the Business Roundtable. A small number of individuals from these institutions exerted influence across a number of decisions and over a considerable period. The senior ministers nominated changed with the election of the National Government, as would be expected. However, a number of others influential in the decisions made during the Labour Government, such as Treasury Secretary Graham Scott, Rod Deane and Treasury official (later Business Roundtable chief executive) Roger Kerr, carried their influence over to decisions made under the new regime. Once again, the results of this chapter emphasise the power certain officials can wield over policy decisions and directions, and that officials can be more influential over certain policy decisions than even prime ministers.

Privatisation

In 1984, the New Zealand state had considerable ownership of infrastructure and trading enterprises including banks, insurance, hotels, telecommunications, transport and heavy industry (including oil-based industries). These trading enterprises accounted for 12 percent of GDP and 20 percent of investment (Treasury 1984a, 275). Starting with the largely uncontroversial public float of shares in Petrocorp in 1987,[1] the Labour Government embarked on a rapid and widescale programme of privatisation, which was continued by the National Government after 1990 (Table 5.1). During the 1990s, the New Zealand privatisation programme was the largest in the OECD in terms of sale receipts as a percentage of GDP (RBA 1997).

Of the actions of the Labour Government, privatisation was one of the most controversial and possibly electorally damaging, coming as it did in the face of explicit promises not to sell certain assets; most notoriously the broken promise made by David Lange in the electoral campaign of 1987 not to sell Telecom (the telecommunications arm of what had been the Post Office).[2] Relations between the parliamentary and extra-parliamentary Labour Party were also severely strained over

Table 5.1 Corporatisation and sale of state assets in New Zealand[1]

1986
- State Owned Enterprises Act 1986 establishes nine state owned corporations: the Government Property Service, the Airways Corporation, Forestcorp, Landcorp, New Zealand Post, Post Office Bank, Electricorp, Telecom and Coalcorp. (SOE Act comes into effect 1 April 1987)
- Decision announced to sell government's interest in NZ Steel

1987
- Government announces it will sell shares in the Bank of New Zealand and Petrocorp. (15% of Petrocorp sold by tender, 15% by float)
- Budget (18 June) announces the Government will sell all its shares in New Zealand Steel, and shares in the Development Finance Corporation, Petrocorp and Air New Zealand. The budget also announces the Government Property Services Corporation and Forestry Corporation will issue State enterprise equity bonds (a form of non-voting public share holding) equal to 25% of total paid-up capital, while other SOEs will be authorised to do the same
- Government 'Economic Statement' of 17 December announces a programme of ongoing asset sales with the intention of reducing public debt by one third by 1992, with the benefits of sales assessed on a case-by-case basis

1988
- NZ Steel sold to Equiticorp
- Sale of Petrocorp, with remaining 70% to Fletcher Challenge
- Health Computing Service sold to Paxus Information Services
- DFC sold to National Provident and Salomne Brothers
- Bank of New Zealand 26% sold to Fay Ritchwhite, 16% floated, (57% government share sold to National Australia Bank in 1992)

1989
- Postbank sold to ANZ Banking Group
- Shipping Corporation sold to ACT (NZ) Ltd
- Air New Zealand sold to consortium of New Zealand and foreign companies
- Landcorp Financial Instruments sold to Fletcher Challenge
- Rural Bank sold to Magneton Holdings.
- Communicate NZ sold to DAC Group Ltd

1990
- Government Printing Office sold to Rank Group and others (1989–91)
- National Film Unit sold to TVNZ

- State Insurance Office sold to Norwich Union
- NZ Telecom sold to American and New Zealand consortium, with 30.9% now floated
- Tourist Hotel Corp sold to Southern Pacific Hotel Corp (NZ) Ltd
- NZ Liquid Fuel Corporation, Synfuels Stocks and Current Assets, and Maui Gas sold to Fletcher Challenge and others
- Forestry Cutting Rights sold to a variety of companies (1990–92)
- Export Guarantee Ltd sold to State Insurance Office (an ex-SOE)

1991
- NZ Railways Corp (Bus Services) sold to co-operative of NZ operators
- Housing Corp Mortgage sold to TSB Bank Ltd, Postbank, Mortgage Corp of NZ and others (until 1999)

1992
- Studies on four SOEs commissioned by Government to reach decision on privatisation
- Government Supply Brokerage sold
- Taranaki Petroleum Mining Licenses sold to Petrocorp/Southern Petroleum and others
- New Zealand Timberlands sold to ITT Rayonier

1993
- New Zealand Rail Limited sold to Wisconsin Consortium
- Wrightsons Rights sold to domestic and international institutions

1994
- Government Computer Services sold

1996
- Various airports sold to local authorities (until 1998)
- Maori Development Corporation holdings sold to the Maori Development Corporation (sic)
- The Radio Company Ltd sold to NZ Radio Network Ltd
- Forestry Corporation of NZ Ltd sold to consortium of Fletcher Challenge, Brierley's and Citifor Inc
- Works and Development Services Corporation NZ Ltd sold to Downer and Co and Kintas Kellas

1998
- Capital Properties NZ Ltd, first instalment of public share float

1999
- Contact Energy sold, with 40% to Edison Mission Energy Taupo Limited and 60% public float

Notes
1. Accurate to 30 June 1999. Sources: Bollard and Mayes 1993; Treasury 1999 and various budget statements. As at 30 June 1999 sales had raised $NZ19,102,878,000.

the privatisation programme and the way it was handled by the Government, with extra-parliamentary concerns having been largely ignored, or in some cases, treated with contempt.[3] Controversy also arose over how the sale of some of the assets was handled, with the possibility that some, such as the Rural Bank and the Government Printing Office, were sold well below their true market value.[4] The Government also found itself facing a legal battle over the collapse of the Development Corporation Fund after its sale. Many key sales were made during the recession of the late 1980s and early 1990s, when demand and therefore the price gained for the sales was possibly lower than might have been achieved at other times. Privatisation was largely initiated by the Treasury, and was supported by key ministers and business leaders. Table 5.2 shows those persons nominated by respondents as influential on privatisation, including Ministers Douglas and Prebble, Treasury Secretary Scott, State Services Commissioner Rod Deane and business leaders Kerr and Trotter.

The privatisation process can be seen as having two stages. The first was corporatisation, the second was privatisation, which itself grew out of the corporatisation process. Corporatisation was first announced in the *Economic Statement* of December 1985 and formalised in the State Owned Enterprises Act 1986. SOEs were moved from traditional departmental management structures to ones that attempted to make

Table 5.2 Persons nominated as influential on privatisation

Name	Votes	Position	Name	Votes	Position
R. Douglas	51	Min Fin	Andrew	6	Treas official
Prebble	46	Ass Min Fin SOEs	Fernyhough	6	CE SOE/Consultant
Scott	27	Sec Treas	Myers	4	Bus Leader
Deane	16	State Serv Comm[1]	Fay	3	Banker
Trotter	15	Bus leader/NZBR	Duignan	3	Treas official[2]
Kerr	13	NZBR	Lange	3	PM (1984–9)
Caygill	12	Min Fin	Palmer	3	PM (1989–90)
Gibbs	10	Bus leader	Elworthy	2	Fed Farmers
Cameron	9	Treas official	Rodger	2	Min SOEs
Chetwin	9	Treas official	Wilkinson	2	Treas official[3]

Notes

1. Previously deputy governor of the Reserve Bank, took over as State Service Commissioner in 1986. He left in 1987 to head the State Owned Enterprise, Electricorp, and later became the chief executive of Telecom.
2. Left the Treasury in the mid-1980s and now works in the private sector.
3. Left Treasury in the mid-1980s and now works in the finance industry.

them behave more like commercial enterprises. This involved, according to Deane (1989, 118):

> the need for SOEs to concentrate upon their commercial objectives; to be run as successful businesses; to be as transparent as possible in their operations by providing full and ongoing information about their activities in a normal commercial manner; to function within the competitively neutral environments free of regulatory favours and inhibitions; to be appropriately monitored to ensure adequate accountability; and, *in some cases, to be privatised to ensure the attention of a maximum degree of efficiency* (emphasis added).

Like many of the reforms under the Labour Government, the corporatisation process was pushed through remarkably quickly, with policy formation concentrated around key ministers and officials who were often operating outside official channels. There was some resistance from the existing public service, if not always because of the direction of the change, at least because of the speed and extent of it.[5] Dr Roderick Deane, who had already been involved in the SOE process, was brought from his job as Deputy Governor at the Reserve Bank to head the State Services Commission largely to bring about modifications to its corporate culture and make it more supportive of the changes.

While the corporatisation process generated some controversy, especially from those under threat of losing their jobs (Russell 1996), as far as the Labour Government was concerned it was probably privatisation that was the most contentious. It was certainly not prefigured in the manifesto of 1984, which, if anything, gave support for state involvement in the economy and ownership of assets. Similarly, the speed of transition from corporatisation to privatisation suggests that there was never any real intention to allow corporatisation to bed-in and deliver positive results; rather it was merely 'polishing the family silver' in preparation for sale. This is implied by a former departmental chief executive:

> [We] started to corporatise, and then deregulated the industry, and we set it all up in such a way that privatisation could occur. And no one talked about it. And indeed the meetings were so secret we used to have them at Roger Douglas's house. Not publicly [seen as first step to privatisation] but privately it was . . .
>
> [Deane] was the great advocate for saying what we have got to do is form all these companies under the Companies Act so the Government could subsequently sell shares under them, and

then just have a little Act, which was the SOE Act 1986, which just linked the regular Companies Act into government ownership. The reason the SOE Act was so small was we just used the usual private sector legislation. The Labour Party were neurotic about us doing that, because they thought we were setting that up for privatisation, so the Ministers all said 'don't lets talk about privatisation'.

It would probably be unfair to claim that in the minds of all the Labour Cabinet, the SOE corporatisation process was just a first step towards privatisation. Certainly a number of respondents, including some of their fellow Cabinet colleagues,[6] believed that privatisation was in the minds of Douglas and Prebble early on in the corporatisation process (or even before). However, Douglas says he did not have any secret agenda to privatise state assets, but rather came to see privatisation as a procedure where the advantages of corporatisation could, in his view, be locked in and protected from governments that might feel the need to intervene in the future.[7]

The initial drive for privatisation seems, instead, to have come from the Treasury.[8] According to a former Treasury secretary, some officials in the Treasury had been advocating privatisation since the mid-1970s, although this was done privately and their thoughts were not committed to paper. By the time of *Economic Management*, however, this support for some degree of privatisation had become explicit (Treasury 1984a, 293–4). Treasury files show that, even before the SOE Act had come into effect, the Treasury was talking of the sale of some state assets (Treasury 1986). However, while it is certainly true that some officials had a clear view about the desirability of privatisation and of corporatisation as only a step towards it, for others in Treasury there was a gradual movement towards this position. As a head of department in 1996, (previously a senior Treasury official) says:

> I was running the part of Treasury that [set up corporatisation as well as privatisation]. As the SOEs were being set up, it became increasingly clear that there would be enormous efficiency gains in the process of separating regulatory, social and commercial functions, and setting up the commercial functions in business form and setting them up in competitive markets. But the potential gains would be limited because of the lack of contestability and market [discipline] and control. [We went] on thinking about can we replicate financial market discipline, the answer was yes,

up to a point, but you only get the full benefits with privatisation.

Once this Treasury position on privatisation had firmed, the Treasury quickly became a strong advocate of moving SOEs to a position where they could be sold. According to one ex-chair of an SOE, for the Treasury 'price didn't matter per se, because future governments might change their minds and not sell things. So the quicker it got done the better.' The setting up of independent boards, staffed from the private sector, was also important as a number of these new chief executives came to be advocates for moving the SOEs into private hands. This, along with advice from officials and a barrage of support from the business community and from the Business Roundtable, was an important factor in the 'social learning' that the Labour Cabinet was going through. A number of Cabinet members came to support the privatisation of some state assets, even if this was not always support for privatisation as a whole.[9] According to David Lange:

> If you're talking about the influence of people such [as the] Roundtable it comes through on these issues, which were issues of gentle maturation of position and changing of position and evolution of position. [Privatisation] is where you start to see Roger Kerr and the Roundtable moving in. They didn't actually set the agenda but provided the taste and the appetite for it and they also provided the macho challenges. And it was appropriate for the time, because we were a very dramatic Government and we did all sorts of dramatic things, and we smiled a lot and showed a lot of confidence and showed we hadn't been rubbished by the [share market crash]. There are some things you can't rationally explain.
>
> I was an advocate for selling some things, [such as] Railways, Tourist Hotel Corporation [and] Air New Zealand. There were some people who had their little hit list of what they wanted to get rid of, and other people who had lists of what they regarded as strategic worth, such as the Post Office. And so again the BRT [NZBR] started. And their mates that used to provide comment on Morning Report [a widely listened to news show on the publicly owned National Radio] who had never made a bob in business but became business experts on Radio New Zealand.

The growing debt problem, particularly with the movement of a number of producer board debts onto the government balance sheet and the need to recapitalise assets, was a factor that convinced some Labour ministers of the desirability of selling a number of assets. It was cited as the justification for such actions in the Government 'Economic Statement' of December 1987.[10] However, for other ministers, and a number of officials, efficiency arguments were more important.[11] Further reasons were given in the 1988 'Budget Statement', including: that ministers did not make good business owners and would be better to concentrate on social and economic policy objectives; that with privatisation there would not be draws on government funds; and that risk to the government would be minimised. Those in the Cabinet who were, or became, wholly convinced of the benefits of privatisation, such as Douglas and Prebble, were important in convincing others that privatisation was the way to proceed. No one else in the Cabinet presented such a closely argued alternative. It would be a mistake however, to see asset sales as simply something driven by Douglas and Prebble in the face of a compliant Cabinet. It is worth noting that even after Douglas had been replaced as Finance Minister and Prebble fired as SOE Minister, the Cabinet continued along the privatisation path with the most controversial sale of Telecom coming in the last months of the Labour Government.[12]

The Reserve Bank Act 1989

The Reserve Bank Act 1989 made a requirement of the practise the Bank had been following since 1984: that of formulating monetary policy principally to combat inflation, rather than targeting other possible considerations such as employment or output (RBNZ 1990b; 1990c). The Bank was given greater autonomy in this pursuit, with the government role in monetary policy largely limited to publishing inflation targets (0–2 percent) which the Governor of the Bank contracted to achieve within a certain time frame.[13] Table 5.3 shows those individuals nominated by respondents as influential in initiating and developing the Act. These include a number of Ministers such as Douglas and Caygill, former Reserve Bank deputy governor Rod Deane, Treasury Secretary Scott and a number of other Treasury and Reserve Bank officials. The Act showed the influence of Chicago School and New Classical arguments regarding the conduct of monetary policy, as well as the policy framework that influenced public sector reform in general and encouraged moves to isolate policy instruments from 'opportunist' politicians.

After the heavily interventionist and highly regulated style of monetary policy control by Muldoon in the 1970s and early 1980s, monetary policy under the new Government was largely left to the Reserve Bank and became solely directed at controlling price levels, with firm anti-inflationary monetary policy that was continued even in the period immediately following the 1987 share market crash (RBNZ 1990a). This singular focus on inflation was despite section eight of the Reserve Bank Act as amended in 1973, which articulated broadly Keynesian goals. According to the Act:

> the Minister may from time to time communicate the monetary policy of the Government, which shall be directed to the *maintenance and promotion of social and economic welfare . . . the highest level of production and trade and full employment,* and of maintaining a stable internal price level (emphasis added).[14]

The conduct of monetary policy after 1984, the development of the Reserve Bank Act and argument justifying it after it had been passed, reflected the influence of Chicago School and New Classical prescriptions (Dalziel 1993; O'Shaughnessy 1997; RBNZ 1992a). These schools argued that output and employment should be eliminated as policy objectives and that inflation should be the sole policy target. They focused on creditability and setting of monetary policy instruments (see Appendix Two). For example, the Treasury (1984, 115) had noted the 'fundamental (monetary) source of inflationary pressure' and the importance of the credibility of anti-inflationary policy in their post-election briefing notes. In a similar vein, Douglas and a number of officials argued that the previous monetary policy framework had contributed to New Zealand's poor performance in constraining inflation (O'Shaughnessy 1997). The

Table 5.3 Persons nominated as influential on the Reserve Bank Act 1989

Name	Votes	Position	Name	Votes	Position
R. Douglas	32	Min Fin	Kerr	6	NZBR
Deane[1]	21	SSC, CE Electricorp	Nicholl	6	RBNZ official
Caygill	20	Min Fin 1988–90	Neilson	4	Ass Min Fin
Scott	19	Sec Treas	Palmer	4	Dep PM, PM
Prebble	13	Ass Min Fin	Richardson	4	Shadow Min Fin
Brash	14	Gov RBNZ 1988–	Wilkinson	3	Treas/Banker
Fancy	11	Treas official	de Cleene	2	Min Tax
Russell	8	Gov RBNZ	Duignan	2	Treas/Bus
Grimes	7	RBNZ official	Lange	2	PM

Notes
1. Former deputy governor of the Reserve Bank.

mix of targets and the lack of separation between the government and the Reserve Bank meant, they argued, that there was a possibility that politicians could be tempted to interfere with monetary policy for the sake of electoral advantage. This in turn meant the credibility of the Bank in clearly demonstrating its commitment to conduct monetary policy in the pursuit of price stability, was undermined. As Douglas noted in a Cabinet memo:

> The lack of a single statutory objective, coupled with the perception that past governments have frequently switched the target of monetary policy from one objective to another has increased the real costs of disinflation since individuals are not easily convinced that monetary policy will remain consistently directed at controlling inflation (cited O'Shaughnessy 1997, p. 139).

Officials also drew on the experiences of central banks in other countries and empirical research on the link between bank independence and levels of inflation. Although, as the Bank admitted, 'empirical evidence was never taken to be fully conclusive' they saw it as 'at least suggestive that a more autonomous central bank would be helpful' (RBNZ 1992a, 208).

The design of the Act also reflected the general move within the public sector to tighten management and accountability structures, which themselves reflected the influence of Public Choice and New Institutional economics. As a Reserve Bank official noted:

> . . . another important aspect of the environment of the time was the major reforms in the public sector more generally. These included, in particular, establishing clearer objectives to public sector organisation, clearer accountability for the attainment (or otherwise) of those objectives, individual performance-based contracts for chief executives, and more management and financial economy within agreed policies and budgets. The details of the Reserve Bank's arrangements are analogous in many respects to these features of public sector reform (RBNZ 1992a, 208).

The Reserve Bank was also eager to consolidate and extend their powers of prudential supervision, in light of the massive changes to the banking system since financial deregulation (including the growth in the number of registered banks) and in response to changes that had been made to the monitoring regime in 1986 (RBNZ 1990d; 1992b). When passed, the new Act allowed the Bank to prescribe standards or guidelines for the registration of banks. This included introducing the capital adequacy system adapted from that developed by the Basle Committee on Banking Supervision.[15]

While strongly supported by the economic policy bureaucracy and while certainly reflecting the debates (theoretical and otherwise) of the time, according to a number of respondents, including Douglas, much of the credit for the initiation and design of the Act belongs to Douglas. According to one senior Reserve Bank official, Douglas was responsible for the basic principles of the Act such as the inflation target, the accountability regime, and the desire for a framework to guarantee the independence of the Bank. These moves, in Reserve Bank folklore, were seen as an attempt to 'Muldoon-proof' the Bank.[16] The Reserve Bank then set up a team under the leadership of Peter Nicholl to develop the proposals further, and Peter Neilson, then an Associate Minister of Finance, visited a number of countries to study Reserve Bank regimes and was given the responsibility for overseeing the development of the legislation.

The Reserve Bank worked closely with the Treasury, and while there was a general agreement between the two on the direction the Act should take, and both were working within a broadly Chicago School and New Classical framework, there was considerable debate over detail and about what management structure the Bank should finally take.[17] One Reserve Bank official described the role of Treasury as obstructive in the process and another downplays the role of Treasury in actually driving the process. Nevertheless, the New Zealand Treasury differed from the position the British Treasury had taken in similar debates in the United Kingdom in the past, in that they were strongly supportive of a move to an independent Reserve Bank and an independently operated monetary policy. The Bank too was generally very happy with the move to a more independent framework, because, as a former Reserve Bank Board member noted:

> the Bank seemed to have been deeply affected . . . over that whole Muldoon transition, they just saw the money disappear and they couldn't do anything about it. There just didn't seem to be mechanisms in place when someone just didn't seem to be reasonable. So they desperately did want a mechanism [for independence].

There was some internal debate over whether the Reserve Bank should have more broadly based aims rather than just targeting inflation in the medium term. In addition, a number of submissions to the Select Committee considering the Bill, including some from academic economists, either disagreed with the notion that monetary policy did not have long-run effects on employment and output, or argued that the Bank should take into account short-run effects on these variables, as was usual in a number of other countries (O'Shaughnessy 1997). The general argument was lost partly on theoretical grounds, because as one Treasury official said:

> Inflation primarily is a monetary phenomenon. [The belief that monetary policy can not really influence employment or output] while not universal . . . was certainly broadly the international perspective.

According to a Reserve Bank board member, the Reserve Bank was also not keen on having other targets apart from inflation, partly because it did not see itself as having any expertise in these other matters. There was also some debate about the appropriate inflation target, but the 0–2 percent band was decided on because, according to one Treasury official, 'ideally we should aim at price stability, you shouldn't . . . just accept some international average'.

A number of people were consulted outside the bureaucracy including academics such as Frank Holmes, Charles Goodhart (a monetary policy expert from the London School of Economics), and the former deputy governor Rod Deane. The Reserve Bank Board, which included such persons as Margaret Wilson and Peter Elworthy, was also kept closely informed.[18] The process began during late 1985 and took over three years, with the actual Bill being drafted early in the process. The result, according to a governor of the Reserve Bank, 'was a framework which in the end was homegrown; it didn't replicate anyone else's model exactly.'

By the time the Bill was introduced into the House, the Labour Caucus was also strongly supportive, despite the misgivings a number of academic and other critics voiced in submissions to the Select Committee considering it. In the Cabinet, only Moore had not supported the Bill, but he was talked around very quickly. Both sides of Parliament also supported the Bill, although there was some debate over whether to broaden the objective away from a single focus on inflation.

The National Government's 1991 Budget

Only six weeks after their election, the National Government introduced the 19 December 1990 'Economic and Social Initiative'. Despite the election result being seen by some as a rejection of Rogernomics by the electorate, this 84-page document continued the macroeconomic disinflation begun by the Labour Government (Vowles and Aimer 1993).[19] In the face of a 'fiscal crisis' and a projected deficit of 4.8 percent of GDP for 1991–92 (the Labour Government had predicted a small surplus) this fiscally contractory stance was taken, despite the worst recession in New Zealand since the Great Depression. The statement imposed significant cuts in welfare benefits (up to 25 percent in some cases) and tightened eligibility, leading to projected cuts of $1.275 billion in the yearly welfare budget and large cuts in other areas (Bolger et al 1990). It also set up a number of ministerial taskforces to study welfare, housing, health and education (overseen by the Prime Ministerial Committee on the Reform of Social Assistance) and prefigured a study of the pension scheme, then called Guaranteed Retirement Income. As with budgets under the Labour Government, the 'Economic and Social Initiative' and the 1991 Budget which grew out of it were initiated and developed by a group of mostly Treasury officials, ministers and select business leaders. As Table 5.4 shows, those nominated as influential included: senior Ministers Richardson, Bolger and Birch; along with Treasury officials such as Secretary Scott and Deputy Secretary Horn; Kerr from the Business Roundtable; and other business leaders.[20]

Unlike many of the policies followed by the previous Labour Government, some of the policies followed by the new Government were prefigured in their election manifesto. This is certainly true in the case of the Employment Contracts Act 1991 (see below), and there is a constant theme in the manifesto of looking at fiscal constraint, redesigning the welfare state and making people more self-reliant, without being more specific about what this meant in practice (National Party 1990). However as Nagel (1998, 250) has pointed out:

> [While] sophisticates who read manifestos could therefore anticipate most (but not all) of the liberalizing policies National would pursue in office . . . the party's campaign centred on the slogan 'Creating a Decent Society', and most voters appear not to have clearly understood National's intentions.

There were also a number of election promises that were clearly not followed by the Government: the superannuation surtax was dramatically increased in the second reading of the Budget, despite an election promise to reduce it.

The so-called 'Mother of All Budgets' followed on 30 July 1991 and delivered on some of the promises contained in the economic statement. In a series of documents remarkable for the scope of the changes they introduced, the Government: signalled that it intended to tighten superannuation eligibility with a rebatement scheme that was later relaxed in the face of a large degree of opposition; introduced major changes to the management of the public health system and introduced targeting for health, including some user charges (some of which were later removed); moved public housing into an SOE to be managed on commercial grounds; introduced major changes to the Accident Compensation scheme; and made changes to education (Richardson 1991). These cuts, along with cuts to defence, led to a downward revision of the projected fiscal deficit by $2 billion in 1991–92 (actual deficit was $2.5 billion) and $3.8 billion in 1992–93 (actual deficit was $1.8 billion) (OECD 1993, 31–2; 1994, 40–41).

In opposition the shadow finance minister Ruth Richardson had become a supporter of the economic direction taken by the previous government and had worked, along with other National Party market liberals such as Simon Upton, to move the party along in a similar direction. There was pre-election consultation outside the party with, according to Birch, 'anybody who would listen'. Richardson used the Business Roundtable, the Employers' Federation and senior business people to recruit her party colleagues to the new direction through such things as meetings and seminars. The market liberals in the party were largely successful in bringing about this change, and by the 1990 election the National Party had decided to pin back the welfare state, attack the fiscal deficit and deregulate the labour-markets.

Table 5.4 Persons nominated as influential on the 1991 Budget

Name	Votes	Position	Name	Votes	Position
Richardson	53	Min Fin	Kerr	8	NZBR
Scott	28	Sec Treas	Upton	6	Ass Min Fin
Bolger	16	PM	Fancy	4	Treas official
Birch	12	Min Lab	M.Prebble	4	Treas official
Shipley	9	Min Soc Welfare	Deane	2	CE Electricorp
Horn	8	Dep Sec Treas	Myers	2	Bus/NZBR

According to Richardson, Martin Haines (an economist attached to Richardson's office) and 'her team' (her office staff) had put together what would be the December package in 1989, and while the 'Treasury [were] my faithful agents in implementation . . . they did not craft the agenda.' A Treasury official, Iain Rennie, had been seconded to the National opposition as was usual practise, but according to Richardson, was 'very important in terms of the information base, not in terms of the direction or the determination'. Rennie was, however, highly influential in persuading less-than-enthusiastic members of the Cabinet before and after the election to support the new policy directions, especially in the case of Jim Bolger. There was also consultation with such people as Roger Kerr of the Business Roundtable.

Only two weeks after the election, Richardson had outlined the broad thrust of the economic statement in a memorandum to the Cabinet Strategy Committee (Richardson 1990).[21] The speed at which the economic statement was unfolded meant many of the changes were directly initiated from the Cabinet and in the beginning the Treasury were largely involved in implementation.[22] According to one head of department, then a senior Treasury official, Richardson had very firm, clear new ideas and also felt she had to show herself to be on top of the bureaucracy. However, Treasury too had advocated fiscal restraint through some cuts in welfare, education and health in their post-election briefing notes to the incoming government. They had already been working on a number of issues, such as: housing; the curtailment of the welfare state, including reducing eligibility and benefit levels; and the coverage of superannuation (Treasury 1990a; 1990b ch. 8). As a former secretary to the Treasury says 'it was a bit like 1984; there was a marriage between the sort of things they had been thinking about and the sort of things we had been thinking about.' The economic statement was formed largely from this interaction between the Cabinet and Treasury, and there was little consultation outside these two groups. Like Labour in 1984, the sense of crisis induced by the fiscal blowout gave the incoming National Government, at least in the minds of some of its ministers, a mandate to make drastic and rapid changes, and induced the sense of urgency necessary to drive these changes through in the face of less than total support from some members of Cabinet and the now very large National Caucus.

The budget process began where the economic statement left off. A large scale review of expenditure was carried out by the Expenditure

Control Committee chaired by Cabinet Minister Doug Kidd, which scrutinised the votes of the departments, with most of the detail handled by the Officials' Committee on Expenditure Control. Policy development was carried out by the Prime Ministerial Committee on the Reform of Social Assistance, which according to Shroff (1993) met 23 times between 30 April and 30 July 1991. Unlike most of the Cabinet during the first term of the Labour Government, there was a degree of scepticism regarding some of the new directions contained in the economic statement and the 1991 Budget. Richardson actively recruited Cabinet members to the cause, because as she said 'unless there was a community of interests in the Cabinet I couldn't possibly have had the reach with the budget.'[23] The budget process was often highly interactive, with Ministers giving an indication of what they wanted to achieve and officials responding with ideas and options. This process would often involve discussion between the Finance Minister and other Ministers and (mostly) Treasury officials over such things as the state of the economy, what the overall fiscal strategy should be, what other priorities should be, and how these should be implemented. The Secretary of the Cabinet and Clerk of the Executive Council describes the formal process (overseen by the Minister of Finance):

> Cabinet committees consider the detail and Cabinet decides the big picture ... Officials prepared papers on individual expenditure and policy issues for consideration by various Cabinet Committees. Committees either agreed them for recommendation to Cabinet or sent officials away for further work. When groups of policy or expenditure decisions were considered ready they were submitted to Cabinet for decision. Cabinet in some cases required further work at official or committee level before taking final decisions on material for inclusion in the budget. At the final stages of the budget process everything moved in a tightly coordinated sequence—preparation of the Estimates, final expenditure and policy decisions by Cabinet, drafting of budget legislation, printing of the Estimates and drafting of the budget speech (Shroff 1993, 7).

While there was an appearance of some consultation within the various committees, actual consultation outside the Treasury and the Cabinet was limited. This failure to consult on policy decisions (rather than just merely expenditure reduction) that would affect departmental responsibilities 'used to rankle somewhat' with other departmental chief executives, according to one chief executive. As another chief executive of a department describes it:

In social policy there was involvement from the social policy departments, but I think not as much as they probably should have been. It was like the [1984 Budget]. Treasury kept things to themselves [and Richardson] was intent on keeping major control over it. She didn't want any security [leaks].[24]

The Employment Contracts Act 1991

The Employment Contracts Act 1991, prefigured in their election manifesto and introduced by the National Government in the 19 December 'Economic and Social Initiative', extensively deregulated the labour-market, moving away from the active state involvement and sponsorship of collective negotiation that had persisted since the late nineteenth century (Walsh 1992; 1993). Instead, the new Act provided for individual contracts of employment between employer and employee, and removed statutory recognition of trade union registration. Voluntary unionism was introduced, with individual employees able to choose bargaining agents who did not necessarily have to be union officials (subject to employer veto over which potential bargaining agents can enter the workplace to obtain authorisation). The Act was largely the initiative of employer groups, especially Kerr from the Business Roundtable and Marshall from the Employers' Federation, with Ministers such as Birch and Bolger, officials, and members of the extra-parliamentary National Party also being nominated in Table 5.5 as influential.

Table 5.5 Persons nominated as influential on the Employment Contracts Act 1991

Name	Votes	Position	Name	Votes	Position
Birch	41	Min Lab	Bell	5	Emp Fed/National[2]
Marshall	24	Employers' Fed	Martin	5	Dept Lab
Kerr	22	NZBR	McKenzie	5	Sec Lab
Richardson	17	Min Fin	Brook	3	NZBR
Myers	10	Bus leader/NZBR	Kiely	3	Nat Party
Bradford	8	Nat back-bencher[1]	Gibbs	2	Bus leader
Bolger	8	PM	Knowles	2	Employers' Fed
Jones	8	Employers' Fed	Stockdill	2	Dep Lab
Scott	7	Sec Treas	Rowe	2	Employers' Fed
Trotter	6	Bus leader/NZBR			

Notes
1. Previously a senior official in the Employers' Federation.
2. Seconded by the Employers' Federation to the National party.

Business groups, especially the Business Roundtable, had been strongly advocating some move towards individual contracting since before the time of the debate over the 1987 Labour Relations Act. The Treasury had also been pushing for further liberalisation of the labour-market, including discussing individual contracting (Treasury 1990a).[25] The main impetus for what would be a radical change, however, came from Roger Kerr and the Business Roundtable. Kerr hired a Cambridge educated scholar, Penelope Brook, who produced a Hayekian influenced book on labour-market and individual contracting called *Freedom at Work*, which developed further the philosophical basis for the changes (Brook 1990). Roger Kerr was also important in convincing the Employers' Federation to back the individual contracting line. What was called a draft 'bill' or 'act' by a number of respondents was produced in the private sector, either by the Business Roundtable or the Employers' Federation. Whether this 'bill' was anything beyond a statement of principles or drafting instructions is, however, doubtful.[26] Realising that it was extremely unlikely that the Labour Government would move to deregulate the labour-market as much as they wished,[27] the Business Roundtable and the Employers' Federation started to lobby hard on the opposition benches. According to a senior Employers' Federation official:

> We had a series of fortnightly lunches [with] Bill Birch, Ruth [Richardson] and a couple of others . . . and we would go through each section of the labour-market and simply have an informal discussion about what happened in the present time and why it happened and what needed to change.
>
> We had quite a lengthy process. Basically what we had to do was to make people who had not had any experience in the labour-market understand the practicalities, there was Roger [Kerr] and myself and Anne Knowles. We worked through issue-by-issue because it was important for them to come to grips with the philosophies. We had to get them to understand the principles for inclusion in their election manifesto. There was a draft bit of legislation that was able to be given to them. They then worked through that.

Once the National opposition was convinced of the desirability of moving in the direction suggested, a group consisting of Paul Bell and Peter Kiely was set up in Bill Birch's office to develop the ideas further. Paul Bell had been seconded from the Employers' Federation, while Peter

Kiely was a partner in the law firm Hesketh Henry and had a decade's experience in industrial law. Kiely was also a member of the National Party Executive and deputy general counsel to the Party.[28] Bell and Kiely liaised frequently with Kerr and the Business Roundtable, and Anne Knowles from the Employers' Federation. The group worked through the series of policy principles that had been drawn up and debated though a number of National Party conferences (such as voluntary unionism and no right to strike in support of multi-employer contracts) and the general principles of the Employment Contracts Act were decided on before the election. The policy paper was developed further by Paul Bell, and what Walsh and Ryan (1993) call 'legal drafting instructions' were presented to Department of Labour officials by the new Minister of Labour only five days after the election.

While some Department of Labour officials were less than impressed with the quality of the initial drafting instructions and found it necessary to devote considerable work to developing them further, as Walsh and Ryan (1993) document, these initial drafting instructions set the agenda for future policy development. At first the process was to be in steps, building on the existing Act, but this was abandoned in favour of a totally new industrial relations act. According to one Cabinet Minister:

> We found the moment we took office, Bill [Birch] reverted to his more normal . . . incremental [approach] as lets just take one step at a time . . . in which Bill brought to the Cabinet table a half-baked . . . reform. [Richardson] trumped his card by tabling [her] own draft . . . drawn up in the private sector, a lawyer was engaged to do that . . . you should probably talk to Roger Kerr,[29] he is a key actor in all of this. And at that critical Cabinet meeting, [her] approach, let's do it once, let's do it all properly, prevailed over Bill's incremental approach.

Max Bradford, the chair of the select committee on the Bill and a former Employers' Federation official, also saw an important role for the select committee in simplifying the bill, without changing its basic principles. The basic principles that had been advocated prevailed in the Act. However, the business community, Treasury and some in the Cabinet like Richardson were not able to convince the Minister of Labour to do away with the specialist Employment Court. Strongly argued papers from the Departments of Labour and Justice, and submissions to the select committee, including from unions, favoured retention of the court. While maintaining the Employment Court was seen as a defeat by some employer groups, the radicalism of the Act and the speed at which it was introduced surprised and delighted many of them. As one corporate chairman and leading member of the Business Roundtable says 'We were somewhat surprised at the pace at which it happened—[it was] very much [a victory].'

Conclusion

Chapters three to five have analysed economic policy-making in New Zealand. In chapter three, the simplicity of the institutional structure of New Zealand and the broad processes of economic policy-making were demonstrated, while chapters four and five investigated a number of key economic policy decisions in detail. Economic policy-making was highly centralised and personalised, with a few key institutions such as the cabinet, Treasury, the Reserve Bank, the Business Roundtable and the Department of Prime Minister and Cabinet being most important. Of the decisions studied, the intensive consultative process involved in the Labour Relations Act 1987 saw an exception to the usual concentration of influence, with a greater range of individuals and institutions having been important, and with the Department of Labour having played a central role. However, in the Employment Contracts Act, the Department of Labour played a less significant role. While important in developing legislation and arguing against the abolition of the Employment Court, the Department was largely reduced to implementing the agenda set elsewhere. This chapter has analysed four key economic policy decisions: privatisation, the Reserve Bank Act 1989; the Employment Contracts Act 1991 and the 1991 Budget. Privatisation was driven by Treasury, cabinet and business leaders. The Reserve Bank Act 1989 was initiated by Roger Douglas and developed by a number of ministers, the Reserve Bank and Treasury and reflected the influence of Chicago School and New Classical theoretical ideas, as well as the general policy framework surrounding public sector reform. The Employment Contracts Act 1991 was initiated by the Business Roundtable and developed by a number of ministers, National Party officials and government officials, and reflected neo-liberal ideas. The 1991 Budget was initiated and driven by a number of ministers (especially Ruth Richardson), Treasury officials and business leaders.

Within the broad policy area of economic policy, a relatively stable and long-lived policy community, containing individuals located in key institutions, such as Treasury secretary Graham Scott, Roger Kerr from the Business Roundtable and Roderick Deane, along with senior ministers, exercised influence over a number of decisions and over a considerable period of time. Social and other ties, trust and consensus on policy directions, were facilitated between members of the policy community, before and during the process of economic policy decision making. This underlines the importance of micro- and decisions-level studies, and the importance of personal relationships between individual actors, in understanding broader issues of policy-making. In some of the earlier decisions examined, certain officials, such as Deane, Wilkinson, Cameron, Scott and Kerr, exercised a greater influence over policy decisions than did some of their public service superiors and senior ministers. As these individuals were promoted to positions within and outside the public service, sometimes by members of their 'policy community', this influence continued, even after the change of government in 1990. This was especially true of Scott, Deane and Kerr. In economic policy-making, formal structures, such as cabinet and officials' committees, were sometimes bypassed under the Labour Government, with policy being made by small groups of ministers and officials. Under the National Government, greater use of formal structures, such as cabinet and officials' committees, was made.

6
Economic Policy-making in Australia during the Labor Government

In Australia's sometimes complex federal system, influence in policy-making can be diffuse. While the federal cabinet is responsible for economic policy decisions and influence can be concentrated around key ministers, this dominance is not absolute. While cabinet often dominates the House of Representatives, the existence of the Senate, an upper house of almost coequal power, limits its ability to control the legislative process.[1] At the same time, the six states and two territories contain governments of their own, with considerable powers in economic policy, and policies often need to be developed with their consultation and agreement. Policy-making structures in the federal capital of Canberra can be complicated. A number of powerful departments and bureaux limit the ability of one department (such as a Treasury) to dominate economic policy formation.

During the Labor Government, attempts were often made to introduce policy change through negotiation and consultation. This was reflected in consultative mechanisms such as the Economic Planning and Advisory Commission (EPAC) which was established to facilitate interest group participation. The trade unions played a key role in policy formation through the incomes policy known as the Accord. Union influence on policy directions spilled over from the Accord to other aspects of policy, with the Australian Council of Trade Unions Secretary Bill Kelty wielding as much influence over economic policy directions as did some other non-economic ministers.

The federal government is the leading partner in economic policy-making within the Australian federation. It has control over monetary policy and external trade, it can make labour-market law for the States, and, as well as controlling its own spending priorities, it has a large role in fiscal policy in the states, in that it controls a large amount of public sector revenue and so can influence their fiscal policies. By far the greatest proportion of revenue from taxation is gathered by the federal government which has had a monopoly on income tax collection since 1942. State and local governments raise only 28 percent of total public sector revenues, while accounting for 46 percent of current outlays and 76 percent of capital outlays. The power of the federal government over the states is increased by its ability to target money to certain spending areas under Section 96 of the Constitution. Attempts, of varying success, are also made to provide cooperative solutions to policy problems through meetings and agreements between the state and federal governments such as premiers conferences and the Council of Australian Governments, which was established in 1992 (Commonwealth-State Relations Secretariat 1998). A notable example of this was the agreement between the federal, state and territory governments on the adoption of the National Competition Policy to promote efficiency in the public sector and to reduce costs for private business (Harman 1996). While important in economic policy, the federal government is not all-commanding, and where powers are not reserved exclusively to the federal government in the Australian Constitution, they are shared concurrently with the states, with residual powers also accruing to the states (Galligan 1995). This gives the states, and indeed territory governments, a significant role in economic policy formation and implementation. Given the overall importance of the federal government, however, this chapter will focus mainly on economic policy-making at the federal level.

The cabinet

In the Australian version of the Westminster system, executive power rests with the cabinet, with the prime minister sometimes having a pre-eminent position within that cabinet. Collective responsibility, where cabinet presents a united front and takes responsibility for its decisions, at least in public, is a convention of cabinet government, and was prominent under the Hawke Government (Davis et al 1993, 81).[2] In

Table 6.1 Institutions nominated as influential on economic policy 1983–93[1]

Institution	Votes	Institution	Votes	Institution	Votes
Treasury	76	Line depts	12	ALP	4
ACTU	63	Media	12	Industry dept	4
DPMC	44	EPAC	11	NFF	4
RBA	41	Bus assocs	9	Think-tanks[6]	4
Mins offices[2]	36	Academics[4]	7	Environ movement	2
Finance	34	MTIA	7	IR Commission	2
BCA	30	ACOSS[5]	6	Private consultants	2
Cabinet[3]	29	Private corps	6	State governments	2
Indus Comm	15	ACCESS econ	5		

Notes

1. Respondents were asked, 'Which groups or institutions do you think were particularly influential in economic policy as a whole during 1983–93?'
2. Contains 12 PMO and 11 TO.
3. Contains three Expenditure Review Committee.
4. Contains five ANU associated academics or centres.
5. Contains one 'welfare lobby'.
6. Contains Centre for Independent Studies, Centre for Policy Studies and Institute of Public Affairs.

1987, the 26 commonwealth departments were consolidated into 16, each represented in cabinet by a minister who was assisted by up to two junior ministers.[3] Strong party discipline gives the executive a dominant position in the House of Representatives, enabling it to dominate the initiation and development of legislation.

Ministers do not make policy alone, however, and while they may have strong beliefs and policy agendas they wish to implement, they take advice from, and are influenced by, a large variety of institutions and individuals. These other influences can sometimes be as important as the minister in initiating and developing policy, and can play key roles in implementing and evaluating policies. Strategic location will often be an important factor in this policy influence, with the formal roles of the central agencies and the Reserve Bank in economic policy-making ensuring that they will always be important in economic policy decisions.

This chapter examines the key institutions and processes of economic policy-making. Tables 6.1 and 6.2 show those individuals and institutions nominated as influential by respondents. Figure 6.1 gives a model of economic policy influence, with the 'inner circle', consisting of the cabinet, the central agencies, the Reserve Bank, the ACTU and the ministerial offices, being most important during the Labor Government. The 'first tier' illustrates those institutions outside the 'inner circle' that could be influential on certain issues and at certain times. This category includes the Business Council of Australia (BCA), the Industry Commission, EPAC, line departments and a broad category of 'business associations'. The 'second tier' includes those institutions whose influence is even less regular and variable or concentrated in select areas, such as the media, academics, a number of think-tanks, consultants, the ALP, the Industrial Relations Commission and very select interest groups such as the Australian Council of Social Services (ACOSS).

The central agencies

The Treasury

The 1986 *Commonwealth Government Directory* described the role of the Treasury as:

> ... advis[ing] and assist[ing] the Treasurer, and through him (sic) the Government, in discharge of his and its responsibilities in relation to economic, fiscal and monetary matters. The Department's main responsibilities lie in the field of general economic management. As necessary, the Treasury fills the function of the central co-ordinating body within the portfolio.

The Treasury's important role in economic policy-making proceeds from a number of factors. First, 'its traditional function of financial controller enabled it to be involved in the whole gamut of governmental activities' (Whitwell 1986, 20). While the role of financial controller is now shared with the Department of Finance, the Treasury's role of overseeing economic policy generally gives it a role in coordinating projects and commenting on and 'pulling-apart' 'pet' ideas and funding initiatives of other departments. Second, the Treasury is able to present itself, or attempts to present itself, as having a broad picture of the economy and representing the 'wider community interest' rather than one sectional interest or sector, as may appear to be the case for some other departments (Higgins and Borthwick 1990, 45). Third, with its relatively large number of university graduates, especially in economics and business, and its rigorous training and selection processes, the Treasury has managed to portray itself as the elite of the public service.[4] Fourth, the development of the 'Treasury line' and the strong unity amongst Treasury officials, has meant that Treasury officials are able to argue a consistent line in policy debate in contrast to other departments that may have a larger degree of internal disagreement (Whitwell 1986, 16–24). Fifth, the Treasury has often maintained control over information, sometimes trying to deny other departments access to key economic data, although this lessened during the second half of the 1980s (Langmore 1988). Critics of the Treasury have claimed that it will try to dominate economic policy-making by delivering cabinet submissions late or at cabinet meetings, so as to not allow other ministers or departments time to prepare responses (Langmore 1988). Finally, the close relationship that the Treasury can have with the treasurer, who usually has a high rank in cabinet, can mean the Treasury view is strongly advanced in cabinet. The success with which the Treasury view is advanced can vary—Keating as Treasurer had a close relationship with the Treasury, especially in the earlier years of his tenure, and was able to present their views strongly in Cabinet, whereas, during Malcolm Fraser's Government Treasury was less successful.[5]

The Department of Finance

The Department of Finance was created in 1976 when the financial management and expenditure control functions were split off from Treasury. This was, according to Weller (1989, 74) 'designed to break the monopoly of information that Treasury held, to provide alternative sources of economic advice, and to centralise the expenditure control function'. According to the 1986 *Commonwealth Government Directory*, the Department of Finance functions:

> as the co-ordinating body in respect of the Commonwealth's financial administration. The Department is responsible for the collection, preparation and analysis of financial and staffing estimates by all departments, and for examination, review and evaluation of expenditure and staffing proposals, principally from the viewpoint of their resource implications (Commonwealth of Australia 1986b, 1).

While the Department was created partly to counter Treasury's power and provide different views on economic policy, it often prescribed similar views to that of Treasury so that 'there have generally been two voices in Cabinet arguing similar briefs, rather than one' (Higgins and Borthwick 1990, 44). This homogeneity of opinion can be overstated and there were at times genuine disagreements between the two

Table 6.2 Persons nominated as influential on economic policy 1983–93[1]

Name	Votes	Position	Name	Votes	Position
P. Keating	72	Treasurer/PM	Johnston	8	Gov RBA
Hawke	56	PM	Sedwick	8	Sec Fin
Kelty	48	Sec ACTU	Carmichael	7	Vice-Pres ACTU
B. Fraser	46	Sec Treas/Gov RBA	Hughes	7	TO
Walsh	28	Min Fin	Ferguson	6	Pres ACTU
D. Russell	25	TO	Howe	6	Min SS/Health/Hous
Garnaut	23	PMO/Academic	Phillips	6	Dep Gov RBA
Button	22	Industry Min	Codd	5	Dep Sec DPMC
Dawkins	22	Min Trade/EET/ Treasurer	Fitzgerald	5	Sec Fin
			Ralph	5	BCA/Business
Higgins	20	Sec Treas	J. Edwards	4	TO/PMO
M. Keating	20	Sec Fin/DPMC	Gregory	4	Academic
Willis	16	Min IR/Fin/Treasurer	Kerrin	4	Min Ag/Treasurer
Morgan	14	Treas official	Visbord	4	Dep Sec DPMC
Crean	12	President ACTU	Blewett	3	Min Health/Trade/SS
Cole	12	TO/ Sec Treas	Bond	3	Business/Fraudster
Abeles	10	Business/BCA	Charles	3	Secretary Industry
Stone	10	Sec Treas	Hilmer	3	Business/Academic
T. Evans	9	Sec Treas	K. Henry	3	Treas official

Notes

1. Respondents were asked, 'Can you name the individuals you think were particularly influential in economic policy during 1983–93?' Down to three votes.

departments. However, it may be that having two departments backed by senior ministers presenting broadly similar neoclassical views meant that there was a greater likelihood that such views would be adopted. As well as advising on economic policy from a similar neoclassical framework to that of Treasury, as Campbell and Halligan (1992, 48–9) point out, the Department of Finance's focus on expenditure control suited the climate of fiscal constraint during the 1980s. Along with its key role in the Expenditure Review Committee (ERC) and budget process, as noted below, Finance administered the Financial Management Improvement Program (FMIP) and pushed for greater flexibility in budget and resource allocation processes (Campbell and Halligan 1992, 48–9).[6] Finance was also important in the corporatisation and privatisation debate.

The Department of Prime Minister and Cabinet

The Prime Minister's Department was established in 1911 and became the Department of Prime Minister and Cabinet in 1971. The main goal of the department is to serve the prime minister by informing and advising on 'those matters requiring the Prime Minister's attention as the Head of Government and the Chairperson of Cabinet' (DPMC 1990, 18). This includes coordination of government administration, giving assistance to cabinet and its committees, providing policy advice and administrative support to the prime minister and facilitating intergovernmental relations. The Department has also had a role in the status of women and multicultural affairs (Commonwealth of Australia 1993). The Department is divided into a number of divisions (some of which have changed their name and function over time) to provide advice and coordination. In 1990, for example, these divisions were Economics; Industries, Trade and Resources; International and Social Policy.[7] The Economics Division maintained a general overview of micro- and macro-economic policy, and was especially strong in microeconomic policy. Its level of expertise was increased by the recruitment of a number of Treasury trained economists. The DPMC is also important in coordinating and brokering issues between departments and trying to get departments, including line departments, to sign on to new policy directions and coordinate policy advice.

The power of the DPMC can vary with the prime minister. Under

Figure 6.1 Institutional influence in economic policy-making in Australia 1983–93

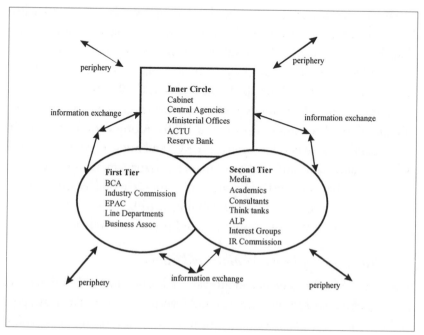

Malcolm Fraser, it was very powerful and a rival to Treasury, and this continued under Hawke, especially in the early years of his Government where the Department was a major contributor to economic policy. For example, Deputy Secretary Eddie Visbord was an important contributor to the financial liberalisation debate and the early budgets, and the DPMC was a strong supporter of floating the dollar. Under Prime Minister Keating the Department again became powerful as Keating sought to distance himself from his previous incarnation as Treasurer and relied heavily on the DPMC for economic policy advice and support.

Relationships between the central agencies

There were a number of official forums of cooperation between the central agencies. Each agency, along with representatives from the Reserve Bank and the Australian Bureau of Statistics, is a member of the Joint Economic Forecasting Group. According to Higgins and Borthwick (1990), this group met three or four times a year as quarterly national accounts become available and made projections based on the policy settings then current. The budget forecasts, which Treasury undertook by itself for reasons of security, built heavily on these forecasts. The Committee of Budget Officials with representation from the three central agencies, met to prepare advice for the ERC 'on Budget outlays, timetabling and process; and [was] also a forum for exchanging views on broad fiscal strategy' (Higgins and Borthwick 1990, 48). This was a not a very formal process and during the budget round the committee would meet every two or three weeks. Outside the budget round it met infrequently.

Generally, the three central agencies worked together during the Labor Government, although there were significant periods where there was some disagreement, such as over the float of the dollar and during the tax debates in the mid-1980s. A former deputy secretary of DPMC described the relationship as follows:

> Our relationship with Treasury was pretty complementary. We took a big interest in structural policy micro-issues where Treasury traditionally haven't played a large role in those. Treasury . . . from the mid-80s to early 90 were mainly dealing with macro-issues. They were interested [in micro-issues], they had a division, but we put more resources into those issues. Finance were always interested in the money. If we wanted to grease the wheels of microeconomic reform, Finance would always oppose that because it involved spending money.

Ministerial offices

Ministerial offices, with personally appointed advisers to the minister rather than (necessarily) departmental officials, largely began operations under the Whitlam Labor Government (1972–5). They reflected that Government's concern to increase the power of the ministers in dealing with departments that were suspected of having neither the expertise nor the inclination to implement the Government's agenda (Walter 1986). The system was continued by the Fraser Coalition Government (1975–83). Soon after the election of the Hawke Government, appointments to ministerial offices were formalised through the Ministerial Staff Advisory Panel. The growth of ministerial offices through the 1980s reflected both the fact that staff performed some roles previously carried out by senior public servants and were 'routinely involved in departmental processes' (Campbell and Halligan 1992, 203) and, according to one respondent, that the move to the new parliament building in 1988 allowed greater space for ministerial staff.

Ministerial advisers have a more explicitly political role than bureaucratic advisers—they are fundamentally the creatures of their minister and 'no matter how lofty their own aspirations are, they . . . must couch their advice in terms of the Minister's needs' (Walter 1986, 2). Ministerial advisers can be policy initiators and developers of considerable importance, as well as prompting and briefing the minister on important issues. Because of these roles, and the fact that staffers sometimes provide a nexus between the minister and the career bureaucracy and act as a filter of information for the minister, there is 'some evidence that ministerial staff exert considerable influence in setting agendas' (Ryan 1994, 155). While the advisory resources of the offices are tiny compared to that contained in the departments, the high quality of some of the staff and the closeness of the staff to the minister can mean this imbalance of power is reduced. Some ministerial staff also see their advisory role as compensating for the poor quality of advice from the department (Ryan 1994; Walter 1986, 148–50).

Hawke inherited a sophisticated office structure from Fraser, which he reorganised into three groups with specialised staff. Of the approximately 17–18 staff, eight were in the Administrative and Coordinating Group, six were in the Advising Group and three were in the Media Relations Group (Campbell and Halligan 1992, 64–5). In the Prime Minister's Office, Hawke employed Ross Garnaut, an ANU economist who was 'a dedicated anti-protectionist and pro-market economist . . . whose influence on Hawke was never remotely matched by any subsequent economic adviser' (Kelly 1994, 58). As trust between the Government and the bureaucracy grew, Hawke's office moved from being staffed mainly by political appointees to a position where most of its staff came from the career bureaucracy.

As Keating had taken over as shadow treasurer shortly before the 1983 election, he inherited some of Ralph Willis' staff. One of these staffers, John Langmore, did not fit with the new policy direction taken by Keating and the Government and soon departed. Keating also had in his office long-time aide Barbara Ward, a future Treasury official, and Greg Smith who had a background in advising the ALP. Tony Cole, a career Treasury official, a future chairman of the Industry Commission and Treasury secretary, became his private secretary. Former academic Dr Barry Hughes became his economics adviser. Later during the life of the Government, Dr Don Russell, a former Treasury official, became an economics adviser in Keating's office, and was extremely influential on Keating.

While having the ministerial offices staffed by career bureaucrats may have meant that the offices came to reflect the views of the departments, it may also be that influence worked both ways. The more explicitly political nature of the work in ministerial offices changed the way certain officials viewed policy. According to a former Treasury official who spent some time in the Treasurer's Office:

> You might go in with the Treasury line. But you had to take political things into account and so expand away from the purist line. On some occasions you might pull back from something you believe, you might repackage it to make it more palatable, or look for other ways to achieve it.
> It does affect you—you get exposed to a broader range of issues. Treasury has a Treasury line and they are not real keen if people try and buck the orthodoxy.

Time spent in a ministerial office meant some bureaucrats found it difficult to return to the bureaucracy. Others, in contrast, found it was not detrimental to career advancement within the bureaucracy. Tony Cole, for example, returned to the bureaucracy and moved steadily up the ranks to head the Industry Commission and then the Treasury, while Greg Smith moved to a senior position in Treasury.[8] As time in a ministerial office may change the way individuals view policy, it may be that the ministerial offices exerted a subtle influence over the bureaucracy when their former staff were placed in high positions.[9]

Cabinet committees and the budget process

Much of the work of the cabinet is carried out by cabinet committees. During the early years of Hawke's Government, committees grew to be particularly important and the number of decisions made by the full Cabinet decreased (Weller 1990). The two most important committees in economic policy-making during the Labor Government were the Structural Adjustment Committee and the Expenditure Review Committee. The first, the Structural Adjustment Committee, existed 'to focus on [the] development of Government policy on a range of issues relevant to improving the growth capacity of the Australian economy, including micro-economic reform' (Commonwealth of Australia 1991, 2). General principles for the development of certain policy issues covered by the Structural Adjustment Committee, such as the operation of government enterprises, were supplied by the cabinet and then worked through by the committee, subject to cabinet endorsement. The committee was supported by task groups of officials from the Department of Prime Minister and Cabinet (Codd 1990). The committee was an important forum for raising issues of trade liberalisation and microeconomic reform programmes.

The second important committee, the Expenditure Review Committee, existed:

> to examine expenditure proposals in the light of the overall fiscal strategy, to advise Cabinet on budget expenditure priorities and to initiate reviews of expenditure under individual programs (Commonwealth of Australia 1991, 1).

Under the Labor Government, the Expenditure Review Committee had a central role in economic policy-making. As well as reviewing expenditure it was also a major forum for the discussion and development of macroeconomic policy, superannuation and revenue issues. Its influence was such that it 'effectively [became] the crucible for all important government priority settings' (Higgins and Borthwick 1990, 50). During the early years of the Labor Government, the members of the Committee were the Prime Minister Bob Hawke, the Treasurer Paul Keating, Ralph

Willis (a future treasurer), John Dawkins (another future treasurer) and the Minister of Finance Peter Walsh. Brian Howe (Social Security) and Gareth Evans (Resources and Energy) were later additions.

The role of the ERC was central to budget development. Early in the budget process, the Treasury advised the Treasurer on what the fiscal envelope or strategy should be, drawing on the forecasts of the Joint Economic Forecasting Group (JEFG) and parameters set by the previous year's budget. This advice may or may not have been accepted by the Treasurer. A former treasurer describes how the ERC process began with the preparation of this budget strategy in February:

> A budgetary policy is determined by cabinet, which is always brought by the Treasurer. That would always be approved by the prime minister before it was brought to cabinet. There was agreement about what the budget objective would be. This provided a framework in which the budget's put together. It brought a bit of discipline into the budget targets.
>
> The ERC was always very important. It was the body which actually delivered the expenditure side of the budget. Sometimes the ERC would discuss the budget strategy, but more often it was taken to the full cabinet. So a strategy was developed in full cabinet and the ERC job was to deliver the expenditure side of that strategy.

Once the targets were agreed upon, the departments and the ERC would work on developing savings. The line departments would prepare submissions on possible savings, which would be coordinated between the departments and Finance before going before the cabinet or the ERC. The three central agencies; Treasury, Finance and DPMC had key roles in the ERC process, with the DPMC coordinating the business of government, Finance preparing detailed budget estimates and the Treasury taking overall responsibility for the integration of budget and general economic policy (Higgins and Borthwick 1990, 50). A former finance minister Peter Walsh describes the ERC process as follows:

> Savings papers—Cabinet memoranda which, unlike submissions, did not carry recommendations were then prepared by Finance in consultation with the relevant Department(s). These Memos contained a range of options [and] were circulated to ERC and other relevant Ministers.
>
> Finance prepared and circulated to ERC Ministers 'Green Briefs' . . . which contained the Finance view and arguments on each memo, some of which would have been disputed by other

Departments in an agreed memo.

On rare occasions the Committee would have private meetings—only politicians present—but usually, one personal staff member of the Prime Minister, Treasurer and Finance Minister would be present, plus Cabinet note takers, one Treasury official and two Finance officials . . . The portfolio Minister could also have officials or staff present and usually did. (Walsh 1995, 103–4).

The process where cuts were delivered was long-winded and political—and often entailed going through proposals 'line-by-line'. While ministers would often read the memos from the line departments, the 'finance greens' were usually more widely read, giving the Finance Department a powerful role in setting the framework and sequencing of the budget. While the process was dominated by Finance, it would often work closely with the Treasury in the background to try to develop a common perspective.[10]

Hawke's chairmanship of the committee was characterised by attempts to build consensus, including involving relevant ministers in discussions where specific portfolio spending decisions were being examined.[11] Ministers could appeal to the full cabinet if they did not agree with expenditure decisions, but this was seldom done so that 'ERC decisions [became] de facto Cabinet decisions' (Walsh 1995, 103). The decisions of the cabinet and its committees were in part the outcomes of interplays of personalities and alliances. In the early stages of the Labor Government, the relationship between Hawke and Keating was very strong and this gave them the ability to achieve many of their policy aims.[12] While in general there was a broad consensus for the liberalisation of economic policy in Australia, there were some disagreements over policy directions in the Cabinet particularly from the 'left-wing' Ministers such as Brian Howe and Susan Ryan (Education). Ministers could also resist attempts to reduce the resources of their own portfolio. As a result, the ERC process became, at times, extremely rigorous and sometimes unpleasant. Susan Ryan describes it as follows:

> Most of the time it was intensely adversarial . . . highly aggressive, very unpleasant. Walsh in particular was extremely aggressive, he would suddenly produce these figures we hadn't seen before. I would bring in my own aggressive fellows—so we would have shouting matches.

While there were certainly strong personalities, Keating being a prime example, economic policy development was not always dominated by one or two people in the face of a compliant cabinet, and instead key cabinet ministers could be involved in policy development from an early stage, particularly through the ERC. This is in contrast to how the previous Coalition Cabinet under Prime Minister Malcolm Fraser had operated, as Fraser largely concentrated decision making around himself and his office. While Hawke tried to keep a watching brief over what was happening in the various ministries and liked to ratify decisions in Cabinet and in committees, Keating as Prime Minister saw his role more as an initiator of key policy and didn't see the need to keep abreast of what was happening in other ministries or engage in the policies being developed by other ministers. Keating, on the issues he was concerned with, was less likely than Hawke to try and build a consensus within the Cabinet. The budget process during the Labor Government is summarised in Figure 6.2.[13]

The Reserve Bank

The Reserve Bank is in charge of the formulation and implementation of monetary policy and provides general economic advice, especially on macroeconomic policy.[14] It also provides a general overview of the operation of the financial markets and the financial system (Reserve Bank

Figure 6.2 Making the budget during the Labor Government[1]

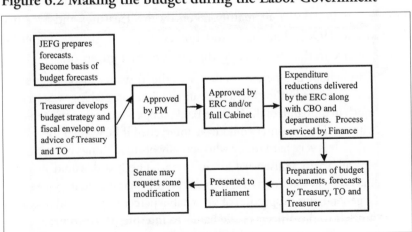

Notes
1. CBO is committee of budget officials. JEFG is Joint Economic Forecasting Group.

1987). The Bank was particularly important in the debate over financial deregulation and the float.

The way monetary policy was conducted changed over the life of the Labor Government. From 1976 to 1985, monetary policy was targeted at the growth of a number of monetary aggregates. These were abandoned after it was found, as in a number other countries including New Zealand, that partly due to financial deregulation any 'relationship between money . . . and nominal income that might have existed in earlier times was rendered an increasingly unreliable guide for policy by the financial deregulation of the 1980s' (Fraser 1994, 20). A transitional period where monetary policy was targeted at a checklist lasted until the early 1990s. This checklist included:

> interest rates, the exchange rate, monetary aggregates, inflation, the external accounts, asset prices and the general economic outlook—in short an amalgam of instruments, intermediate and final policy objectives, and general macroeconomic indicators (Macfarlane 1997, 26).

During 1993, the focus of monetary policy shifted to inflation, although the Bank still saw its role as also doing what it could 'to smooth the business cycle' (Fraser 1994, 21). Since the departure of Bernie Fraser as governor in 1996, it is possible that the focus on inflation-only has hardened.

There has been some debate over the level of independence of the Bank. For most of the 30 years after the Reserve Bank Act, monetary policy was implemented as if the Bank had no independence, with monetary policy decisions mainly taken by the Treasurer and Treasury (Macfarlane 1996). The Bank did however gain a greater degree of independence in the 1980s. According to a former governor:

> Throughout this period the law said the Treasurer made interest rate decisions but for the most part the decision making was very much in the hands of the Reserve Bank, subject to us carrying people with us. The Treasurer could have intervened if he wanted to.
>
> It is very hard to say who actually decided things because it was all a very consensual arrangement. The board would meet and come to some sort of agreement [as to] what should be done—in general, not in specifics of say a half a percent up . . . and it was just left to the officers of the banks to interpret those things.
>
> We would talk to the Treasurer [Keating] about the outcome of the board's deliberations and what we thought ought to happen

about interest rates. He would often have his own view, and the Treasury would have its own views. These things would get knocked around a bit. I can say this categorically, the Treasurer never instructed the Bank about what it should do about interest rates. He never sought to twist the board's views. He was quite impeccable in that sense. He was a very persuasive man, so we all talked together.

By the early 1990s, the Bank was asserting that it had a high degree of independence as outlined in the Reserve Bank Act. According to the then governor, Bernie Fraser, the Bank was to carry out this independent role 'in close consultation with the Government—to exercise independence with consultation' (Fraser 1993, 4). The relationship between the government and the Bank was further clarified by the Statement on the Conduct of Monetary Policy issued on 14 August 1996 which stated the government's understanding of the high degree of independence enjoyed by the Bank and gave support to the Bank's inflation target of 2 to 3 percent on average over the business cycle (RBA 1996).

As well as directing monetary policy, the Reserve Bank also played an important role under Labor in giving general economic policy advice. The governor would liaise with the secretary to the Treasury, as required by the Reserve Bank Act, and the Bank, through its general research programme and submissions to such things as the Campbell Report, would contribute to the framework of general economic policy. The Bank would also directly advise the government on general economic policy issues. According to a former governor:

> The machinery was that the Reserve Bank board always meets at least once a month. The board meeting minutes used to be extremely brief, partly because . . . we had to be careful that no more people knew what we had in mind. Following the meeting, the governor has a [verbal] debriefing session with the treasurer to tell roughly what the Bank thought about things, what should be done, a bit of chit-chat about policies generally.

The debriefing process later broadened out to include some Treasury officials, depending on the personalities involved. According to a former Reserve Bank secretary:

> Under Hawke, a meeting would be set up in the Bank's Canberra office. The governor, deputy governor, head of research and head of financial markets would be there and the equivalent Treasury

people. The head of research would show the slides that were shown at the board meeting. Then there would be a general discussion on the board meeting and where it had got to. There were occasions when the governor would feel he needed a private word with the treasurer without the others.

The Reserve Bank also sent a letter to the treasurer before each budget outlining the policies it wished to see implemented, and provided general economic advice in its annual report. Governor Bernie Fraser, Bob Johnston's successor, occasionally advised the treasurer directly on economic policy-making. Fraser had a close relationship with Keating, possibly because of the trust built up while Fraser was the Secretary to the Treasury. This was reflected in the direct contact Keating had with Fraser, which often involved unrecorded conversations over the telephone.[15]

The Australian Council of Trade Unions

The Australian Council of Trade Unions wielded influence on economic policy through its formal role in the Accord process as well as influence over economic policy generally, due to its ties, personal and otherwise, with members of the government. Bill Kelty, Secretary of the ACTU throughout the period of the Labor Government, wielded key influence over policy directions.

The ACTU was formed in 1927 and is the only peak council for the trade union movement with nearly all unions, especially the major ones, affiliated (Derry, Plowman and Walsh 1997; Harcourt 1994). The ACTU is supported by industrial, research, administrative and printing staff. It also has specialist advisers in a number of areas such as occupational health and safety, and childcare. With the help of its affiliates, the ACTU coordinates national campaigns on a number of issues such as equal pay, and occupational health and safety. The ACTU publish a number of reports each year and have carried out a number of research projects: one of the more significant of these being *Australia Reconstructed,* a report published by the ACTU and the Trade Development Council (Department of Trade/ACTU 1987). Carried out in August–September 1986, this study led to a number of recommendations including the use of 'positive industry policies' to restructure industry in the face of international pressures. While the approach seems to describe some of the early Button plans, later industry policy deviated considerably from this recommendation and instead followed a non-interventionist model, although *Australia Reconstructed* had some influence on the restructuring of unions (Anthony 1993; Rafferty 1997).

As chapters seven and eight explain in greater detail, the ACTU had an extremely close relationship with the Labor Government. As well as the formal ties developed though the Accord and through the union affiliations to the ALP, there were strong personal relationships forged between union officials and Labor politicians. These relationships were facilitated by the previous union experience of Hawke and Willis, and the later movement of former ACTU presidents Simon Crean and Martin Ferguson into federal parliament. The most important relationships were those between Kelty and Hawke, and Kelty and Keating. Kelty wielded immense influence on the Labor Party in opposition before 1983 and throughout the term of the Labor Government. His and the ACTU's support for Hawke was a factor in wrestling leadership of the Labor opposition away from Bill Hayden. Over time, Kelty formed a strong relationship with Paul Keating, and his power was probably greatest when both Hawke and Keating courted his influence in their leadership dispute of 1991–2.[16] Kelty's influence spread beyond the Accord process to other areas of economic policy-making, so much so that he was described by one respondent as having 'a seat under the cabinet table'.

Line departments

While not in the front line of economic policy change, the line departments played an important role in economic policy-making. The various incarnations of the Industry Department, Trade, Primary Industries, Social Security, Industrial Relations, and Education and Training departments,[17] amongst others, all had their own interest and expertise in economic policy both within their sectors and in economic policy broadly, and contributed research and policy advice in these areas. This expertise in economic policy was encouraged by the growth in recruitment of economists to senior positions (Campbell and Halligan 1992, 55). A number of departments also had research bureaux with varying degrees of independence, sometimes producing research work of high quality. These included: the Bureau of Industry Economics[18] under the aegis of the Industry Department; the Agricultural and Resource

Economics[19] attached to the Primary Industries Department; and the Bureau of Transport and Communications within the Department of Transport and Communications.

Traditionally there was considerable tension between the line departments and the central agencies and this continued to some extent in the early 1980s. Industry, for example, was sceptical of the moves towards economic liberalisation in the early days of the Labor Government. This strain had lessened considerably by the end of the 1980s, partly due to the amalgamation of departments in 1987, which contributed to the breaking down of traditional enmities and departmental ethos. Another factor was the spread of economics-trained chief executives and senior officials (a number with PhDs) through the departments, and the movement of a number of key officials through central and line departments. (These factors contributed to a similar view on policy issues.) Relationships were also stronger if line departments shared similar approaches to policy formation to those held by the central agencies. According to a former senior DPMC official, the relationship:

> with line departments depended on whether we had the same analytical framework. If we didn't, then we weren't getting on well. If we did, then fine. You had secretaries of the departments who got on reasonably well personally and I think it is a time that people saw the problems of the economy in a certain way. If you both get on well in a certain way and have a similar approach, it follows . . . the departments will get on well. It was different in the 70s and early 80s.

Views of the influence of line departments on economic policy vary. One chief executive of a line department claims that:

> Over that period, most line ministries played an equal part in policy initiation and policy review and were certainly equal partners in the process. I think that is a significant development compared to the previous Australian experience. I've worked in both [line and central]. There has been far greater consistency and depth in the influence from the line ministries.

The Economic Planning and Advisory Council

The Economic Planning and Advisory Council was set up under the Economic Planning and Advisory Council Act 1983 to provide a variety of sources of economic advice to the government, including medium and longer term policy assessments, and to allow for community participation in the development of economic policy advice. It was established in response to the new Labor Government's and Hawke's preference for consensus and for developing policy change through negotiation and consultation, and as part of the Accord agreement. It also reflected distrust of the Treasury by some Labor Party members (Singleton 1985). Serviced by an office of around 40–50 that supplied secretariat and research services, the Council was chaired by the prime minister and contained the treasurer, the minister for Industrial Relations, state premiers, and representation from the unions, business, and social policy groups such as ACOSS. Reports could be initiated and prepared on any aspects of economic policy to advise the government, but although it prepared pre-budget submissions, the EPAC did not have direct input into economic policy-making. Research would be prepared by the office and circulated to the council. The treasurer and occasionally other ministers would then brief the council on the state of the economy. Growing out of the discussion, EPAC reports would be prepared and released.

Views on the influence of the organisation differ. Singleton (1995) is sceptical of its influence on policy, although it served as a 'symbol' of consensus and a channel of communication. Reasons for this lack of influence include the following. First, the economic bureaucracy resented any threat to its influence that the EPAC provided, and worked to undermine it by limiting information and attacking its resource base— successfully pushing cuts that saw its staff numbers fall from 42 to 25 in 1986. Second, key groups, such as the unions, preferred to work outside the EPAC process and deal directly with the government through their Accord and personal ties, as did some other organisations, business people and groups, while some groups within the organisation found their views were less valued than others.[20] Third, there was also some scepticism regarding the independence of EPAC from the federal government and its ability to be genuinely critical of policy directions (EPAC/ Cooper&Lybrand 1994, 48–50; Singleton 1995). Due to this 'semi-independence', the council discussions and EPAC reports sometimes worked more as a selling outlet for government policy rather than as a generator of, or critique of policy. This emphasis on selling policies to the council rather than consulting on them grew with Keating's influence on economic policy, as he was less convinced of the value of building consensus than Hawke.

The EPAC's influence was important in: allowing the views of participants to be at least heard (if not always heeded) by the government; providing a useful source of research; and contributing to a milieu that favoured the use of research-based policy advocacy and the seeking of common ground by participants. While the EPAC's influence faded, from its heights early in the life of the Labor Government, as Ministers built up their own networks, it enjoyed something of a revival during the recession of 1992–3 when the usual sources of advice were temporarily discredited.

In 1994, the Economic Planning Advisory Council was replaced by the Economic Planning Advisory Commission. This organisation was more explicitly a research body without the direct representation of interest groups and the focus on consensus. Its functions were 'publishing studies on medium-term issues, coordinating Budget submissions, and undertaking taskforce work' (Commonwealth of Australia 1994, 383). The Director at the time saw this new EPAC as moving to work on social issues and potentially challenging the Industry Commission on industry policy. After the 1996 election, EPAC was combined with the Industry Commission and the Bureau of Industry Economics on an administrative basis. This body became the Productivity Commission under the Productivity Commission Act 1998.

The Industry Assistance Commission and its successors

The Industry Assistance Commission (IAC) developed out of the Trade Board which was set up to examine tariffs regimes and which, under Chairman G. A. Rattigan after 1963, became a strong promoter of trade liberalisation (Freedman and Stonecash 1997). The independent and often hard-line approach to removing trade protection by the commission and its successors, often quoted extensively by the media, was an important contributor to the elite intellectual climate that encouraged trade liberalisation in Australia, and a move away from government intervention in the economy (Capling and Galligan 1992).

The IAC conducted regular reports into the assistance offered to particular industries and its effects, which allowed for some consultation and public input. In 1987, the IAC was transferred from the Department of Industry, Technology, and Commerce to the Treasury. This, according to one minister, was instigated by Keating, as he wished to move the IAC out from John Button's control, both because he believed Button was not making sufficient use of the organisation and because he believed the liberalisation process would be speeded up if the IAC was placed in a more supportive environment. After 1988, again on the instigation of Paul Keating, the IAC moved from being a 'body concerned with industry assistance to one with a wider role in analysing all industries in terms of their efficiency' (Prasser and Paton 1994, 123). In 1989, the Industry Assistance Commission amalgamated with the Inter-State Commission on transport matters and the commonwealth's Business Regulation Review Unit to form the Industry Commission.[21] The Industry Commission was later absorbed by the Productivity Commission, as noted.

Business and business associations

The fragmentary nature of Australia's business associations has at times limited their effectiveness in influencing public policy. Australia has a plethora of sometimes competing and overlapping business associations. For example, in 1983, there were three major peak groups in business: the Confederation of Australian Industry; the Australian Chamber of Commerce; and the National Farmers' Federation. By 1993, this had risen to six national groups including: the Australian Chamber of Commerce and Industry; the Business Council of Australia; the Australian Chamber of Manufactures; the Metal Trades Industry Association; the Australian Mining Industry Council; and the National Farmers' Federation. Alongside these national groups exist several hundred non-affiliated business and trade organisations. This has meant that 'no single association enjoys a dominant and unchallenged position as the voice of business' (Matthews 1994, 203). According to one departmental deputy secretary, disunity has at times lessened the impact of business associations on policy decisions:

> For a good part of the time [employer groups] were relatively speaking out in the cold. Largely for . . . cultural reasons but also for a good part of that period they weren't particularly coordinated, coherent, and one could say they didn't deserve to be particularly influential. They were fragmented and divisive amongst themselves, they did not have their act together as a concerted lobby group.[22]

As McEachern (1991) argues, this disunity often allowed the Labor

Government to play off one business association against another if certain groups disagreed with certain policies.

The Business Council of Australia was probably the most influential business group during the Labor Government. It was formed in the wake of the Economic Summit in 1983, which, according to a former BCA president:

> From businesses' point of view . . . was a disaster. It was a popularly held belief that the communique from that Summit was probably written before it even took place. Business was not unified. The business organisations did not get together. It is generally accepted that business was rolled. Business came away determined that this would not happen again.[23]

Formed from a merger of the Australian Industries Development Association and the Business Roundtable, the Council contained (at different times) 75–80 of the chief executives of Australia's largest companies. The BCA carried out research, published a monthly magazine and distributed communiques on a number of issues including fiscal constraint, structural adjustment and industrial relations. The BCA also funded the Industrial Relations Study Commission headed by Fred Hilmer, which published reports on the desirability of the move away from centralised wage bargaining towards enterprise bargaining. These had some influence on the debate (or at least the language of the debate) over the liberalisation of the labour-market (see chapter eight).

Initially the BCA was strongly supported by the Labor Government which wanted to deal with just one face of business, rather than the many associations. This relationship was further strengthened by Hawke's friendships with his business 'mates', such as air transport magnate Peter Abeles. The BCA did, however, resist moves by the Government to formally incorporate them into the Accord process and to co-opt them into limiting the growth of executive salaries. Despite the promising beginnings, over the life of the Labor Government, the relationship between the Government and the BCA waxed and waned (McLaughlin 1991).[24] A former president of the BCA for example, was generally sceptical of the direct impact of the BCA on public policy, seeing its influence as being more indirect and working largely by influencing ideas over about a fifteen year period. In contrast, John Dawkins, former minister (at different times) for Trade, Finance, and Employment, Education and Training, saw the BCA as particularly important. He noted:

While it was important to have the BCA as part of the cheer squad, it was useful for other reasons for the BCA to not be identified as author of the policies and sometimes to appear as a critic of the Government's performance.

What the BCA did was to add to the respectability of the reform programme and most particularly strengthened the case for dramatic fiscal tightening in the mid 80's.

But the BCA achieved three other successes.

Firstly, because of the cross sectoral nature of the BCA's membership, other business groups keen to promote special interests became much less influential in the broad policy debate. This had the not unwelcome effect of demoting the influence of the CAI [Confederation of Australian Industry].

Secondly, the BCA put the Coalition parties in an almost intolerable political position. With the central areas of policy undisputed, the Liberals were forced to argue at the margin . . . or venture into more adventurous and ultimately into politically fatal territory, such as . . . the GST.

Thirdly, because the BCA by the late eighties had cast itself in the role of policy pacesetter and critic of the Government's process, it assisted the Government's efforts to maintain the support of most of its own constituency (Dawkins 1994, 4).

Other influences in economic policy-making

There are a host of other influences on economic policy-making. Interest groups can be incorporated through consultative machinery such as the EPAC, they may actively seek to influence policy through lobbying, by publishing research and reports, by making submissions on legislation and other government activities, through personal contacts with politicians and key policy makers, or by seeking to influence public opinion. The Association of Social Services, for example, sometimes wielded important influence over its areas of expertise, both through lobbying and by being directly consulted by government. The Australian Labor Party has a formal role in developing policy for a labor government, but this formal role did not always mean great influence in practice, although it was at times a strong moderating influence over the government, playing an important part in slowing the sale of federal assets. If the Labor Government was not as careful in following ALP policy as critics such as Jaensch (1994) and Maddox (1989) would have liked, it was at least skilful at bringing the party along in policy changes (if sometimes after the policy decision had been made).

The media, while probably not important in establishing the agenda of economic change, played a role in pushing for the extension of economic policies and in selling them to the general public.[25] While fostering debate to some extent, the media was probably not as critical of policy directions as some respondents, including some journalists, would have liked. The Industrial Relations Commission played an important role in the settling of industrial disputes and in the implementation and modification of particular Accord agreements.[26] Certain academics, aside from influencing the intellectual climate, also occasionally had direct input into policy formation and were given places on consultative machinery such as the EPAC, and placed in ministerial offices (see chapter two). Think-tanks also attempted to influence the climate of public debate by carrying out extensive research and/or policy advocacy on particular issues. Important examples include the Tasman Institute, the Centre for Independent Studies (CIS), the Australian Institute for Public Policy, and the Institute of Public Affairs. These, which consistently espoused neo-liberal and pro-free trade policies, arguably had a considerable degree of influence on policy directions (Marsh 1991; Stone 1991).[27]

Management consultancy and contract research bodies and individuals became increasingly important during the 1980s in the provision and implementation of policy advice. Many of the larger accountancy firms and financial institutions carry out contract research, as do a number of consultancy firms, some of which include former public servants.[28] Most of these consultants consistently advocate a neo-liberal or market driven approach to policy and management issues. The growth in the use of management consultants by government coincided with the increasing focus on management efficiency and cost cutting, especially in the public sector. Consultants also supplemented policy advice less able to be provided by a shrinking public sector. It is debatable to what extent management consultants were important in setting agendas and initiating policy advice. Often government will engage consultants expressly because they will be more responsive to stated government policy directions (than for example, the public sector bureaucracy) and because the type of policy recommendations they deliver are often predictable before the event. Management consultants also allow the circumvention of intractable public servants who may not give such agreeable policy advice.

Public inquiries and royal commissions, such as the Campbell Inquiry discussed in chapter seven, also provide a source of advice for economic policy-making (Weller 1994). Public inquiries provide a formal mechanism for consultation, for generating submissions and for studying policy issues in detail. As well as generating policy advice however, public inquiries can be '"symbolic" acts of showing concern, coopting critics and delay,' shifting blame, and allowing governments to undertake policy u-turns and absolve themselves from honouring election promises (Prasser 1994, 9). For example, the Martin Inquiry set up by the Labor Government, did not generate new policy initiatives but repackaged the Campbell Inquiry in such a way that it was more palatable to Labor supporters in the face of a Party platform that was explicitly against financial liberalisation.

The role of parliament in policy should not be overlooked. While the executive is largely responsible for initiation of legislation and dominates the legislation process, parliament can be important in its moderation and adaptation. The senate, for example, has been able to extract significant concessions, point out 'errors' and limit aspects of government-sponsored legislation, including budget legislation such as in the case of the 1993 Budget which the Senate refused to pass until certain amendments were made (Mulgan 1996).

Conclusion

Economic policy-making in Australia under the Labor Government was characterised by some diffuseness of influence and the gradual introduction of policy by negotiation and compromise. Economic policy-making in Australia is concentrated to some extent around an 'inner circle' consisting of the cabinet, ministerial offices, the central agencies, the Reserve Bank and (under Labor) the ACTU. These organisations had the most important roles in the development of economic policy and were most influential over the form that it took. This influence was not unchallenged, however, and other government departments and agencies, think-tanks, consultants, business associations and other groups could also be important in certain issues and on certain decisions. Under the Labor governments of Hawke and Keating, there was some effort made to incorporate interest and functional groups into policy formation through the establishment of the Economic Planning Advisory Council, although this role was often symbolic with the EPAC sometimes acting more as a seller of policy than its generator. The role of the Australian Council of Trade Unions in economic policy-making and change was central during the Labor Government, with the ACTU's (and especially Kelty's) influence extending beyond the incomes policy known as the Accord, to cover a variety of economic policy areas. Prime Minister Bob Hawke's approach to policy change was to explain and gain support for policy directions, rather than impose them on an unwilling Cabinet and population. At the same time, Australia's rather complex federal system, with governments in the six states and two territories, and two houses of parliament at the federal level, encouraged the introduction of policy changes through compromise and negotiation. Chapters seven and eight analyse a number of key economic policy decisions and show how influence in policy-making differed between decisions.

7

Economic Policy Decision Making in Australia from Financial Liberalisation to the 1984 Trilogy Commitment

Soon after the Labor Government came to power in 1983, it liberalised Australia's financial markets, introduced the first of a number of wage agreements known as the Accord and committed itself to the 'fiscal responsibility' that was to be both a theme of much of its tenure, and a distinguishing feature from the previous Labor Government of Gough Whitlam. This chapter investigates in detail four key economic policy decisions made during the early years of the Labor Government and finds influence in economic policy decision making to be relatively diffuse, and to differ somewhat according to the decision in question. This diversity of influence reflects, in part, the considerable complexity in institutional arrangements and in economic policy-making found in Australia's federal system, as well as the political, personal and ideological dynamics of policy-making in Australia. In financial liberalisation, following in the wake of the Campbell and Martin Inquiries, a number of key ministers, the Reserve Bank, members of the inquiries, officials and staffers were important. The 1983 Budget was influenced by ministers, staffers, officials from the central agencies, and ACTU officials. Accord I was dominated by a few key ministers, staffers and ACTU officials, with the bureaucracy playing little role beyond implementation. The budget Trilogy of 1984 was largely drawn up in Hawke's and Keating's offices and implemented by a supportive bureaucracy.

This study of decision making in Australia illustrates a number of important factors in studying policy networks and policy as a whole. As suggested in much policy network literature, although not usually found in this study of New Zealand decision making, influence and those involved in particular policy areas or decisions differed somewhat, with different networks forming around different decisions. For example, the Accord process, a key component of the Labor Government's economic policy, was dominated by political and union figures, with little bureaucratic input beyond implementation. Financial liberalisation saw a wide range of committee of inquiry members, including academics, as important, as well as politicians and public servants. Also of importance were the personal relationships built between policy makers during the making of particular decisions, highlighting the importance of micro-level studies. In particular, the relationship developed between ACTU Secretary Bill Kelty and Paul Keating, largely through the Accord process, had considerable impact on wider issues of economic policy and on political infighting and power struggles within the Government. Similarly, relationships between Keating and key officials such as Tony Cole, Don Russell and Bernie Fraser had an important influence on the direction of economic policy, with trusted individuals providing important advice over a range of policy areas.

Choosing policy decisions

As noted in chapter four, when studying decision making one can look at whether decisions are 'representative' of decisions made or 'important' decisions that affect numbers and resources of people. This study seeks to understand which individuals and institutions were influential in economic policy-making during a period of economic policy change. Therefore, the selection need only be 'representative' of economic policy and 'important' in terms of the direction of economic policy. The eight decisions selected for study were: Accord I and VI; financial liberalisation;[1] the 1983 Budget; the Trilogy Commitment and the 1985–6 Budget; the 1988 May Statement; 'One Nation' and privatisation of federal assets. The Accord process was central to the economic policies of the Labor Government. Because of this, the first Accord, which laid the groundwork for the following Accords was selected. The first Budget in 1983, while expansionary, established the new Labor Government as significantly different to the Whitlam Government by showing itself as being committed to 'responsible' fiscal and economic management. The Trilogy Commitment made in the 1984 election campaign and delivered in the 1985–6 Budget was the first to explicitly commit the Labor Government to a fiscal discipline that would last until the early 1990s. The 1988 May Statement was selected because it set out the first major across-the-board tariff cuts and a scheme of microeconomic reform, the aspects of the Labor Government's economic policy that critics often refer to pejoratively as economic rationalism. Accord VI was selected because it was the first to explicitly adopt a commitment to enterprise bargaining and provided a further move towards decentralised wage bargaining. The 'One Nation' statement stands out as the newly elected Prime Minister Paul Keating's first major economic statement and introduced, after a number of years of fiscal restraint, a Keynesian fiscal boost. The privatisation of federal assets was important because it signalled a major break with Labor Party policy and tradition.

There were a number of economic policy decisions that could have been chosen for examination such as the tax debate, the major changes to the machinery of government, or other Accords or parcels of microeconomic reform. To some extent the choice had to be arbitrary given the number of changes introduced by the Labor Government and the inability of an analysis such as this to adequately cover them all. The criteria for choosing were as follows: first, was the decision the first to introduce a new trend into economic policy? For example, while the 1991 statement may have also delivered significant tariff cuts, the 1988 statement was the *first* to introduce across the board cuts. Second, is it hard to imagine the period of economic reform without the decision? For example, it would be possible to imagine the economic reform without the major changes to the machinery of government made in 1987. Third, was the decision selected distinct enough (such as being passed into legislation) to be easily studied? For example, the endless debates about tax and the tax summit seemed very difficult to come to terms with in a short study. Finally, and most importantly, the aim of the study was to give an overall 'picture' of changing economic policy. A range of policies across the economic policy spectrum and over almost a decade were chosen to achieve this. This chapter examines in detail Accord I, financial liberalisation, the 1983 Budget and the 1984 Trilogy Commitment.

Accord I

The first Accord set up a prices and incomes policy agreement between the union movement and the Labor Government that was to last, through various quite different incarnations, until the end of the Labor Government in 1996 (Table 7.1). It was a key plank of Labor Party policy going into the 1983 election and was part of the then Labor Party

Table 7.1 The Accord in Australia 1983–96

Accord I: February 1983
- largely negotiated before election
- included range of social and economic reforms (including increase in Medicare) offset against wage restraint
- full wage indexation implemented

Accord II: September 1985
- based on a wage-tax-superannuation deal to cope with the fall in the Australian dollar
- real wage discounting of 2% traded-off for tax cuts and increased superannuation

Accord III: March 1987
- abandonment of wage-indexation
- two-tier wage increase:
  -general increase of $10.00
  -extra 4% dependent on efficiency improvements at the enterprise level

Accord IV: August 1988
- start of award restructuring whereby unions review awards for structural efficiency measures, encouraging multi-skilling and avoiding demarcation disputes
- 3% plus $10 6 months later, if improvements in 'structural efficiency'

Accord V: August 1989
- wages increases of $20–$30 in two instalments dependent on showing progress on award restructuring and willingness to continue process
- wages-taxes trade-off

Accord VI Originally February 1990
- first accord to explicitly embrace enterprise bargaining
- tax cut of average $10.80 per week
- negotiated general wage incr, incr superannuation schemes and enterprise bargaining rejected by Industrial Commission
- instead Commission granted selected 2% rises (although softened stance on enterprise bargaining in October 1991)

Industrial Relations Act 1992
- Industrial Commission's power to limit enterprise bargaining reduced

Accord VII March 1993
- enterprise bargaining largely replaced pursuit of general wage increases mainly on productivity gain basis, subject to safety net of small annual increases for less powerful unions

Accord VIII June 1995
- proposed wage adjustments of $9–12 per week and $11–14 for low paid workers between July 1997–July 1999
- legislative changes to unfair dismissal laws
- further encouragement of enterprise bargaining
- overtaken by change of government in 1996

strategy to fight inflation and unemployment simultaneously, rather than the 'inflation first' monetarism of the Fraser Government. The first Accord, as with most of the following Accords, was a mainly political document. It was initiated and developed by key (including at the time shadow) members of Cabinet, mostly what Button calls 'ACTU alumni',[2] trade unions officials and ministerial staff, with the Canberra bureaucracy playing little role beyond implementation.[3] Table 7.2 shows individuals from these institutions nominated as influential, such as ACTU officials Kelty and Simon Crean, Ministers Hawke and Willis, and ministerial staffers Langmore and Hughes.

The first Accord consisted of a wide range of economic and social reforms, including a prices and incomes policy. It provided a commitment to the maintenance of real wages over time through full wage indexation. This full wage indexation was implemented by the Arbitration Commission in four national wage case decisions from March–June 1983 to September–December 1984 (Stilwell 1991). It also encompassed a range of supporting policy commitments including: the establishment of a pricing authority to assess price rises sought by corporations and public authorities; the introduction of Medicare; restructuring of the income tax scale to ease the tax burden on low and middle income earners; and a range of commitments covering industrial relations legislation, industrial development, technological changes and occupational health and safety.

As Singleton's (1990a) extensive study shows, the Accord had its roots in the late 1970s when the Labor opposition committed itself to 'develop and implement a policy . . . with the understanding and cooperation of the trade union movement . . . which will encompass prices, wages, incomes, non-wage incomes, the social wage, and taxation reform' (ALP 1979c, 42, cited Singleton 1990a, 118). However, this incomes policy took more than three years to be finalised. After a lengthy series of negotiations the Australian Labour Advisory Council[4] produced a Draft Discussion Paper on Economic Policy which was in many respects a draft of what became the final Accord. This draft Accord was based on:

> a consultative, co-operative relationship aimed at simultaneously tackling unemployment and inflation through the operation of an agreed prices and income policy which at the same time enabled both parties to satisfy their philosophical and economic objectives; the desire to produce an equitable result, to facilitate redistribution and to maintain living standards (Singleton 1990, 138).

The July 1982 conference of the Labor Party endorsed a move to develop an income and price policy with the unions, and in August the ACTU executive, at a joint press conference with Labor leader Hayden, agreed to the draft Accord in principle. However, negotiations again became strained after the ACTU offered the Fraser Government a wage pause and it was not until December that representatives of the ALP and the ACTU met to further develop proposals. In January 1983, the ACTU executive decided in principle to develop further a prices and incomes policy. However, two further events occurred before the final Accord was negotiated. First, a snap election was called for March, forcing the two parties to quickly get together to formulate a package to use against their common foe. Second, in February former ACTU president Bob Hawke replaced Hayden, in a coup that was backed by Kelty and the ACTU leadership. Hawke's leadership made the successful negotiation of the Accord more likely, partly because personality problems had existed between Hayden and the ACTU leadership and partly because Hawke, as former ACTU president, was known and trusted to deliver on promises made to the union movement.[5] A major effort was made to develop the Accord further, which involved, according to William Mansfield, 'a very substantial effort to then finalise the draft document'. A special unions conference of the ACTU was held which ratified the outcomes of the negotiations and committed the union movement to working within the confines of the Accord. On 21 February 1983, the ACTU gave its support to the 'Statement of Accord by the Australian Labor Party and the Australian Council of Trade Unions Regarding Economic Policy'.

The Accord was a major commitment for the union movement to make to a government.[6] The support of a number of important union officials such as Laurie Carmichael, from the left-leaning Metal Workers

Table 7.2 Persons Nominated as influential on Accord I

Name	Votes	Position	Name	Votes	Position
Kelty	44	Sec ACTU	Langmore	3	TO
Hawke	40	PM	Hughes	3	TO
Willis	36	Min IR	Marsh	3	ACTU
P. Keating	19	Treas	McDonald	3	ACTU
Crean	15	Vice-Pres ACTU	Abeles	2	Bus/BCA
Carmichael	7	Vice-Pres ACTU	Hayden	2	Minister
Dolan	5	Pres ACTU	M. Keating	2	Dep Sec Fin, Sec IR
Fitzgibbon	3	Vice-Pres ACTU	Weaven	2	ACTU

Union, delivered a number of key unions to support the Accord. Carmichael and officials Tas Bull and Tom McDonald were important in insisting that the Accord be broadly based and deal with social issues and industry policy. Dissent, while voiced, was mostly kept behind closed doors and the union movement managed to maintain a remarkable degree of discipline throughout the eight accords.

The Accord was finally negotiated between a small select group at the highest political level. Ralph Willis, a former research officer in the ACTU, and the opposition shadow treasurer, who became Industrial Relations Minister in the new Government, sees his role as central. According to Willis:

> I was the architect of it. It was put together by myself, Bill Kelty and Jan Marsh. It wasn't just we three [but] we were the three that did most of the work. Towards the end, when it was being put together, a lot of other people had to become involved [such as] the Labor Party and the shadow ministers because we were getting into the areas of social security, health policy, education, industry policy etc.

The Accord was a key plank of the Labor Party's election campaign. As well as showing the electorate that the Labor Party had the support of the union movement, it provided, according to Willis:

> a credible anti-inflation policy. What we were looking at, was the then Fraser Government's policy of letting the economy take off then having inflation boost up by high wage claims and them hitting all the panic buttons on monetary and budgetary policy . . . a totally disastrous policy.

The government bureaucracy played little part in the Accord process, past implementation. According to a senior Department of Industrial Relations official:

> We had a role in implementing it. Once they came in it was how to translate what was in the Accords into the wage system. For example, on superannuation and agreements about the general size of increases, this department prepares and presents submissions in the national wage cases. We were important in getting what they had agreed on . . . as part of the wage system and more recently the changes in the industrial relations legislation. Then in Treasury the shifts in superannuation [were developed] as we move through the Accords. As the Accords became wider [and included] social wage issues, it involved more work with other departments in terms of childcare [and] maternity allowance.

While much of the bureaucracy was initially sceptical about the Accord process, Treasury was particularly doubtful as to its usefulness and this view did not change until Stone left as Secretary. By that time there seemed to be positive outcomes from the Accord, and some Treasury officials saw the wage restraint obtained as worth the trade-off for the perceived loss of flexibility they thought further liberalisation would have delivered. According to one departmental chief executive who was then in the Department of Finance, Finance became reconciled to the Accords and although they 'wouldn't have recommended it [they] came to see it as something that could be used to their own advantage.'[7]

While the bulk of the Cabinet was supportive of the general Accord, some were not involved in its development. Even though Ministers might attend the Australian Labor Advisory Council (ALAC), this was characterised by Button as 'a discussion group that kidded itself that it was implementing the Accord'. This lack of involvement was to the extent that they were not fully aware of what had been agreed to by the Government. While Susan Ryan was consulted on the social wage and education, according to Button he was unaware of some things that were actually in the Accord:

> I don't know if there was any formal sort of agreement entered into. I've never known that. In my situation as Industry Minister I suddenly became aware of the detailed contents late 1983, early 1984. It was used heavily against me 'cos it contained a provision that there should be no cuts in tariffs while unemployment remained above five percent . . . which I must say, at the time of the election and for some while thereafter, that I was totally unaware of.

The Treasurer, Paul Keating, was particularly suspicious of the Accord. According to Willis 'the Treasurer . . . thought [the Accord] was a load of crap basically because he had never been involved and his department was very sceptical.'[8] According to Willis, Keating began to support the Accord process only after:

> we hit the fence 1985–6 with a need for a major devaluation of the Australian dollar, the need therefore for a real wage reduction. [Otherwise] we would get a major devaluation inflation cycle. Through the Accord a reduction of real wages [was managed]. The way that was done was to have a compensating tax cut and the Treasurer was intimately involved in that. That got him onside

with the Accord and he became a key player in the Accord from that time on.

Keating also formed a friendship with Kelty and began to dominate other Accords, partially sidelining other ministers such as Willis.[9]

The first Accord agreement was sold to the business world at the National Economic Summit held in the House of Representatives chamber in April 1983. In a carefully orchestrated campaign, including speeches by Hawke and Kelty, business leaders were convinced to support the thrust of Labor's economic policies, including the Accord. The Summit communique, written, according to one respondent, mostly by businessmen Alan Coates, Peter Abeles and Bill Kelty from the ACTU, supported the return to centralised wage fixing entailed in the Accord, and noted the union's commitment to wage constraint. It was endorsed by all participants at the Summit, with the exception of Bjekle-Petersen (Kelly 1994, 65–6). A Prices Surveillance Authority was established which did not legislate for price control, but instead used moral suasion to try to influence price increases. There were also a number of failed attempts by members of the Labor Government, especially Hawke and Willis, to get business to agree to exercise restraint on executive salaries.

Financial liberalisation

The election of the Labor Government in 1983 saw a run against the Australian dollar and a subsequent 10 percent devaluation. Further speculation continued against the dollar as funds flowed in again once the Labor Government had proved itself to be reasonably business-friendly. Partly in response to this continual speculation, the Australian dollar was floated. This was followed by a series of measures over a number of years that progressively and extensively deregulated the financial sector (Table 7.3).

Financial deregulation largely followed the recommendations found in the Campbell and, subsequent, Martin Reports. It was initiated and developed by a group of officials mainly from the Treasury, the Reserve Bank, the Department of Prime Minister and Cabinet, members of the inquiries, staffers from the Prime Minister's and Treasurer's offices, and key Ministers Hawke and Keating. The float was delayed by several months partly because of the opposition of Treasury Secretary John Stone. Table 7.4 shows individuals from these key institutions nominated by

Table 7.3 Financial liberalisation in Australia[1]

1983
- Devaluation—10%
- Float of dollar
- Abolition of exchange controls

1984
- Increase in number of non-bank financial institutions authorised to trade in foreign exchange
- Banks allowed to pay interest on call deposits and fixed deposits
- Approval of 16 banks with foreign ownership to trade in Australia

1985
- Interest rate ceilings on bank loans less than $100,000 removed, except in the case of housing

- Liquid Assets and Government Securities (LGS) convention replaced by Prudential Primes Asset Ratio (PAR)[2]

1986
- Interest rate ceiling removed for new home loans

1988
- Statutory Reserve Deposits (SRD) system replace by Non-callable Deposits (NCDs) system[3]

1989
- Distinction between savings and trading banks removed

Notes
1. Sources: Boehm 1993, Budget Statements 1983–93.
2. Trading banks were required to deposit a proportion of the their funds (known as the SRD ratio) in Statutory Reserve Deposits accounts with the Reserve Bank.
3. The non-callable deposits system required all banks (including savings banks) to deposit 1 percent of total liabilities in Australia with the Reserve Bank.

respondents as influential, including the Governor of the Reserve Bank R. Johnston, Ross Garnaut from the Prime Minister's Office, Treasury Secretary John Stone, as well as senior ministers such as Prime Minister Hawke and Treasurer Paul Keating.

The Australian Financial System Inquiry delivered its findings in an 800 page report in 1981, after two and a half years of work. Known as the Campbell Committee after its chairman J. K. Campbell, the Inquiry recommended a comprehensive series of measures to deregulate the financial markets. Recommendations included removing government regulation of interest rates, dismantling exchange control mechanisms and allowing a managed float of the dollar, and reducing the barriers for new banks (including foreign owned ones) to enter the market (Australian Financial System 1981). While the coalition Treasurer at that time, John Howard, was generally favourable to Campbell's findings, the Prime Minister Malcolm Fraser was not, and few of the recommendations were implemented.

Both Prime Minister Bob Hawke and the Treasurer Paul Keating were generally in favour of liberalising financial markets, influenced in part by their own views and the views of their offices, and by advice from officials in the Treasury, the Reserve Bank and the Department of Prime Minister and Cabinet. There were, however, a number of not unimportant barriers in moving to liberalisation. First, the Labor Party had traditionally been an advocate of regulation of the financial markets and had, in opposition, stated its disagreement with the recommendations of the Campbell Report, both in a resolution at the 1982 party conference and in its 1982 policy platform (McCarthy and Taylor 1995). Second, before the election Keating himself had gone on record as being in favour of regulation of the financial markets. Hawke and Keating managed to get around these policy commitments by setting up yet another inquiry to further examine financial deregulation. Known as the Review Group of the Australian Financial System (the Martin Review Group), this was largely intended to repackage and sell the recommendations of the Campbell Inquiry to a sceptical Labor Party and electorate.

According to one respondent, the new committee was the Treasury's idea. Vic Martin was then asked to chair the committee by the Secretary to the Treasury, partly because he was known to be in favour of financial liberalisation. Richard Beetham, then at the Treasury, drew up the first

Table 7.4 Persons nominated as influential on financial liberalisation

Name	Votes	Position	Name	Votes	Position
P. Keating	50	Treas	Dawkins	3	Min Fin
Hawke	25	PM	Hughes	3	TO
Johnston	24	Gov RBA	M. Keating	3	Dep Sec Fin
Garnaut	17	PMO	Martin	3	Chair Martin Inq
Stone	13	Sec Treas (until 84)	Moore	3	Dep Sec Treas
T. Cole[1]	10	TO	Walsh	3	Min Res & Energy
Phillips[2]	10	RBA official	Willis	3	Min IR
Visbord	9	Dep Sec DPMC	Button	2	Min Indus
B. Fraser	8	Sec Treas(1984–9)	I. Castles	2	Sec Fin
Campbell	6	Chair Campbell Inq	Coates	2	EPAC/Campbell Inq
Higgins	6	Dep Sec Treas	Graham Evans	2	PMO
Morgan	6	Treas official	Fitzgerald	2	Dep Sec Fin
Sanders	6	Dep Gov RBA	Holmes	2	RBA official
Valentine	6	Acad/Campbell Inq	Kelty	2	Sec ACTU
T. Evans	5	Treas official	P. Swan	2	Academic
Beetham	4	Treas/Martin Inq	Ward	2	TO
Argy	3	Treas/Campbell Inq			

Notes
1. Former Treasury official, future Treasury secretary.
2. Deputy Governor of the Bank 1987–92.

draft terms of reference and was also a member of the committee. Academic Keith Hancock was included, partly because of his good standing with the Labor Party.[10] The terms of reference that the committee were to examine were: recent developments in the financial sector; the regulation of the bank and non-bank financial sector; the need for special arrangements for the funding of capital works and for the housing and small business sectors; and additional forms of domestic borrowing for the government. These terms of reference were to have regard to: 'the Government's social and economic objectives, particularly the need for an adequate supply of finance at a reasonable cost'; the recommendations of the Campbell Report; and the 'objective of improving efficiency and maintaining stability in our financial system' (cited Lim 1984, 26).

Commissioned in May 1983, the Martin Group reported on 22 February 1984. Its report was slightly shorter than the Campbell Report and had less analysis, and although it had similar conclusions to the Campbell Report, it arrived at them by different means; ones 'more palatable to the Labor Party' as one respondent termed it. Like the Campbell Report it recommended a number of deregulatory measures including lifting bank interest rate controls and deposit maturity controls, the abandonment of some direct controls in the monetary policy, and allowing the entry of more banks into financial markets.

Cabinet as a whole played little part in financial liberalisation, which was dominated by Hawke and Keating and key officials, and largely presented to the rest of Cabinet as a *fait accompli*. According to Susan Ryan, then minister for Social Services, financial liberalisation was:

> one of the very rare decisions that were made between the PM and Treasurer and then announced. There was surprise . . . at the extent of it. It was something that Treasury had been advocating for some time . . . It was not a novel proposal. I think there was a fair bit of surprise that it had been taken so swiftly and so completely. And there was, generally from non-economic ministers like myself, a question mark about what this would mean.

While much of the programme was worked out by Hawke and Keating and their advisers, foreign banks and governments had lobbied hard to persuade Keating to allow the entry of foreign banks into Australia. Initially the aim was to allow a number in gradually; however, it became difficult to allow some in while excluding others, so Keating surprised some of his advisers by deciding to invite 16 foreign banks to enter in 1985. Existing banks had mixed views on deregulation and the float, with some strongly against the entry of the larger-than-expected number of foreign banks.[11]

Moving to the float

The float of the dollar was announced on 9 December 1983, before the final report of the Martin Group.[12] There had been some attempt to obtain an interim report from the committee supporting the float but this had been unsuccessful. The float was carried out only after several months of discussion and debate, with the Reserve Bank playing the key advisory role, overriding the objection of Treasury Secretary John Stone.

Much controversy has arisen between Hawke and Keating regarding who was first to advocate floating the dollar.[13] McCarthy and Taylor (1995) claim that Keating was keen to float on taking office in 1983 and that he set about disarming opponents in the Treasury and the Labor Party. Hawke has claimed, in interviews on television and in his memoirs, that the float was in fact his initiative with Keating hesitant, while Keating has asserted his primary role (Edwards 1996, 543–8; Hawke 1994, 239–41).[14] However, a number of respondents have seen this debate as less than useful. Tony Cole, a future Treasury secretary, then in Keating's office, says:

> In my view [the debate between Hawke and Keating] is irrelevant. There was never a time when I didn't think [that both] wanted to float the dollar. It was a topic immediately after the election. The only debate was about the timing [and] that was determined by events rather than by either of them. It would have occurred earlier if Stone hadn't been opposed to it.[15]

The role of the Reserve Bank is the key to understanding the swiftness of the financial deregulation, and the floating of the dollar despite Stone's opposition. By the late 1970s the Reserve Bank had come to support deregulation of financial markets, including floating the dollar, both through its experience of operating in the market and through theoretical developments. The Governor of the Bank at the time of the change of government, Bob Johnston, had been appointed by the previous Treasurer Howard in 1982, partly because he was a supporter of deregulation. According to a former governor, there were a number of reasons for the Reserve Bank moving to support a float:

> We had come to the view . . . in the 70s and into the 80s . . . that the regulated system couldn't be retained for two reasons. [First] the

exchange controls affected the honest and honourable, and those people who were not in those categories went their own way.

Secondly, with the change of government in 1983, we had put the existing exchange mechanism to the ultimate test having had a floating peg arrangement. We had to have a devaluation in the aftermath of the election. We couldn't very well go back to the old system. Once you had broken away from saying never . . . it is very hard to get people to believe you. We were being speculated against in 1983, I suppose if we had been bold and moved the rate aggressively and pre-empted the market, we might have been able to hold it. But it really wasn't possible to believe officials could do a thing like that.

And we had the worldwide example of other countries. We were in a diminishing minority of countries that had a fixed rate.

We [would have] some discrete changes. There tended to [be] a log jam, a delay and then a massive change in rates. People would wake up and find the rate had changed six or seven percent.

So we had both theory and practice telling us the existing system wouldn't hold.

The process where an actual decision was made to float took several months, despite the continued pressure from the Reserve Bank and other officials. As Edwards (1996, ch. 7) documents in some detail, the understanding amongst most key players soon after the election was that the float was desirable. Following the election, there was a series of papers sent from the Reserve Bank to the Treasurer. These included a 29 July memorandum to Keating arguing against the pegged system and a 20 September paper, which further discussed problems with the existing system. There were also papers sent to the Reserve Bank board discussing reform options, including a dirty float.[16] Treasury produced a paper of its own arguing against the float.

During October, there were a number of meetings between the Treasurer and officials. One was held in the Canberra offices during late October attended by officials from the Treasury, the Bank and the Treasurer's and Prime Minister's offices. Keating chaired the meeting and Hawke did not attend (Edwards 1996, 223). According to Hughes:

> I thought we had agreed in October in a meeting held in the Reserve Bank in Canberra . . . to float the dollar, more or less there and then, but all that had happened in that stage was that the forward rate was set free and the stock rate was still fixed . . . I thought that was a crazy idea and said so.[17]

(This decision to float the forward rate was endorsed on 27 October.)

The main reason for the delay in moving to a full float was the reluctance of the Treasury, especially the Secretary John Stone, to support a float.[18] According to one respondent, then a senior Treasury official, there 'was considerable scepticism in the Treasury that changes were needed . . . it wasn't just from Stone. It seemed to me to be useful to have this further policy lever. I wasn't convinced that the thing was breaking down.' Further down the ranks of the Treasury, however, there was some support for a float, with Ted Evans openly supporting it to the Treasurer, and in front of Stone. There was also some delay, as both the Treasury and the Bank needed time to sort out how the new regime would be implemented.

After continual debate about the merits of floating and attempts to reach a common position, the Governor of the Reserve Bank became frustrated with the process and initiated a meeting on 8 December to try to reach a final agreement. This was also encouraged by an expected inflow of new capital on Friday (it was then Thursday). As Edwards documents, a meeting was held in Hawke's office that evening, attended by Hawke and Keating and a number of staffers and officials (excluding those from the Reserve Bank) and a decision was made to float. Keating called Johnston and told him to close the markets. A meeting was held on the Friday morning in Hawke's office, after Keating had met with Johnston and other Reserve Bank officials who advised removing exchange controls. The meeting was attended by officials from the Treasury including the Secretary John Stone and the two Deputy Secretaries, Des Moore and Dick Rye. From the Department of Prime Minister and Cabinet came Eddie Visbord. The Reserve Bank was represented by the Governor, John Phillips and Don Sanders. There were also a number of staffers from the Prime Minister's and Treasurer's offices, such as Ross Garnaut, Greg Smith, Tony Cole and Graham Evans. This meeting was essentially to give Stone his last chance to argue against a float of the dollar. He was opposed by Johnston as well as Visbord, Garnaut and most of the assembled officials that were not from Treasury. According to one person who attended the meeting Visbord was particularly 'gung-ho' about proceeding with a float. Keating appeared to be open-minded about what to do next, at least according to one participant at the meeting, but Hawke appeared to have already made up his mind. Stone was not able to convince the assembled Treasurer and Prime Minister that a float should not go ahead and by the time the meeting was finished it had been decided to proceed. The Cabinet endorsed the decision later in the day and a press conference was called to announce the decision. The exchange markets opened on Monday under the new regime.

In summary, financial liberalisation was a programme driven by a part of the public sector bureaucracy (especially the Reserve Bank) and championed by the Treasurer and the Prime Minister. It also drew on the Campbell and Martin Inquiries into the financial system. Parts of it, such as the float, were carried out in spite of opposition from key sectors of the public bureaucracy, in this case the Treasury. Where impediments to its introduction existed, such as party platforms and election promises, the Martin Inquiry was used to repackage the changes in a form that would be more acceptable to its opponents.

The 1983 Budget

Introduced at the tail end of a severe recession, the first Budget of the Labor Government, delivered on 23 August 1983, included a large fiscal stimulus. This was not as large as many commentators might have anticipated, however, and deficit projections were curtailed from the $9.6 billion expected under the budgetary settings inherited from the Coalition to $8.3 billion (Keating 1983). The first Budget was significant because it distinguished the new Labor Government from the Whitlam Labor Government of 1972–5. Whitlam's Government had expanded fiscal deficits dramatically during its short term in office and managed to get itself offside with business and the government bureaucracy, especially the Treasury. The new Labor Government, by projecting itself as 'fiscally responsible', despite some expensive election promises, was able to start off with a good relationship with the bureaucracy and position itself as a government that would be more economically responsible and more amenable to business. The 1983 Budget was initiated and developed by a group of ministers, officials from the Treasury, the Department of Prime Minister and Cabinet (DPMC) and Finance, staffers from the ministerial offices, with input from the union movement. Table 7.5 shows those individuals nominated as influential, such as Ministers Hawke, Keating and John Dawkins, Treasury Secretary John Stone, Bill Kelty from the ACTU, Eddie Visbord from the DPMC and Ross Garnaut from the Prime Minister's Office.

The fiscal deficit projections made by the coalition Treasurer John Howard during the election campaign were generally known by the economic policy bureaucracy in Canberra to be extremely conservative. As well as the usual Treasury projections, the DPMC had also carried out its own projections that showed the new Government would be facing a huge fiscal deficit. Whether or not Labor in opposition knew the extent of the deficit, and it is likely something had been leaked from the bureaucracy,[19] they made a number of election promises that would have increased the deficit. However, on the day before the election Hawke did say that if the fiscal situation was worse than expected, some of these promises would have to be revised.

On the Sunday after Labor's election victory, John Stone and Dick Rye of the Treasury went over to the Lakeside Hotel to talk to Keating and Hawke and a number of their staffers. As well as advising the new Government that they should devalue (which they subsequently did), the two Treasury officials presented a minute that contained the news that the fiscal deficit was expected to blow out to $9.6 billion in 1983–4.[20] This deficit forecast started a debate within the Government on how to deal with the fiscal problem. A number of Labor Ministers and staffers, such as Willis, Kerrin, Langmore and Hughes wanted to continue with a fiscal stimulus of varying degrees, with some of the more left leaning of the party wanting the deficit to expand considerably. Ross Garnaut from the Prime Minister's Office wanted to make significant cuts to the deficit, as did officials such as Visbord from the DPMC and Stone and other

Table 7.5 Persons nominated as influential on the 1983 Budget

Name	Votes	Position	Name	Votes	Position
P. Keating	28	Treasurer	Hughes	5	TO
Hawke	24	Prime Minister	T. Cole	4	TO
Stone	16	Sec Treas	Carmichael	3	ACTU
Dawkins	9	Min Fin	Fitzgerald	3	Dep Sec Fin
Kelty	9	Sec ACTU	G. Smith	3	TO
Visbord	7	Dep Sec DPMC	D. Rye	3	Dep Sec Treas
T. Evans	6	Treas official	Castles	2	Sec Fin
Garnaut	6	PMO	Dolan	2	Pres ACTU
Morgan	6	Treas official	Higgins	2	Treas official
Walsh	6	Min Res&Energy	M. Keating	2	Dep Sec Fin
Willis	6	Min IR	Langmore	2	TO
Crean	5	Vice-Pres ACTU	Moore	2	Dep Sec Treas
B. Fraser	5	Dep Sec Treas	B. Ward	2	TO

Treasury officials. The view that the deficit would be cut came to be shared by Hawke and Keating, who according to Tony Cole 'were determined to come in . . . lower. They didn't care so much how much lower—it was the symbolism of starting to address the problem.' If the election promises had been followed, on Treasury estimates, this would have added an extra $1.5 billion to the deficit (Edwards 1996, 196). The Treasury also claimed that an economic recovery was already on the way so that the need for fiscal stimulus was lessened. The position to reduce the deficit was outlined to Cabinet on 16 March and was followed on 29 March in a joint submission from Keating and Dawkins which argued for a deficit of $8.5 billion to be delivered by expenditure cuts. This would mean that many election promises would have to be abandoned. Keating and Hawke then set about bringing the Labor Caucus and Cabinet onside for the changes, a process that was largely successful. According to Button, 'I don't think the Budget strategy was disputed much . . . I didn't give much argument over the Budget strategy, [although] some people might have wanted to spend more . . . on welfare issues'.

Following the Economic Summit that discussed the extent of the deficit and gained support for what would be the general thrust of Labor's policies, Keating delivered the May Statement that announced a number of new initiatives costing $0.5 billion. This was to be followed by the Budget. The Treasury worked closely with the Treasurer's Office in the development of the broad parameters of the Budget, with Treasury officials David Morgan and Ted Evans spending considerable time in the Treasurer's Office going over what should be in the document. According to one Keating staffer, the Treasury's influence was particularly strong in the first Budget because Keating was 'still learning'. In the 1983 Budget, the DPMC also played an important role in advising on broad economic directions and policy options, possibly to a greater extent than was to be usual in subsequent years.[21]

Once the target of $8.5 billion was accepted, the existing government programmes were examined to see which ones could be eliminated and to make room for some of Labor's own priorities. The process of delivering expenditure cuts was handled through the Expenditure Review Committee. According to a Keating staffer, the ERC was 'like the inquisition' where ministers would be grilled and cajoled into producing savings in their departments. In this budget, Hawke was very active in the ERC process and supported Keating and the Finance

Minister in achieving cuts. According to one minister, this was a very political process because there was:

> tension between programmes you might think could be cut because they are not achieving much but have huge constituencies. There were a lot of the programmes where the money was not tightly managed by the Commonwealth . . . and you couldn't say what they are achieving. But whenever you touch one of those programmes you find a political uproar.

The Labor Government's handling of the budget process quickly won over the economic policy bureaucracy because, according to a then senior Treasury official, the 'reaction in Treasury at the end of the exercise was pretty good—we were relieved, even impressed, by the start the new Government had made.'

The preparation of the budget documents was carried out in the Treasury buildings and budget documents could not be taken out of the Treasury building due to security concerns. This meant the Treasurer's staffers involved had to work in the Treasury buildings. Partly because of this security concern, Keating had his own office in the Treasury buildings which was only used during the preparation of the budget documents. According to one staffer, Keating wrote the Budget speech himself 'a line a day'. In between the speech writing, ministerial staffers Barbara Ward and Tony Cole went through the draft papers, working closely with Treasury officials.

The Budget was delivered on 23 August. Few of Labor's election promises survived, although there was a 'substantial reordering of priorities' with money being shifted from the previous Government's programmes to fund some increases in education spending, welfare and the promised changes to Medicare (Keating 1983).

The Trilogy Commitment and the 1985–6 Budget

The Trilogy Budget Commitment—to not increase tax-take beyond the 1984–5 share; to reduce commonwealth expenditure as a proportion of GDP; and to reduce the size of the fiscal deficit—was a major commitment to fiscal restraint on the part of a government going into an election. It set the scene for the major cuts in government spending and the fiscal surpluses delivered in the late 1980s by the Labor Government. The Trilogy was largely a political decision on the part of

Table 7.6 Persons nominated as influential on the Trilogy Commitment and the 1985–6 Budget

Name	Votes	Position	Name	Votes	Position
Hawke	22	Prime Minister	B. Fraser	3	Sec Treas
P. Keating	22	Treasurer	Kelty	3	Sec ACTU
Garnaut	7	PMO	Morgan	3	Treas official
Higgins	6	Dep Sec Treas	P. Barron	2	PMO
Walsh	5	Min Fin	Graham Evans	2	PMO
Stone[1]	4	Sec Treas to 1984	Hughes	2	TO
Dawkins	4	Min Trade	Russell	2	TO
T. Cole	3	TO	G. Smith	2	TO
T. Evans	3	Treas official			

Notes

1. Stone had retired from the Treasury by the time of the Trilogy Commitment. It is possible that his higher ranking, compared to Fraser, may be partly due to some respondents believing he was still Secretary at the time

the Prime Minister and the Treasurer and their staff, and was supported by a few key ministers and officials. Hawke and Keating along with members of the PMO such as Garnaut, and Treasury officials such as Chris Higgins are nominated as influential in Table 7.6. The Trilogy was a policy commitment made in the heat of an election campaign and in response to tax cut promises made by the opposition and their attempted scare campaign over possible introduction of a capital gains tax by the Labor Government. It also, however, drew on several months of discussion of fiscal restraint and on a background of central agency support for fiscal restraint and smaller government.

Garnaut had written a memo to Hawke advising against lax fiscal restraint in the 1984 Budget and arguing against allowing spending to rise as a percentage of GDP (Kelly 1994, 144). This is what in fact happened with spending expected to rise to 31.1 percent compared to 30.5 percent in the previous year. According to Garnaut, the Prime Minister's Office was unhappy about the 1984 budget as they felt they had missed a chance at cutting back expenditure growth. This encouraged a general feeling that the budgetary process had not been firm enough, and the PMO strongly advised Hawke to put in parameters for future budgets to put pressure on reducing the fiscal deficit. After a report presented on 3 September 1984, Hawke gained Cabinet support for a commitment that spending would fall as a percentage of GDP.

Neither Hawke nor Keating wished to close off the option of tax reform. While Labor was generally in favour of a capital gains tax, introduction of this had been ruled out during Labor's first term. In Cabinet, and in public, Button had talked about the possibility of introducing a capital gains tax and Hawke did not want to rule this out in the election campaign. At the same time, the Leader of the Opposition had been making great play of the fact that Labor would be expected to introduce a capital gains tax as well as death and gift duties (Ellercamp 1984a). The response of the Prime Minister's Office was to make a commitment to not increase the overall tax burden, but with a concurrent commitment to not increase the fiscal deficit. Part of this process was the production of the nine point plan, which drew on earlier promises made during the election campaign.[22] This included a commitment that the tax burden would not rise as a percentage of GDP. Tony Cole describes how the nine point plan was developed by the Prime Minister's and Treasurer's offices:

> the objectives were what Keating called 'to end the tax blackmail' [and] try to get through the election campaign without ruling out tax changes that needed to be considered. The plan was a combined exercise of two offices sitting around—Graham Evans, Peter Barron, myself and Greg Smith . . . Garnaut . . . Barbara Ward. We were looking ahead at the medium and longer term. The exercise was how do we get though the election without promising not to do anything.

In discussions between Hawke and his office, these commitments—to not increase spending as a proportion of GDP, to not increase the overall tax burden and not increase the fiscal deficit—evolved into the Trilogy Commitment. According to Cole, the Trilogy Commitment was not as restraining a promise as it seemed because:

> The Trilogy promise of no increase in taxes as a share of GDP— well if you projected on the basis of the taxes we had and what was going to happen to tax revenue unless we hiked rates enormously, taxes were going to go down as a share of GDP. So it wasn't a restraining promise.

On a radio programme on 19 October, Hawke unilaterally announced that he supported a tax summit (Ellercamp 1984b). This allowed him to enter the election campaign without ruling out further tax reform. The nine point plan was announced on 30 October, at the same time as the detailed proposal for a tax summit (Ellercamp 1984c).

The calling of a tax summit did not gain the support of all the staffers, with one noting the Trilogy Commitment 'was well thought out until Hawkey . . . promised the tax summit.' On 14 November Hawke reaffirmed his commitment to the three promises he now called the 'Trilogy Commitment' (The Australian 1984). The Trilogy Commitment allowed the Labor Government to regain the front foot in the election campaign against Peacock's scare campaign of tax increases.

The Trilogy Commitment was very much Hawke and Keating's initiative and according to Button 'was not discussed as such in Cabinet in any detail.' After the election, the budget process through the ERC, was according to Garnaut, a 'nitty-gritty' one with Hawke and Keating and the key members of the ERC maintaining pressure to deliver cuts during a grinding process. Garnaut sat in the ERC when Hawke wasn't there to maintain the pressure. The central agencies were generally very supportive of the process and developed spending reduction options based on the Trilogy Commitment. According to one departmental chief executive:

> I was personally involved in trying to allocate spending targets out to the departments that would meet the Trilogy objectives. It was really quite a strong focus and all those [central agencies] were quite actively involved. We would meet, sometimes weekly if not more often, as key cabinet submissions were put forward. We used to give joint advice—at least coordinate. We recognised the three of us agreeing was quite critical—probably at its peak in 1985.

The 1985–6 budget delivered on the Trilogy Commitments and led to a projected fall in the 1985–6 budget deficit of $1.8 billion during 1985–6 (Keating 1985, 3).

Conclusion

This chapter has examined economic policy-making at the decision level and found that influence, while concentrated to some extent around the cabinet and key policy-making institutions, is relatively diffuse (especially when compared to New Zealand) and can differ somewhat depending on the decision in question. The membership and stability of policy networks forming around decisions differed somewhat, in contrast to the highly stable and long-lived policy community that dominated the broad area of economic policy in New Zealand. Policy changes such as financial liberalisation or fiscal restraint were signalled through the skilful management of committees of inquiry, in the case of financial deregulation, or signalled before the election, in the case of the Trilogy Commitment. In contrast to the Whitlam period, Caucus avoided the open and damaging policy debates for much of the earlier period of Hawke's Labor Government, reflecting both the Cabinet precedence on policy matters decided upon while Labor was in opposition, and the skilful political management of the new Government. Non-financial ministers were sometimes closely involved in economic policy formation (if not always initiation), with the exception of financial liberalisation, especially through the ERC process discussed in the previous chapter. Once again, this contrasts with the economic policy-making (and especially the budget) process in New Zealand, where policy was most often dominated by the few finance ministers. During financial liberalisation—coming in the wake of two committees of inquiry—a range of ministers, officials, staffers and members of the Reserve Bank were important. The 1983 Budget was influenced by ministers, staffers and officials from the central agencies, as well as ACTU officials. Accord I, as were most subsequent Accords, was dominated by a policy community consisting of a few key ministers (most with previous ACTU experience), staffers and ACTU officials, with the bureaucracy playing little role beyond implementation. The Budget Trilogy of 1984 was largely drawn up between Hawke's and Keating's offices and implemented by a supportive bureaucracy. The next chapter will look at four further key decisions; the 1988 May Statement; Accord VI; the 'One Nation' statement and privatisation.

8

Economic Policy Decision Making in Australia from the 1988 May Statement to Privatisation

This chapter investigates four key economic policy decisions: the 1988 May Statement that introduced major tariff reductions; the Accord VI in 1990, the first Accord to explicitly adopt and endorse elements of enterprise bargaining; the 'One Nation' statement of 1992 which delivered a fiscal stimulus in the face of a severe recession; and the privatisation of federal assets. Key figures, such as the Secretary of the ACTU Bill Kelty, the Treasurer and then prime minister Paul Keating, and a number of other ministers and senior officials sometimes exercised influence over more than one decision; however, as in the previous chapter, patterns of influence differed somewhat in each decision. The 1988 May Statement showed the influence of Industry Minister Button and his department, as well as other ministers and officials. Accord VI was dominated by a few select ministers, staffers and union officials, with bureaucrats playing little role past implementation. The 'One Nation' statement was largely developed by Keating, Dawkins and their staffs, plus a few trusted public servants. Privatisation, supported by the central agencies, only occurred when ministerial support coalesced with political opportunities.

How and why decisions were made did not reflect merely a technocratic response to particular policy problems. The influence of personal relationships, the beliefs of particular agencies and individuals, and the political battles fought by politicians all impacted on what and how decisions were to be made, and who was to be involved in the decision-making process. The political agenda in some ways conditioned what the policy problem was, and even to some extent delimited what the solution would be, such as in the case of the 'One Nation' statement. Skilful political manoeuvring was needed to introduce change without undermining support, such as in the case of the sale of federal assets despite initial extra-parliamentary opposition. Trust relationships built up by key ministers with their staffers, such as Keating's relationship with former members of his office, sometimes continued once they returned to the bureaucracy. For example, former staffers Tony Cole and Greg Smith of the Treasury were heavily involved in the 'One Nation' project even though the rest of the Treasury played a marginal role.

Tariff cuts and the May Statement

The 1988 economic statement delivered the largest tariff cuts since Labor Prime Minister Gough Whitlam's across the board 25 percent reduction in 1973. Tariffs above 15 percent were to be reduced to 15 percent over four years while tariffs between 10 and 15 percent were to be reduced to 10 percent. This resulted in a calculated reduction in the average effective rate of assistance from 19 to 14 percent by 1992–3 (Capling and Galligan 1992, 151). The May Statement also introduced a package of reforms, including changes to the business tax regime, reduction in assistance to the rural sector and deregulation of the telecommunications industry. The tariff cuts and the May Statement were initiated and developed by a coalition of senior Cabinet Ministers and officials. These included the

Table 8.1 Persons nominated as influential on 1988 May Statement

Name	Votes	Position	Name	Votes	Position
Button	17	Min Industry	Kerin	3	Min PI
P. Keating	17	Treasurer	Sedgwick	3	PMO, Dep Sec Fin
Garnaut	10	PMO/Academic	Willis	3	Min IR
Hawke	10	PM	Fitzgerald	2	Sec DEET[1]
Dawkins	7	Min Trade/EET	T. Evans	2	Treas official
B. Fraser	4	Sec Treas	C. Higgins	2	Dep Sec Treas
Russell	4	TO	Sims	2	PMO
Charles	3	Sec Indus	Walsh	2	Min Fin
M. Keating	3	Sec Fin			

Notes
1. Formerly Secretary for Trade.

Industry Minister, the Treasurer and the Prime Minister and their respective departments, and the ministerial offices. Individuals, such as Ministers John Button, Keating and Hawke, Ross Garnaut, and Treasury Secretary Bernie Fraser, are shown in Table 8.1 as having been nominated by respondents as influential.

While dramatic, the tariff cuts introduced in the May Statement were part of a trend within the Labor Government to open up the economy to international forces. There was also a consensus within the economics profession and the economic bureaucracy that trade protection should be relaxed, while the Industry Assistance Commission and its predecessors had been arguing for trade liberalisation for almost two decades. According to a one-time secretary of the industry department:[1]

> I guess a lot of elite opinion realised that this case-by-case tariff setting had really served its purpose and there wasn't any future in it, [such as] people around the central departments [and] . . . the Industry Assistance Commission . . . although they had a vested interest in the case-by-case basis. Some of the key people at ANU . . . the Peter Lloyds and Ross Garnauts etc. So there was a general disposition.

When the Labor Government was elected, the direction they would take regarding trade protection was unclear. Their 1982 policy document 'New Directions for Australian Industry' seems to offer support for continuing trade protection. While Hawke had advocated reducing protection as a member of the Jackson Committee, after taking power and in the face of a severe recession, he did not seem to be keen on cutting tariffs (Capling and Galligan 1992, 117). For example, according to one cabinet minister, the first Accord included an agreement not to cut tariffs while unemployment remained above five percent. Soon after the election, however, certain members of the Government made it clear that the previous regime of tariff protection was under threat. According to one former chief executive of a Metal Trade Industry Association (MTIA), shortly after the 1983 election:

> The MTIA and the major unions had a famous meeting with John Button. Button came over. The unions opened up on what they wanted in tariffs and he said 'Forget it. Dreamland stuff. This is the new Government, we are opening up the economy.' You could have heard a pin drop.

What was of particular importance was the introduction of the

1984 Motor Vehicle Plan, one of a series of plans that included the Steel Industry and the Textile, Clothing and Footwear Industry plans.[2] According to a former secretary of the industry department, the Motor Vehicle Plan, 'gave a clear indication to industry that tariffs were going to go down.' The industry plans themselves included reductions in barrier protection over time, and promoted developments in worker and management efficiency. Government support, including measures such as bounties and worker retraining, was contingent on adequate performance of management and unions (Capling and Galligan 1992; Gerritsen and Singleton 1991). These plans were 'all part of the same thread' that would lead to the 1988 and future tariff cuts. This thread, according to the same chief executive, was that 'industry was going very badly, high cost, all that sort of stuff, [and we] had to lower tariffs to put pressure on them. But do it in an orderly fashion over time.' The plans were also important because they incorporated the unions and were seen as a method of accustoming the unions to trade liberalisation.

Along with Button's industry plans, others in the Government were also preparing the way for future tariff cuts and for public acceptance of the cuts. Hawke's economic adviser Ross Garnaut was a strong advocate of trade liberalisation, and in February 1985 Hawke noted in a speech to the Centre for European Policy Studies:

> From Australian Industry we seek acceptance of the need to reduce protective walls around the small domestic market. And in this we have had some success. It is enlightened self-interest to recognise that protective measures impose a cost for the economy as a whole. They put upward pressure on prices in the protected market and through the rigidities and distortions which they introduce they will ultimately reduce employment and export opportunities.
>
> We have to break loose from the notion, inherent in the negotiation framework, that one's own trade liberalization is a concession granted to others (cited Snape 1997, 4)

At the same time, John Dawkins, the Trade Minister in 1984, was also looking at the potential for opening up the economy, as his trade officials advised. The Department of Trade produced a series of papers looking at the domestic impediments to trade competitiveness. A committee process set up by Dawkins in 1986 discussed, amongst other things, trade, tariff and microeconomic reform policy issues. This committee had a range of members and was attended by people such as

Geoff Miller, Button, Garnaut and Ted Evans, and occasionally Willis. A range of papers were produced with the long-term aim of changing public perceptions on the need for trade liberalisation. The committee became the Structural Adjustment Committee in 1987, which, as well as being the major forum for discussing trade liberalisation issues, was also important in putting together and overseeing a programme of microeconomic reform, some of which appeared in the 1988 May Statement. The DPMC was also important in pushing for further tariff cuts and microeconomic reform.

The gradual industry-by-industry approach to lowering protection gave way to general tariff cuts when the Australian dollar began to depreciate in 1987–8.[3] According to a former departmental chief executive there was immediate pressure from all 'the usual suspects' such as the central agencies, and a number of media commentators, for some major across-the-board tariff cuts. A decision was made in April 1988 to cut the car tariff to 35 percent by 1992, and, in the same month, Button advocated across-the-board cuts in tariffs to the Structural Adjustment Committee. Button describes the move away from the industry-by-industry process as follows:

> I had separately decided we should embark on across-the-board tariff cuts because a piecemeal process . . . was a bit messy . . . and then of course Keating as Treasurer was very keen[4] . . . or the Treasury was keen on tariff cuts as a matter of principle. There were very deep-seated hatreds, within the economic bureaucracy in Canberra, of manufacturing because manufacturing had been so highly protected. Manufacturers had been successful in pressuring governments to retain high tariffs and I guess as an institution, a competing contender for influence over governments, Treasury didn't like that.
>
> I think Hawke was at that stage [supporting the cuts] for a different principle. [He was] terribly keen on internationalising the Australian economy and saw tariff reductions as a key part of that.
>
> My motivation was [that] manufacturing was a stagnant sector and had to be pushed along. You really had to point them outwards, make them look at the world market, technology dictated that. My motivation was all about performance of the manufacturing sector.

The various ministers and their officials debated at what level tariff cuts would be set. According to a former industry department chief executive:

> All through April a game was being played between Keating and Button. Keating wanted to become PM and Button didn't, so everything had to be seen through the glasses of 'how do I make myself prime ministerial material'.
>
> The game basically was: any tariff reduction John Button was going to propose, Treasury and Keating were going to propose something lower. There was a leaking game going on to the press. Keating was deliberately trying to make himself the hard man. Button was more interested in their real effect—he had to look industry in the eye.

Hawke was important in managing the process and keeping it on track, supported by others in the Cabinet who were in favour of tariff cuts, or at least not opposed to them. According to one respondent, the Agricultural Minister John Kerin was also important because, as he had previously supported some farm sector changes and wanted an even-handed approach to reforms, he threatened to resign if tariff cuts were not made. John Button negotiated with industry groups and tried to get them on board for the tariff reductions. While the Confederation of Australian Industry endorsed the cuts, the Australian Chamber of Manufactures and the MTIA were considerably less enthusiastic, with the MTIA reluctantly accommodating itself, only in the early 1990s. The ACTU and Kelty were against the degree of the cuts and argued for their moderation, preferring instead a greater degree of industry policy.

While Treasury and the Treasurer were possibly less important than the DPMC, Industry and other ministers on initiating microeconomic reforms and trade liberalisation, the business tax changes in the 1988 package were developed by the Taxation Policy Division of Treasury and taken by Keating to the Cabinet. Keating managed to get the changes adopted by Cabinet without much discussion. According to one senior public servant:

> I was sitting in the cabinet room when those [tax] submissions went through Cabinet. What was remarkable was that all the submissions were more-or-less ticked—it was almost proforma. I think it was really because they didn't want to take him on and it was just acknowledged that he was in charge of economic policy. He was certainly in charge of tax policy.

The introduction of trade liberalisation by the Labor Government was a process where policy directions were signalled well in advance by the government, before a more gradual process of trade liberalisation gave way to across-the-board tariff cuts. The move towards tariff reduction reflected a widely held belief amongst policy elites and academic economists that such cuts were desirable. Several ministers within the Labor Government and their departments were also pushing for trade liberalisation. The eventual level of tariff cuts reflected to some extent political manoeuvring within the Labor Cabinet.

Accord VI

Accord VI was the first Accord to explicitly incorporate and endorse elements of enterprise bargaining. As such, it was a significant step towards liberalising and decentralising labour-markets further from the highly centralised wage bargaining that had been restabilised in Accord I.[5] Accord VI incorporated a wage–tax–superannuation trade off, a claim for a $12 wage rise to apply from May 1991 and further improvements in employer-funded superannuation. It also made further commitments to the role of industry policy in underpinning economic restructuring and made commitments to promoting equal pay through an equal pay unit in the Department of Industrial Relations. It talked of the importance of maintaining the 'social wage' through the families' package and developments in childcare. Like Accord I, Accord VI was initiated and developed by a small policy community of ACTU officials, ministers and Treasurer's office staff, with bureaucrats playing a minor role. Table 8.2 shows individuals such as ACTU officials Kelty and Crean, Ministers such as Keating and Hawke, and Don Russell from the Treasurer's Office nominated as having been influential.

The negotiation of Accord VI had two parts. The first was negotiated in February 1990 before the election in March and expected to come into play for the next financial year. Intended to introduce a wage rise of 1.5 percent based on the expected September change in the Consumer Price Index (adjusted to 0.7 percent when the inflation figure was lower than expected), this was to be followed by an increase of $12.00 per week after six months. A tax cut, averaging $7.50 per week, was to be introduced in January 1991. Above-award increases could be obtained by workers in individual enterprises if increases in productivity could be

Table 8.2 Persons nominated as influential on Accord VI

Name	Votes	Position	Name	Votes	Position
P. Keating	27	Treasurer	Campbell	3	ACTU/AMWU
Kelty	27	Sec ACTU	I. Ross	3	ACTU
Hawke	12	Prime Minister	Carmichael	3	ACTU
Crean	8	ACTU Pres	P. Cook	2	Min IR
Willis	8	Min Fin, Trans.[1]	McDonald	2	ACTU
Ferguson	7	ACTU Vice-Pres/Pres	Sword	2	ACTU
Russell	6	TO	Weaven	2	Ass Sec ACTU

Notes
1. Formerly Industrial Relations minister.

demonstrated. A 3 percent increase in superannuation, which was to be phased in over three years, was also introduced (Stilwell 1991; Thompson 1992). In November Accord VI was renegotiated and it was announced that there would be a further tax cut of $2.95 per week (making a total cut of $10.80) introduced instead of the first wage increase, although the $12 increase would remain due in May 1991. As Stilwell points out, this partial freeze on wage increases put more pressure on productivity-based agreements at the enterprise level as a means of increasing wages. As such, it reflected the Government's preference for 'negotiations in the enterprise and unique to that enterprise' (*Sydney Morning Herald* 14/10/90, cited in Stilwell 1991, 41).

The Industrial Relations Commission (IRC) dropped a bombshell by refusing to implement the Accord, citing a number of reservations held towards enterprise bargaining.[6] Instead, it gave a 2.5 percent wage increase. The Government and the unions did not, however, accept the IRC decision and decided to follow through on the agreement. Keating was particularly aggrieved stating he disagreed 'most strongly with the conservatism of the commission' while Kelty likened the centralised wage system in Australia to that in Cuba (cited Capling and Galligan 1992, 258). A number of enterprise agreements went ahead and were presented to the Commission as a *fait accompli*, and in the face of this pressure the IRC backed down. Subsequently, amendments were made to the Industrial Relations Act in 1992 to limit the power of the IRC to influence enterprise agreements.

Enterprise bargaining had been discussed and advocated for a number of years prior to Accord VI. The Business Council of Australia, along with other commentators, began to advocate a shift to labour-market flexibility in the mid-1980s (Dabscheck 1990; Thompson 1992, 53). In March 1987, the BCA released a statement advocating a shift to enterprise agreements and later set up the Employer Relations Study Commission designed to look at ways enterprise bargaining could be implemented. Chaired by Stan Wallace, then Managing Director of Amcor, the first report of the Commission, *Enterprise Bargaining Units: A Better Way of Working,* was released in July 1989 (Employer Relations Study Commission 1989). It advocated changing the union movement's traditional craft and industry union structure to a situation where unions had one bargaining unit at each enterprise. This was followed by a second report in 1991 which proposed a series of workplace and legislative reforms, which the committee claimed would reduce the level of industrial action by encouraging greater commitment to industrial awards and agreements (Hilmer et al 1991). The BCA monthly magazine, the *Business Council Bulletin,* continually advocated moving towards enterprise agreements.[7]

While the support for enterprise bargaining from sections of business may have prepared the way for its adoption in Accord VI, enterprise bargaining was adopted only because it suited the two parties to the Accord, that is, the Government and the ACTU. After Keating's conversion to the Accord process, he became a key player in its development and became very close to Kelty.[8] According to Tony Cole, Keating and Kelty had discussed moving to enterprise bargaining some years before Accord VI. Kelty, however, was not keen to move too early as he thought unions were too divided and diffuse and wanted to make progress on amalgamations. As time progressed, however, the ACTU leadership became concerned that trade unions were becoming too centralised and were losing contact with the shop floor. The ACTU also saw it as desirable to respond to the civil and criminal litigation at the enterprise level (Thompson 1992, 53). Possibly the major factor was the pressure that several years of wage restraint had put on the Accord. According to Willis, the enterprise bargaining in Accord VI:

> was reflecting the strains in the Accord. We had wages in a strait-jacket for almost a decade. It is exceedingly difficult to keep wages so constrained. Not just in terms of the overall level, but in terms of relative movements in the various sections of the economy. At some stage natural forces operate. We reached a point where we had to loosen the traces otherwise we would lose the whole show.

It was pressure from the union movement and the ACTU to keep the show together. They didn't want to be overrun by their constituents. [They] wanted a policy that would deliver what we wanted, that is, overall responsible wages outcome, but [that would] give them the capacity to enable their individual constituents to be freer.

According to a one-time vice-president of the ACTU, it was particularly the larger more powerful unions that were pressing to break out of centralised wage bargaining, especially as the Australian economy was booming[9] at the time:

> The popular view was that the Labor Government [and] Keating . . . did a deal with Kelty that subjugated the interest of the union movement. The truth was the unions like Metals . . . were about to break out, and unless flexibility could be built in, we were not going to have an Accord to go into the election. That's not to say that there wasn't academic opinion [and] worldwide trends towards deregulation.

While Willis and others would claim that the support of the BCA and the think-tanks were irrelevant to Accord VI, the union movement did borrow some ideas from right wing think-tanks and use their rationales and rhetoric to justify their own policy aims. As another former ACTU vice-president says:

> I think we were responding to outside pressure. There was a New Right agenda running. The New Right groupings were quite influential. The H.R. Nicholls Society for example, they did create a strong counter-agenda. I actually agree with [some of their] analysis. Their agenda was: no outside parties, no unions, no arbitration. And the ACTU response to that, if that is the buzz-word, we understand some of the arguments for the need for flexibility at the enterprise level and there is an element of truth in them, moreover this is a great opportunity for us. Unions have always had enterprise bargaining—called over award pay. So let's capitalise on this buzz-word and recapture the agenda and concede some of the valid points, but also exploit [it].

By using some of the arguments and rhetoric of the business community, Accord VI allowed Labor and the ACTU to go into the 1990 election with an Accord document.

Negotiating Accord VI

The process for Accord VI, as with other Accords, followed a structured process of negotiation. Preliminary meetings of the ACTU executive discussed the broad framework of the Accord, but according to Bill Mansfield 'that would have been a very broad discussion, I might add'. The actual negotiations were carried out by Iain Ross of the ACTU with the Treasurer's Office, who worked together to produce a draft document, with the bulk of the initiatives coming from the ACTU. The Wages Negotiation Committee, made up of senior officials of the major unions and of the ACTU, then met to finalise the document.

While the Wages Committee was not a rubber stamp to the draft documents, nor was it likely to make great changes to them. The Wages Committee then met with the Government negotiators, including the Treasurer, and finalised a draft agreement on the Accord. This meeting was mainly a symbolic gesture, as the bulk of the Accord would have been agreed beforehand.[10] The Accord document was then taken to a special conference of the unions where it was explained and discussed. This conference was held in Melbourne and each union was entitled to send delegates to vote. Votes were determined by the size of unions, rather than one person one vote as in the ACTU executive meetings. Once approved the document was released.

By the time of Accord VI, government officials were playing more of a role in the Accords. According to a senior Industrial Relations official:

> I remember the discussion over in the Treasury buildings . . . it involved a wage–tax–superannuation trade-off so there was quite a role for Treasury. There was a lot of backroom discussion . . . there was a lot of briefing being done to the Minsters by both Treasury and ourselves [such as] labour costings [and] scenario work on different outcomes from bargaining.[11]

In summary, Accord VI was the first Accord to explicitly adopt and endorse a commitment to enterprise bargaining, and was driven by a small group of Ministers, ministerial staffers and ACTU officials. As with most Accords, there was little discussion of the process with the wider Cabinet and according to John Button, 'I don't recall any serious Cabinet discussion again about this'. Accord VI borrowed the language and rhetoric of business groups and used them to the advantage of the Accord parties.

'One Nation' and fiscal stimulus

The 'One Nation' statement, delivered on 26 February 1992, was a package that contained a significant fiscal stimulus in the face of a severe recession, and made a definite break with the fiscal constraint that had largely been maintained since 1985. It was a highly political document, designed to give tax cuts in the face of the 'Fightback!' policy document delivered by the coalition opposition and was to stand out as the first major policy document delivered by the Prime Minister Paul Keating. It was initiated and developed by select Ministers, the Prime Minister's Office, the DPMC, and select senior public servants. Table 8.3 shows those individuals nominated as having been influential by respondents including Ministers Keating and Dawkins, Russell from the Prime Minister's Office, DPMC Secretary Mike Keating and ACTU Secretary Bill Kelty.

The 'One Nation' statement delivered a fiscal boost of $0.5 billion in 1991–2 and $1.8 billion in 1992–3 (Keating 1992). The statement outlined a number of proposed infrastructure spending programmes to the value of $874 million in 1992–3 and $375 million in 1993–4. These included projected spending on improving rail links, further developing roads, the national highway system and the electricity infrastructure, as well as providing funds for the Building Better Cities programme, the restoration of heritage buildings and educational infrastructure. The statement also introduced: a number of tax changes, including successive reductions in personal income tax from July 1994 to January 1996;[12] accelerated depreciation deductions; liberalisation of foreign investment regulations; a number of microeconomic efficiency measures including liberalisation of aviation markets; further liberalisation of the financial

Table 8.3 Persons nominated as influential on 1992 'One Nation' statement

Name	Votes	Position	Name	Votes	Position
P. Keating	36	PM	Willis	7	Min Fin
Russell	16	PMO	T. Cole	4	Sec Treas
M.Keating	15	Sec DPMC	Button	3	Min Indus
Dawkins	13	Treasurer	Crean	3	Min PI & Energy
Kelty	8	Sec ACTU	Ferguson	2	Pres ACTU
Edwards	7	PMO	M. Gray	2	DPMC official
R. Simes	7	PMO	Howe	2	Dep PM
R. Sims	7	Dep Sec DPMC			

industry; and changes to electricity supply. It also included a one-off payment, to those families eligible for Family Allowance, of $125 for families with one child, increasing to $250 with families with five or more children. The statement argued that as the economy improved, the budget would move back to surplus by 1995–6.

At the time of the delivery of the 'One Nation' statement the Australian economy was in the grip of the worst recession in ten years. The Government had been particularly slow to react to this recession and strongly resisted calls from within the Cabinet and outside the Government for a stimulus to the economy, fiscal or otherwise (Tingle 1994, ch. 4–5). As Button says:

> even as early as 1989 and 1990 there was a disenchantment in the Cabinet which reflected itself in some discussion in Cabinet that was quite heated at times. I was a very hands-on politician [and] I knew what was going on on the ground, I don't think Hawke and Keating at that stage had any idea. So the businessmen would come and see me as early as 1989–90 about the problems they were encountering. I'd say why don't you go and see the Treasurer or the Prime Minister about this, they pull the levers on this, they'd say 'they are tone deaf'—those were their exact words— 'they won't listen'.[13]

There was a very small fiscal stimulus in November of an extra $300 million for 1991–2, but its low level meant it had little impact. As the recession continued, pressure grew, within the Cabinet, for some sort of action.

A further stimulus to action was the release of the 'Fightback!' policy document by the opposition on 21 November 1991 and the subsequent successful leadership challenge by Keating. The 'Fightback!' package proposed a 15 percent goods and services tax and a 10 percent cut in government spending, as well as cuts in income tax and the removal of payroll tax and petrol excise. Keating had already unsuccessfully challenged for the leadership, and according to Edwards (1996, 441), the weak response on the part of the Government (Keating was by now a back-bencher) to 'Fightback!' was part of the reason for the success of his second challenge on 19 December.

Once elected leader, Keating moved to put his own stamp on the prime ministership and respond to the 'Fightback!' document and the recession. The statement countered the promised tax cuts in 'Fightback!' by promising its own. The apparent decisiveness of the statement showed the electorate that Keating was taking charge and responding to the recession, as well as widening his interests beyond that of a treasurer to broader-based ones seen as more suitable for a prime minister. Keating was also distancing himself from the economic rationalism that he had done so much to develop and promote. According to Edwards (1996, 456), Keating convened a meeting with Treasury and DPMC officials on Saturday 21 December, less than forty-eight hours after his victory. The officials were informed that there would be a large statement to address the recession.

According to Willis, while the statement 'would have happened anyway . . . because we were in a recession, the actual form of it, the name of it, bore the Keating mark.' This is a view shared by most respondents—that the 'One Nation' statement was largely the initiative of Keating working with his office and with a few key officials. Many of the initiatives, including the spending on infrastructure that was central to the statement, seem to have been the idea of Keating himself. These were mulled over while he was sitting on the back-bench after his first unsuccessful challenge to the leadership and in discussion with various people, including influential Labor Party figures on whose support he depended to finally deliver him the leadership. Earlier in the recession, John Button had organised meetings which included leading business people. Some of these issues had been discussed there. Keating also seems to have decided on how big the fiscal stimulus should be. According to Dr Mike Keating, then secretary of the DPMC:

> [Paul Keating] was the one who wanted public investment. It wasn't just the quantum. He [gave] the flavour [and] the broad strategy. We had some influence on the quantum, he wanted higher, but that might have been 'cos he knew we would cut him back— maybe he only wanted two billion to start off.

There was also some discussion about whether there should be a more gradual approach or a large multi-faceted statement which would respond comprehensively to 'Fightback!'. Some in Keating's office, such as his economic adviser Dr John Edwards, favoured a more gradual approach. However, Keating favoured the broadside approach and was supported in this by the Treasurer John Dawkins. Edwards, along with elements of the DPMC, recommended a three or four year programme for the statement. This was intended to allow the Government to introduce major tax cuts without major spending cuts to pay for them, because as John Edwards said 'we could take three or four years of fiscal drag and give it back all at once.' According to Edwards:

> the objective of the statement was not to bring about a recovery but to bring forward a recovery, which we thought ought to have been happening anyway. This turned out to be untrue. In theory, the recession was over almost by the time we came to office. But the expansion was feeble and remained feeble for almost another year.[14]

> [The statement] was successful in serving certain political purposes. It eliminated tax cuts as an issue between Keating and Hewson, and left Hewson with the nasties. In fact it probably didn't have a big impact on the economy. [With $2 billion] you wouldn't necessarily expect [that].

Elements of the bureaucracy, such as parts of the Treasury, had not been in favour of a fiscal stimulus. According to Willis, when developing the small stimulus that had been given in the previous year:

> I recall vividly as Finance Minister discussing this with some Treasury officials—I was Acting Treasurer—and they said they didn't see much need for a package but if we had to have one then something around 50 million would be all right. [It was several times this.] It was a drop in the bucket.[15]

Many in the Treasury had believed that automatic stabilisers would take care of the recession eventually and were sceptical, in any event, that a fiscal stimulus would be successful because of a history of time lags in the implementation of fiscal policy. Treasury officials were also worried that increasing the fiscal deficit would impact negatively on national savings. However, the Treasury had lost some of their influence by this period, as several Cabinet Ministers blamed them for the recession. Despite opposition from some of the bureaucracy, according to Mike Keating, 'It was quite clear that [the Prime Minister] wanted a statement and he wanted to kick-start the economy. He wasn't going to debate that. Essentially [Tony] Cole and myself had to turn the bureaucracy around.' In the end, the Treasury was largely left out of the statement (aside from a few trusted people), although it had some role in developing the paperwork and in implementation.

Keating and his officials conducted consultations with the states and persuaded them to agree to the net fiscal spending of $2 billion. A small group, including Mike Keating and Tony Cole, toured the country and talked to business leaders and state governments to develop options on how the money would be spent. The group was specially interested in intensive capital projects that could be started quickly.[16] The state of Victoria was particularly important as it was suffering the worst recession and its Labor Government was starting to look shaky. Victoria was also one of the power bases of the left in the Labor Party and had been an important element for Keating to separate from Hawke in the leadership struggle. 'One Nation' served partly as a pay back for this support. Groups such as the Committee for Victoria, which included senior union officials such as Kelty, as well as a number of business leaders, were important in offering ideas for helping Victoria. This committee, along with the State Government led by Joan Kirner, contributed the ideas for the standard gauge railway and the Melbourne Transport Hub. Some of the members of the options study group, such as Tony Cole, were surprised at how difficult it was in some cases to spend the money. For example, an offer was made to fund roadworks in Victoria, but the Victorian Government tried to charge a commission and disputed how it would spend the money. The options and ideas that were generated in the process were then worked on to make a more manageable list. As a former Keating staffer says:

> The ideas-gathering process came up with vastly more ideas than they could deal with. A few weeks before the statement all of them, that related to the revenue side of the budget [were given to me]. I was acting Deputy Secretary [at Treasury and] I was given a very short time to turn those 40 ideas into a package. I got the 40 down to 11, and I modified eight of the 11 very heavily.

A joint committee of Finance, the DPMC and Treasury brought together the proposals and prepared them for submission to a Cabinet troika consisting of Willis, Dawkins and Keating. The proposals were then worked on through the usual ERC process (although at an accelerated pace), with ministers and their departments being involved where appropriate. The DPMC played the major coordinating role in the process, with, according to a then deputy secretary of DPMC:

> a close involvement in every policy issue that came up. It was in a sense my responsibility. Malcolm Gray [from the DPMC] also had heavy responsibility and Mike Keating as head of department was involved in a range of issues, he had a general oversight . . . and he also had a particular interest in a range of issues—so he got involved in parts in some detail and in other parts he wasn't much involved.

The paperwork for the statement was itself prepared largely by interaction between the Prime Minister's Office, the Prime Minister and the DPMC. The major role in the bureaucracy was played by the DPMC. According to Mike Keating, 'the writing of it [to] give it a coherence—I put a lot of time in myself—it was done in my department. It [the document] had to produce the rationale for the thing, even those famous tax cuts.' The coordinating and drafting function, for the statement, consumed the department, and according to Rod Sims 'took up the entire economic divisions of the department and at least half of the industry trade resources division and would have involved aspects of the rest of the department'. The draft statement was then discussed with other public officials. According a former deputy secretary at the Treasury:

> I represented Treasury and we did a check through the statement. I don't think any officials were important—it was basically a political document. We had a great argument with them because they wanted to put in far more optimistic than justified growth estimates. They won, but they did change them back a wee bit.

The 'One Nation' statement and the fiscal stimulus it contained was a largely political document driven in part by the economic circumstances of a deep recession, but also in response to a political challenge from the opposition's 'Fightback!' document. It was largely the initiative of the new Prime Minister Keating, and was developed along with the Treasurer Dawkins, their staffs, the DPMC and a few trusted senior public servants.

Privatisation

In 1991, the Labor Government floated shares amounting to 30 percent of the equity of the Commonwealth Bank. In November 1991 Aussat was sold to Optus Communications. In 1992, the merger of Australian Airlines and Qantas was announced along with the intention to sell 100 percent of the new airline. The 1992–3 Budget announced a programme of significant sales. Further asset sales announced, and sometimes carried out during the Labor Government, included sale of: part of the shipping company, Australia National Line;[17] the Moomba–Sydney gas pipe line; 49 percent of equity in the Australian Industry Development Corporation, the Housing Loans Insurance Corporation, the Commonwealth Serum

Laboratories and Commonwealth properties (Table 8.4; Waterman 1993; Wettenhall 1997).

Privatisation in Australia was slow in starting compared to the British and New Zealand examples. Instead, it was a piecemeal and gradual process, only gathering momentum in the final years of the Labor Government and then proceeding in earnest from 1990 on, both at the state and federal levels (Table 8.4). By the end of 1997, receipts from privatisation as a percentage of GDP were second only to New Zealand in the OECD (RBA 1997). Privatisation at the federal level was something advocated by the central agencies for a number of years, but it only occured when the support of key officials and ministers coalesced with political opportunities that overrode Labor Party opposition to the sales. Table 8.5 shows those individuals nominated as influential in privatisation, such as senior ministers Keating, Hawke and Kim Beazley, ministerial staffer Don Russell and departmental secretary Mike Keating.

Some support for privatisation had long been part of the ethos of the central agencies. The Treasury, for example, had been advocating some asset sales since the 1970s. While some officials held ideological beliefs that privatisation in itself was a good thing, it was also believed that there would be efficiency gains if some public sector corporations

Table 8.4 Sales of Australian federal assets 1990–97[1]

Name	Type of Sale	Fin Year of Sale
Australian Industry Dev Corp.	Public float and trade sale	1989–90 to 1997–8
AUSSAT	Trade sale	1991–2
Commonwealth Bank	Public float in four tranches	1991–2 to 1997–8
Australian Airlines	Trade sale	1992–3
Qantas	Trade sale and public float	1992–3 to 1995–6
Commonwealth Serum Labs	Public float	1993–4
Moomba–Sydney Pipeline	Trade sale	1993–4
Snowy Mts Engineering Corp	Three trade sales	1993–4 to 1995–6
Aerospace Industries of Australia	Trade sale	1994–5
Avalon Airport Geelong	Trade sale	1996–7
Commonwealth Funds Mgm	Trade sale	1996–7
Australian National (Rail)	Trade sale	1997–8
Brisbane Airport	Trade sale	1997–8
Melbourne Airport	Trade sale	1997–8
Perth Airport	Trade sale	1997–8
Telstra	Public float	1997–8

Notes
1. Source: RBA 1997c. Total of federal government asset sales to 1997 was $30 102 million. Total of state government asset sales to 1997 was $31 166 million.

could be moved into private hands. It was the corporatisation process however, that crystallised the policy framework and allowed privatisation to be carried out. The corporatisation process could involve the adoption of commercial practices by public service departments, but usually meant the 'hiving off [of] departmental functions into new organisational entities, either fully fledged GBEs [Government business enterprises] or budget funded agencies' (Beckett 1994, 242).[18] These GBEs were structured in such a way as to approximate private commercial enterprises. This included: having management board members appointed on commercial strength; being paid at levels close to private sector rates; being given some freedom to manage; being expected to earn commercial rates of return; and community service obligations being clarified and directly paid for, either out of the budget or through different expected rates-of-return (Waterman 1993).

Corporatisation itself was largely driven by the bureaucracy. According to Mike Keating:

> Finance was the one that drove corporatisation. Corporatisation came first . . . it was driven out of the bureaucracy and then it got Walsh's support. Once corporatisation had gone through, and once competition [policy][19] went through, you couldn't use [GBEs] for a social purpose because you would give them a competitive disadvantage, unless a complex system of levies and subsidies through the budget were introduced. Once you have put competition and corporatisation in place, privatisation is almost inevitable.

Table 8.5 Persons influential on privatisation of Qantas and Commonwealth Bank of Australia

Name	Votes	Position
P. Keating	24	Treasurer, PM
Hawke	10	PM
Beazley	7	Min Transport, ET
Willis	7	Min Transport, Fin
Walsh	4	Min Fin
Dawkins	3	Min EET, Treasurer
Richardson	3	Min Transport, Communications
Russell	3	PMO
Button	2	Min Industry
G. Evans[1]	2	Min FAT
M. Keating	2	Sec Fin, DPMC

Notes
1. Minister for Transport and Communications 1987–8.

While the central agencies and elements of the business community[20] were supporting privatisation, there had also been discussion of some asset sales in Cabinet very early in the Labor Government. According to one departmental chief executive:

> I think I recall when the seed of selling Qantas starting sprouting a sprout. It was quite an early ERC meeting, early in the days of the Hawke Government [in 1985]. I remember after midnight when the ERC had exhausted their agenda and run out of ideas and hadn't closed the budget. They had a bit of a think-tank—[the selling of Qantas was raised]—it was a bit of a left field shot by Paul Keating.

On 26 February 1986 Peter Walsh, then Finance Minister, had mentioned in a speech to the *Australian Financial Review* that he had no 'ideological preference for public or private ownership' but that what mattered was what would deliver at lowest cost (Walsh 1995, 107).

Facing the Labor Government, however, were a number of barriers to asset sales. First, the Labor Government itself had previously run an effective campaign against the privatisation plans of the coalition opposition in the South Australian state elections of 1985 and at national level (Kelly 1994, 237–40). While successful in helping to undermine coalition leader John Howard's leadership, this had the effect of largely removing privatisation from the policy agenda for a number of years. Second, privatisation was against the Labor Party platform. Hawke himself had said in a 1985 Chifley lecture:

> What in the name of reason is the justification for breaking up and selling off the great and efficient national assets, like the Commonwealth Bank, Telecom, TAA, Qantas? The fact is that this recipe for disaster represents the height of economic irrationality . . . it is based on a blind and mindless commitment to a narrow, dogmatic and discredited ideology (cited Kelly 1994, 391).

Despite these earlier attacks against privatisation, members of the Cabinet began to push for some asset sales. For some members of the Cabinet there was a gradual move towards the position, as they grappled with being involved in business decisions and dealing with the spending decisions of public corporations.[21] This belief that some privatisation might be a good thing was held largely because of the perceived fiscal benefits of asset sales, rather than any firm belief that privately owned firms would be better run.[22] According to John Button:

My own belief, certainly with the airline sale, certainly with the merger of Australian Airlines and Qantas, that was driven very much by fiscal discipline. You would watch that [fiscal] deficit come in and you got sick of all the bullshit about it—'oh well it's bad this month 'cos of a couple of new Qantas aircraft.' That argument was advanced most strongly by Hawke because of that constant strain on the budget.

In August, after the 1987 election, despite his earlier statements, Hawke called for a new agenda to build a competitive economy; this included advocating some microeconomic reform and asset sales such as Australian Airlines and Qantas. Papers commissioned by Gareth Evans showed both airlines were in difficult fiscal positions and, according to Kelly (1994, 391) by 1987 there was support by some Cabinet members for a sale of 49 percent of Australian Airlines and Qantas. This support for some asset sales was raised outside the Cabinet, according to Bob Hogg, then president of the Labor Party:

In the lead up to the May 1988 Statement, it was floated internally to sell off the Australian Airlines and Qantas separately. It was put most vigorously that it meant the survival of the Government—which was bullshit—and it was pretty primitive stuff. [There was a meeting] Hawke, Keating, Gareth Evans and ten officials.

The Cabinet wanted to go to National Conference to endorse the change, but as Hogg said to them, 'we can have one tomorrow, but . . . you will only get two votes. Literally no one in the room had any idea what the sale of Australian Air and Qantas would realise.' Hogg says he suggested combining the two airlines and rationalising their costs and capital—but he was told that it couldn't be done. Despite Hawke's and other Cabinet Ministers' support for privatisation, further progress on asset sales was delayed by the opposition of the Labor Party, as the sales were in contravention of the Party platform. In April, the Labor Party affiliated think-tank, the Evatt Foundation, published a report that was sceptical of the benefits of privatisation (Botsman 1988). Hawke then suffered a defeat at the ALP National Conference when the issue of privatisation was discussed. It was decided at the conference to allow a partial sell off of the Australian Industry Development Corporation, but on 7 June 1988 it was also decided to set up a committee to study the funding of airlines, effectively ruling out asset sales for the time being. The committee never presented a report, and it took two years for negotiation and pressure to change the mind of the Party and allow the Party platform to be amended.

Within the bureaucracy, work on privatisation continued. In the Department of Finance a Taskforce on Asset Sales was established in 1987 (Wettenhall 1997). This was followed by a second taskforce in September 1992. According to the Department of Finance, the approach of the taskforces was to:

> draw on expertise from within the relevant portfolio Departments and the private sector as appropriate . . . While each sale has its own characteristics, the general strategy for prosecuting sales involves establishing the sales objectives and identifying key sales related issues including precisely what is to be sold, foreign ownership restrictions, transitional and post sale staffing arrangements and employment conditions (where applicable), timing and method of sale and engagement of specialist private sector advisers. Generally, the Task Forces seek to bring competition to sale processes to ensure that the Government receives fair value for the assets concerned (cited Wettenhall 1997, 72).

After the long debates about the merits of privatisation, the Government was given an opportunity to undertake the partial privatisation of the Commonwealth Bank when in 1990 the Victorian State Bank was on the verge of collapse (Tingle 1994, 260–71). After a series of negotiations between the Victorian State Government and the Treasurer (along with his office staff, especially Don Russell), it was decided to sell the State Bank. The State Government of Victoria, a Labor Government (then led by Joan Kirner who had just replaced John Cain) would have been embarrassed by the collapse. The collapse would possibly also have impacted on the support for Federal Government in Victoria. While the State Bank was ostensibly for sale by tender, the two Governments largely decided that it would be bought by the Commonwealth Bank. To pay for the take-over the Commonwealth Bank needed to raise capital by issuing equity. As the sale was to support a State Labor Government and the purchase of the State Bank by the Commonwealth Bank at least meant it was maintained in public hands, the move was not actively opposed by the Labor Party.[23] Announced by Keating on 27 August 1990, a public share issue in July–August 1991 raised $1.3 billion. The Federal Government maintained its shares in the bank, but its voting capital was diluted to 70.25 percent. The partial privatisation of the Commonwealth Bank, an icon of the left of the Labor Party, arguably opened the door to further privatisations. The Government later reduced their shareholding to 50.4 percent with a statutory guarantee that the government would maintain a majority shareholding.[24] Despite this, the rest of the Bank was sold in two share floats, and was completely privately owned by 1997–98.

After the 1990 election Hawke again began pressuring for microeconomic change, including some assets sales. Pressure was maintained on opponents of the sales by the Government with their refusal to allow recapitalisation of the assets (Beckett 1994; Wettenhall 1997). Opponents of privatisation were still fighting a rearguard action, however, and would not grant special dispensation from the Party platform to allow the asset sales, in an attempt to force the Government into changing the Party platform (Gruen and Grattan 1993, 9–10). A special ALP conference was held in September to discuss the issue. After, according to Bob Hogg, 'the normal trading and argument' went on, it was agreed by the conference that the telecommunications industry would be opened to competition and that all of Australian Airlines and 49 percent of Qantas, along with Aussat,[25] would be sold.[26] The Party stood firm on opposing the privatisation of Telstra, however. To endorse privatisation was a major policy change for the Labor Party and according to Hogg the Government 'did go through the Party, to their credit.' Despite the major policy change involved, the special conference 'seemed ultimately pro-forma' and unheated (Gruen and Grattan 1993, 10). The partial sale of the Commonwealth Bank was not formally discussed at the conference. Bob Hogg put the argument that it wasn't the policy of the Labor Party, but as he said 'most people realised that it was either that or let the State Bank go to the wall—so there wasn't much of an internal argument about the CBA—it was done without going through the conference.' The partial privatisation of the Australian National Line was approved at the July 1991 National Conference.

Previously the Government had committed itself to a three year moratorium on policy change, such as continuing to maintain a distinction between domestic and overseas aviation markets, to allow the sale of the two airlines to proceed. However, this commitment was abandoned, meaning that the domestic airline Australian Airlines became less attractive to buyers as it would face competition from Ansett, Qantas and possibly Air New Zealand (Beckett 1994).[27] In 1992, after he had become Prime Minister, Keating proposed in a television interview a merger of Qantas and Australian Airlines and a sell off of 70 percent of the combined companies. Despite the fact that this contravened the Party platform to maintain government majority control of Qantas, it was received largely without controversy. In fact, amongst the Cabinet and Caucus there was a feeling that there might as well be a 100 percent sale (Gruen and Grattan 1993, 10–11). The Government also argued that the combination of the two airlines would give 'operational synergies' and provide a 'seamless' domestic and international aviation market (Beckett 1994, 251). After an attempt to amend the platform by special ballot was blocked by the left, the Government decided to go ahead with the 100 percent sale without seeking Party approval. According to Gruen and Grattan (1993, 11) the sale was tolerated by the Party because it did not want to seem disunited before the coming election. In March 1993, 25 percent of the equity in Qantas was sold to British Airways for $665 million. The full privatisation of Qantas was not completed until July 1995, delayed because of a downturn in the aviation market.

Privatisation, that is, the sale of some federal assets, was something that was strongly driven out of the central agencies and supported by a number of key ministers. While efficiency arguments were important, for most ministers privatisation was supported largely for its perceived fiscal benefits. Strong resistance from the extra-parliamentary Labor Party was a key factor in delaying assets sales for a number of years. It was not until the collapse of the State Bank of Victoria was averted through its purchase by the Commonwealth Bank, with the funds supplied through a partial float of the Commonwealth Bank, that this Labor Party opposition could be overridden.

Conclusion

This chapter has examined four key economic policy decisions made during the Labor Government: the 1988 May Statement; the Accord VI in 1990; the 'One Nation' statement of 1992; and the privatisation of federal assets. The 1988 May Statement was driven by a coalition of senior ministers and their offices and departments, while the 'One Nation' statement was largely developed by Prime Minister Keating and his office, along with the Treasurer, Dawkins, and a few trusted senior bureaucrats. Privatisation was largely driven out of the bureaucracy and supported by a number of ministers mainly for perceived fiscal benefits, but extra-parliamentary Labor Party opposition slowed the sale of federal assets considerably.

Chapters six to eight have looked at economic policy-making in Australia. Partly due to a complex federal system and attempts to build consensus, influence can be relatively diffuse in economic policy-making. This influence differs from decision to decision. As chapter seven shows, in financial liberalisation, the Reserve Bank played a leading role, with key minsters, their offices and the central agencies important, along with members of the Campbell and Martin Inquiries into the financial system. Accord I was generated by ACTU officials, key ministers (often ex-ACTU) and ministerial offices, with the bureaucracy playing little part beyond implementation. The 1984 Trilogy Commitments were initiated by the Prime Minister and the Treasurer along with their offices, and further developed by a supportive bureaucracy.

The examination of economic policy decision making in Australia and New Zealand offers some lessons for the general study of policy-making. First, purely technocratic explanations of policy decisions will always be only partial. Aside from the fact that there is never one answer to policy problems, political factors, the interplay of personalities, institutions and ideology can also be important in policy decisions. Political infighting as Keating tried to wrest the prime ministership, the response to the electoral threat of 'Fightback!' and the rebranding of Keating as Prime Minister, probably explain as much of 'One Nation', as do any technical responses to the serious recession. Personal relationships between key political and union figures explain much of the Accord process, its political success and long life, quite apart from its possible effectiveness as an economic policy instrument. In Australia and New Zealand, the rapid removal of tariffs can be explained partly as an ideological response reflecting the strength of neoclassical economic theories, especially in the face of the apparent success of the Button Plans in reorientating industry to the international market in Australia. Many of the economic policy decisions taken in New Zealand after 1984, show the strong influence of particular schools of economic theory. This influence remained pervasive despite the success of other models, including the Australian Accord. As the final chapter will demonstrate, differences in institutions, personalities of policy makers, electoral and party dynamics, as well as economic conditions, go a long way to explaining policy differences between the two countries.

Second, studies of policy networking that take into account micro-level decision making and the importance of interpersonal relationships, as well as focusing on meso-levels of policy-making (as recommended by Rhodes 1997), will give a better understanding of policy-making. Relationships built at the decision-making level can influence other decisions and the policy arena in general—a dramatic example is given by the development of Kelty and Keating's relationship. Studying discrete aspects of a policy area shows that different policy communities or networks can form around different decisions. These relationships may be overlooked if the study concentrates only on a general or meso-level.

9
Remaking New Zealand and Australian Economic Policy

After 1983 Australia and New Zealand extensively liberalised their economies. In a series of reforms remarkable for their scope, both countries deregulated their financial, capital and other markets, floated their dollars, made changes to the machinery of government, corporatised and sold a number of state assets, and dramatically reduced trade protection. New Zealand radically liberalised its labour-market by introducing individual contracts into employment, while Australia introduced a series of income policy agreements known as the Accord. Macroeconomic policy in both countries generally focused on deflation, although to a considerably greater extent in New Zealand. Drawing on 180 interviews carried out with institutional elites and nominated individuals, as well as primary and secondary sources, and analysing a select number of key economic policy decisions in both countries, preceding chapters have illustrated the broad processes of economic policy change. Economic policies in New Zealand were highly derivative of neoclassical economics and some of its offshoots, whereas, in Australia a less doctrinaire form of neoclassical economics was important, with corporatism and labourism also influential. In New Zealand economic policy change was driven by a select and small number of members of strategically located elite groups. This rather closed 'policy community' often exercised influence over a number of decisions and across a considerable period of time. In contrast, influence in Australian economic policy-making was more diffuse, with a greater variety of individuals and institutions being involved in policy formation. While concentrated to some extent around key institutions, influence differed somewhat depending on the decision being investigated.

This final chapter will summarise and expand on themes developed throughout this study. Economic policy-making in New Zealand has been characterised by a 'crash through' approach with policy introduced quickly, largely without consultation and sometimes contrary to election promises and party manifestos.[1] In contrast, economic restructuring was carried out in Australia through a process of 'bargained consensus' where change was introduced more gradually and where there was an attempt to explain and to develop support for new policies. The New Zealand process of 'crashing through' has often been touted as an exemplar for other countries wishing to restructure their economies. The Australian 'bargained consensus' has, however, avoided the electoral instability and breakdown of political legitimacy suffered in New Zealand. At the same time, the New Zealand economy has generally not performed as well as that of Australia and the other OECD economies, as measured by commonly used economic indicators. It is argued that a 'bargained consensus' approach to economic policy change may deliver better economic policy advice.

'Crashing through' versus 'bargained consensus'

New Zealand: 'Crashing through'

Economic policy-making in New Zealand, during a crucial period of change, was dominated by a small and identifiable group of institutionally based elites largely from four key institutions: the cabinet, the Treasury, the Reserve Bank and the Business Roundtable, with the DPMC important after 1990. Institutional structures in policy-making in New Zealand were simple. Parliament was dominated by the executive, and the Treasury and the Reserve Bank dominated the economic policy-making bureaucracy. The Business Roundtable enjoyed considerable access to, and influence on, politicians and policy makers under both the National and Labour governments. They also had the resources to publish a seemingly endless stream of influential reports on a wide variety of public policy issues.

New Zealand may be similar to other Westminster countries in having its economic policy-making dominated by a few key institutions and individuals, and as such the results of this study might not be surprising. For example, Thain and Wright's extensive study of economic policy-making in the United Kingdom found policy formation was often concentrated around key ministers and officials (1995, ch. 9, 13). Nor is it unusual for public servants, including Treasury officials, to wield immense influence in policy formation, even, in some cases, to a greater extent than their political masters (Egeberg 1995; Goldfinch 1997). While the institutional simplicity of New Zealand has meant there was always potential for a small elite to dominate policy formation, the making of policy as it developed after 1984 departed markedly from what had formerly been usual practice. New Zealand has had a strong tradition of participation in policy-making which had, until 1984, followed a process of consultation, where major interest groups were formally and informally incorporated into policy formation. Governments saw themselves as bound to follow Party manifestos and election promises.

After 1984, the Labour Government, and to a lesser extent the National Government after 1990, moved away from consultative processes of policy-making. Shortly after the 1984 election, an Economic Summit was held with representatives from the unions, business and social groups. However, even before the Summit reported, the economic policy direction had been decided, making the Summit largely a public relations exercise. Policy formation instead came to be personalised around a few key ministers, officials and business leaders and was often made in secret, while party manifestos and party traditions were sometimes disregarded. Both the Labour and National Governments spectacularly broke a number of election promises.

Formal structures that did exist were often bypassed. For example, while the Labour Government had such structures as the Officials' Coordination Committee and the Cabinet Policy Committee to keep departments and others informed, key economic policy decisions were sometimes made by the Minister of Finance, Associate Ministers and key (mostly Treasury) officials working outside official channels, with the Reserve Bank being responsible for monetary policy. There was a greater attempt to use formal processes after the election of the National Government in 1990, with a greater use of cabinet committees and revival of officials' committees to shadow these cabinet committees, as well as the establishment of some consultative mechanisms. Policy formation was particularly centralised during the budget process. As budgets were traditionally prepared in secret, and because of the huge number of policies that could be presented in the second reading of the Appropriation Bill, there was often little time (or attempt) to debate and discuss issues. The Treasury, often ignored during the Muldoon Government, found its power increased under supportive finance ministers and with the removal of some potential public sector rivals.

This change of style in policy-making can be seen as the result of a number of factors. First, the perception of economic crisis supported a belief that usual methods of policy-making were not appropriate and that radical change needed to be introduced. Second, Public Choice theory was influential in developing a belief that interest groups were vested interests that should be excluded from policy-making, and that, in fact, interest group influence had previously contributed to New Zealand's relative decline. Public Choice views of policy-making accorded with the elitist and technocratic views of leading policy makers and politicians. As Finance Minister from 1984 to 1988 Roger Douglas noted in his book *Unfinished Business*:

> Do not try and advance a step at a time. Define your objectives clearly and move towards them in quantum leaps. Otherwise the interest groups will have time to mobilise and drag you down (Douglas 1993, 220–21).

Third, leading policy makers formed a close (and often relatively closed) trust and reciprocity policy community in Wellington as they were educated and worked together. The influence of members of this community increased as they were appointed to key positions within the public and private sector.

Australia: A 'bargained consensus'

Economic restructuring in Australia was introduced more gradually and through greater negotiation and compromise than in New Zealand. Influence in Australian policy-making was also more diffuse than that found in New Zealand. While the cabinet, the central agencies, the Reserve Bank, the ministerial offices and the ACTU were often the most important institutions in economic policy-making during the Labor Government, others, such as the line departments, EPAC and business associations (amongst others) were also important. Influence differed somewhat depending on the decision being studied.

As well as influence in economic decision making being more

diffuse, the processes of economic policy change differed between the two countries. In contrast to the 'crash through' process adopted in New Zealand, the Australian approach involved what Keating and Dixon (1989) called a 'bargained consensus'. This attempted to build and maintain support for the new policy directions by cajoling and using the symbols and rhetoric of consensus and by incorporating key interest groups in policy formation. As Ross Garnaut, a former economics adviser to Prime Minister Hawke describes it:

> Hawke's reform style was gradualist, emphasising intensive public discussion of economic problems and policy alternatives and close consultation with interested parties. Public discussion and consultation was usually led by Government, and vested interests were often coopted to support reform in the process (Garnaut 1994a, 68).

Supporters of the Labor Government might be inclined to overstate the degree to which Labor did carry out this bargained consensus, and there was considerable debate and disagreement over policy directions. On the other hand, there are a considerable number of examples where economic policy was indeed made in this 'bargained consensus' fashion, especially during Hawke's prime ministership. The Labor Government had strongly articulated policies going into the 1983 election and by and large it developed policies based on them. Once in office, it developed support for the new economic directions through the Economic Summit in 1983. Where changes of direction were made, they were often indicated through the use of commissions such as the Martin Report on financial liberalisation, or were actively signalled before the elections, such as in the case of the Trilogy Commitment. Industry plans were based on tripartite negotiations between the government, the unions and employers (Capling and Galligan 1992). Trade liberalisation was prefigured through the industry plans and constant references (including speeches by Hawke) and research on the need to open the economy to external competition. Other pronouncements such as the famous 'banana republic' statement of Treasurer Paul Keating in 1986, were used to garner support for further policy changes. Wide, although hurried, consultation was carried out for the economic statement 'One Nation'. Normal extra-parliamentary party procedures were used, by-and-large, to obtain Labor Party approval for asset sales and there was a general regard for keeping the Party onside during the change process. The Premier's Agreements were developed to obtain support for competition policy throughout the states (Harman 1996). A number of specific consultative mechanisms such as the EPAC were used to sell and build consensus support for the direction of government policy, if not always to actively consult interest groups. Of central importance was the Accord process itself, which directly and openly incorporated the union movement into policy formation. The Labor Government was probably at its weakest when it became insular and turned away from consultation and attempts to build support for government policy, such as during the last days of Hawke's Government during the 1991–2 recession and Keating's second term as Prime Minister.

Explaining the differences

Economic restructuring in New Zealand and Australia, while sharing a number of similarities, also contained a number of important differences. Economic policy change in New Zealand was introduced more quickly, more extensively and showed a greater degree of theoretical purity than found in Australia, and the countries differed on macroeconomic and labour-market policy. The differences in approach to economic restructuring can be explained by reference to a number of institutional, economic, political and personality variables.

Australia's sometimes complex federal system, the existence of a genuine house of review in the Senate with almost coequal powers, and institutional complexity may go some way to explain why change sometimes needed to be introduced by negotiation and compromise. In contrast, once elected, the New Zealand executive faced few constraints on its powers to initiate and put into action policy and legislation.[2] The larger and more complex public policy structure in Australia, with its greater numbers of departments with expertise in economic policy, made the formation of the closed economic policy community found in New Zealand less likely.

The situation faced after the election of the two Labo[u]r Governments was also significantly different. Australia faced a less serious economic situation in 1983 than did New Zealand in 1984 (or at least that was the perception). This suggested a less pressing need for radical reform in Australia. The actions of the New Zealand Prime Minister Robert Muldoon in refusing to devalue on the advice of the incoming Government and the consequent constitutional predicament further cemented this feeling of economic crisis.

The personalities and personal histories of leading politicians were also a significant factor. Hawke's ties with the ACTU and his training as a negotiator meant he was more inclined to seek support for policy directions, rather than impose them (Garnaut 1994a). This was in marked contrast to the elitist and sometimes bullying tendencies of the New Zealand Labour and National Governments.

The structure of the Labo[u]r parties in the two countries was also different. The Australian Labor Party had institutionalised factions within caucus, reflecting state party bases and ideological and policy preferences. These needed to be brought onside for the changes. In contrast, the New Zealand Labour Government Caucus did not contain formalised factions but depended more on personal loyalties (Easton and Gerritson 1996). The New Zealand Labour Government was largely able to ignore the extra-parliamentary Labour Party, although not necessarily without electoral cost.

The relationship of the two governments to the union movement also differed. The Labor Government in Australia had a very close relationship with the union movement. The Labor Government contained a number of ACTU alumni, such as Hawke and Willis, and ACTU presidents Simon Crean and Martin Ferguson later entered parliament. The Accord process, a vital part of the Labor Government's economic policy going into the 1983 election and after, and a 'source of strength for the reform program' (Garnaut 1994a, 68), needed to be maintained through negotiation and compromise and would have been endangered by a 'crash through' approach. Such an approach would also have damaged the friendships between leading Government figures Hawke and Keating, and ACTU Secretary Kelty.

In contrast, the relationship between the New Zealand union movement and the Labour cabinet was usually not close. The New Zealand union movement did not act as the training ground for politicians to the same extent as did the Australian one, with the only Labour cabinet minister with strong union links being Stan Rodger. Rodger was a past president of the Public Service Association, and was ranked only fourteenth out of twenty (Easton and Gerritson 1996).[3] This lack of identification with unions and working class interests was intensified by class shifts within the membership of the parliamentary Labour Party. As Nagel (1998, 241) has pointed out:

> . . . the shift in class composition of the Labour party elite—
> which Muldoonism both responded to and accelerated—produced

a change in the policy preference of its parliamentary leaders. With few exceptions, they no longer had any visceral identification with poor and working class people: their own interests, associations and lifestyles led them to identify with New Zealand's affluent classes; and their leftism lay in non-economic issues.[4]

The New Zealand union movement also had a part to play in its comparative exclusion from policy influence as it lacked the resources and policy expertise held by the ACTU, and it is possible that it could not have delivered the degree of discipline exercised by the ACTU in the Accord process. A further factor was the Public Choice-influenced and elitist beliefs of policy makers in New Zealand that resulted in the exclusion of interest groups, including unions. This was in marked contrast to the labourist and corporatist ideas that underpinned the Australian Accord process and the industry plans and saw a role for unions and interest groups in policy formation. After the New Zealand National Government's adoption of individual contracting in the labour-market, this exclusion of unions from policy formation was complete.

Related to the institutional simplicity and smallness of New Zealand, is its lack of an intellectual culture, and of a tradition of policy and theoretical debate. This allowed theoretically driven policy entrepreneurs to dominate policy change, without the culture and structures that might have led to greater debate over the policies, and then to their modification and moderation. While Australia is not necessarily a paragon of intellectual debate, the greater number of universities, the higher quality media, the inclusion of academic economists (especially ANU economists) into policy debate, and the policy expertise of the union, business and social welfare movements, all contributed to a wider ranging and higher quality debate over economic policy directions. This in turn led to questioning and discussion over policy directions and probably contributed to their modification and moderation.

Political acumen may also explain some of the differences. The Australian Labor Government looked to hold office for a long time and so proceeded cautiously. The New Zealand Labour Government seemed less interested in electoral success and more interested in doing what it perceived to be 'right'.[5] Douglas did not intend to stand again in 1990, and after the Labour Government won the 1987 election it 'became politically reckless, happy to confront the party's supporters in the public sector professions and to attack some of the party's sacred cows by privatising state enterprises' (Mulgan 1997a, 12).

Finally, electoral dynamics also influenced the speed and direction of policy change. In New Zealand, the success of the Bob Jones' New Zealand Party in the election of 1984 (in gaining 12.3 percent of the vote) gave some in the parliamentary Labour Party the belief that they could appeal to the pro-liberalisation constituency of Jones' party in the next election of 1987, even at the risk of alienating its traditional supporters in safe Labour seats (Nagel 1998).[6] The National Party in opposition, at least in the 1987 election, could be painted as the party of the interventionist Muldoon era. Before the 1990 election, the National Party moved to embrace and extend the market–liberal approach of the Labour Government. In contrast, the Australian Labor Party was distinguishing itself from the neo-liberal 'fight inflation first' of the Fraser Government in the election of 1983. It did this partly through the Accord process and the rhetoric of consensus and 'fighting unemployment and inflation simultaneously', including through elements of Keynesian stimulus. The Accord process played a useful role in distinguishing the Labor Government from the opposition. The Labor Government was also able to portray itself as more moderate than the coalition, such as in early debates over privatisation, welfare issues, the debate over a goods and services tax and the 'Fightback!' package in the 1993 election. This gave it an electoral incentive to introduce change slowly and to moderate its position on certain issues.

Comparing the reform programmes: Has the New Zealand approach to policy change delivered better policy outcomes?

Those seeking to carry out restructuring in their own countries may look at the New Zealand experience with a degree of envy. In contrast to the more gradual process in Australia, those advocating economic policy change in New Zealand achieved their policy objectives to a remarkable degree and in a remarkably short time. In such a vein, New Zealand has been touted as an exemplar of economic restructuring and as a model for the world to emulate (Evans et al 1996; Douglas 1993; Richardson 1995). Serious doubts can be raised as to whether this is in fact the case. There are three closely related issues at hand here. First, there are the political and social costs of a 'crash through' approach to policy change that might not occur in a bargained consensus approach to economic change. As this section will argue, the process in New Zealand seriously undermined the legitimacy and stability of the political system. Second, despite the New Zealand process avoiding the influence of 'vested interests' and the, at times, highly theoretically based policies being largely unmodified in the policy process, it is by no means clear that such policies delivered better policy outcomes as measured by commonly used economic indicators. Third, there are good reasons to believe that a 'bargained consensus' approach to policy formation delivers better policy advice and possibly leads to better policy outcomes.

Undermining political legitimacy by 'crashing through'

The 'crash through' approach to policy change in New Zealand, while effective in achieving some of the aims of policy makers and policy entrepreneurs, led to significant opposition, electoral instability and the undermining of the legitimacy of the political system. The new policy directions and the new elitist politics of economic policy-making in New Zealand did excite some opposition, but as Kelsey (1995; ch. 12) points out, opponents were sometimes slow to articulate and organise dissent in the face of rapid policy change and the dissolving consensus, and found it difficult to adjust to exclusion from policy formation. This was especially the case for some traditional supporters of Labour governments such as the trade unions and members of the extra-parliamentary Labour Party. There were also a number of academics who were critical of the new ideologically and theoretically derived policies. However, in a country where public theoretical debate was not much practised and not much valued, and which had previously prided itself on its 'pragmatic' approach to policy development,[7] these academics, as well as being excluded from policy-making, were often ignored or marginalised by a media that was either middle-brow (in the case of print) or approaching tabloid. When policy reversals were made, such as in the case of Roger Douglas's abortive attempt to introduce a flat tax in December 1988 and the abandonment of hospital charges introduced by the National Government in 1991, this was either because of internal power struggles within the Labour Government in the case of the flat tax, or because public opposition coincided with the realisation (even by some of their proponents) that changes were unworkable, such as in the case of the health charges.

While opponents of Rogernomics were largely ineffective in modifying the new policy directions, the volatility of the electorate in the late 1980s suggests that opposition to the new policies and politics of Rogernomics became widespread and intense, especially following the 1987 election. Factional disputes inside the Labour Cabinet led to a number of resignations and sackings of ministers, culminating in the resignation and replacement of Prime Minister David Lange by Geoffrey Palmer in 1989. Palmer himself was replaced by Mike Moore just before the 1990 election. In 1990, the Labour Government lost the election in a landslide to a National Party that seemed to promise a move away from Rogernomics (Vowles and Aimer 1993). However, after the National Government intensified the economic liberalisation programme and broke a number of its own election promises, it too found its support evaporate and its large majority slip to just one seat after the 1993 election. The two-party system that had dominated since the 1930s also suffered stress, with some of the left of the Labour Party, led by Jim Anderton, splitting in 1989 to form the New Labour Party (later part of the Alliance), some of the right (including Douglas and Prebble) later forming the extreme market liberal Association of Consumers and Taxpayers (ACT), while a former National minister Winston Peters formed the populist New Zealand First Party in 1993.[8] Most importantly, the 1993 election also saw the endorsement in a referendum by the electorate of a shift from plurality voting to a proportional system based on the German Mixed Member Proportional system. This was despite the change being opposed both by leading politicians and a well-resourced advertising campaign funded by big business. As Mulgan (1997b) points out, such radical constitutional change is usually found only after severe stress, such as that experienced after a loss of a war or following a revolution, and is normally evidence of a breakdown of political legitimacy. Such a loss of political legitimacy is in itself sufficient reason to have serious reservations about the New Zealand approach to economic restructuring.

In contrast to the New Zealand experience of electoral volatility and loss of legitimacy, change was introduced in Australia during a period of political stability. The Australian Labor Government managed to maintain office for 13 years and Bob Hawke became the second longest serving prime minister in Australian history. Electoral stability may be a measure of success in implementing change without alienating large sections of the population. There was a considerable degree of debate and disagreement over policy directions, especially from some academic quarters, and there were, of course, a variety of reasons for electoral success beyond that of change management. However, it is still remarkable that a Labor Government could introduce quite far-reaching change, that some such as Maddox (1989) claim repudiated Labor tradition, yet still remain in power.[9]

Comparative economic success of the reform process

Despite the political costs of the reforms in New Zealand, it may be that they can be justified by their economic success. As Ormsby (1998, 357) argues:

> It can . . . be confusing to mix arguments based on economic theory with objections to the reforms based on political values.
>
> One objective is to distinguish as clearly as possible the differences between the kinds of arguments that are taking place at these different levels, since it seems the debate over reforms is still bedevilled by confusing arguments about the economic success of the reforms with arguments about their impact on constitutional and social values.

Economic outcomes will, of course, depend on a variety of factors, including external factors[10] and possibly issues regarding the sequencing of the reform process.[11] It is not necessarily clear that a reform process and the policies implemented can be blamed for the success or otherwise of the Australian and New Zealand economies, or any other economy for that matter.[12] It could also be argued that New Zealand's economic performance may have been even worse without the economic changes. However, this later argument assumes to some extent that the comparison is between *no* changes on one hand, and *extensive* change on the other. Instead, it is extremely likely that at least some liberalisation of the economy would have been carried out after 1984. As international experience, especially that of Australia, shows, there are different degrees and directions of economic liberalisation, including in terms of speed and theoretical purity. It is not the general direction of the reforms in New Zealand that is entirely unique, 'but rather their extent' (Dalziel 1999, 6).[13] Given these provisos, there are two factors that suggest that the economic success (or otherwise) of New Zealand is, at least in part, a fair assessment of the reform programme in that country. One is that improving economic outcomes has been one of the stated benefits of the

New Zealand policy revolution and a reason they should be emulated elsewhere (Douglas 1993; Evans et al 1996; Richardson 1995). So even if there are 'democratic and constitutional' concerns with the process itself, it may be that these costs are offset by the economic benefits. Second, the belief by some originators and supporters of the reform process that the laboratory type conditions in New Zealand allow the testing of economic theories as they are put into practice, also gives some credence to the view that the reforms should be judged partly on their economic results.[14] As Evans et al (1996, 185) state:

> After decades of policy errors and investment blunders, New Zealand appears to have finally diagnosed its predicament appropriately and is on a trajectory to maintain its economy as a consistent high performer among the OECD.
>
> New Zealand once again appears to be emerging as a laboratory from which results will animate economic debate and policy throughout the world.[15]

Given both these factors and taking supporters of the reforms at their word, that the reforms should be judged upon economic results, serious doubts can be raised as to whether the New Zealand experience is in fact a model for the rest of the world to follow. New Zealand has *not* performed well as measured by a number of commonly used economic indicators, either in comparison to Australia, or to the rest of the OECD. In particular, as measured on average GDP per capita growth, New Zealand is one of the poorer performing economies in the OECD.

Drawing on the OECD and various other statistical sources and using a number of commonly accepted economic indicators, Appendix Two compares the economic performance of Australia, New Zealand and the OECD.[16] As this appendix shows, New Zealand moved from an unemployment rate well below that of Australia and the OECD, to similar levels of unemployment after 1988. Australia has been more successful in promoting employment over the reform period. Despite the claims made by supporters for the success of the Employment Contracts Act, since 1992 labour productivity growth in New Zealand has been well below that of Australia. For the previous 14 years it had been at similar levels (Dalziel 1999b; Philpott 1999). On price inflation measured by consumer price indices, Australia and New Zealand have performed similarly to the OECD. New Zealand has performed particularly badly in terms of income inequality. In Australia income inequality and poverty rates did not change greatly between 1982 and 1994, while in New Zealand income disparity grew at the fastest rate in the OECD, and poverty increased (Easton 1996; Harding 1997). As Dalziel (1999, 22) points out, the 'per capita real income of low income households in New Zealand fell by *more than three percent in absolute terms between 1984 and 1996*' (emphasis added).[17] Both countries face serious current account deficits.[18]

Importantly, Australia has been considerably more successful in generating economic growth, with the relative decline of New Zealand compared to the OECD and Australia continuing. As Dalziel (1999b, 23) argues, this divergence from Australian growth rates was particularly marked after 1987 when 'compared to Australia, New Zealand sacrificed a large volume of real per capita gross domestic product'. From 1984 to 1994, GDP per capita in New Zealand declined by 10 percent relative to the OECD average (OECD 1996, 3). As measured on a GDP per capita index with the OECD at 100, in 1984 New Zealand's GDP per capita stood at 94. By 1991 it had fallen to 79, before recovering to 86 in 1995, and then falling again to 83 in 1997. In contrast, Australia's GDP per capita had recovered from a low of 94 in 1992 to reach 102 in 1997 (OECD 1999d).[19] New Zealand will need several years of high economic growth to recover ground lost during the late 1980s and early 1990s, and while its growth rates were high during 1994 and 1995, by 1997 the economy had slowed to its lowest level of growth since 1993. In 1998, New Zealand had again entered a recession with its economy shrinking by 0.7 percent of real GDP, compared to growth rates of 5.1 percent in Australia and 2.4 percent for the OECD (OECD 1999b).

Does a 'crash through' approach give better policy?

Although the New Zealand 'crash through' approach has had political costs and has not lead to a better performing economy, it might be that New Zealand's poor economic performance is due to other factors, such as the external factors already canvassed. There might still be reasons to believe a 'crash through' approach leads to better policy advice. Douglas (1990; 1993), Richardson (1995) and a whole host of literature on economic restructuring (see, for example, Williamson 1994a; 1994b) make a virtue of the 'crash through' approach. Public Choice theory states that policy can be influenced by rent-seeking interest groups who pursue regulatory or other governmental action, the benefits of which accrue to the interest groups, but whose costs are widely diffused throughout the general population (see, for example, Olson 1982; 1984; Treasury 1984a, 130–32). Eventually the competition of interest groups leads to policy 'sclerosis'. Avoiding the influence of interest groups and vested interests then, and leaving policy-making to the 'experts', 'technocrats', 'econocrats' or possibly 'philosopher kings', is seen to be the best way of making rational and effective policy. A related approach is the argument that there are 'facts' that can be distinguished from 'values'. According to Ormsby (1998, 357), facts are settled 'empirically, by recourse to observation and measurement, the second by relying on a variety of moral conventions and constitutional arrangements'. This section shows that claims that there can be disinterested 'expert' policy makers, determining empirical 'facts' in contrast to society determined 'values', are fallacious and the political and ideological nature of policy-making is highlighted. It will argue that, despite claims to the contrary, there are good reasons to believe that in many cases policy is better made through debate and compromise.

Making policy without consultation means the aims of policy makers can be achieved largely without compromise. There can be costs if the second (or third) best option is delivered because of political expediency or through the influence of vested interest groups. For example, some that would have preferred a goods and services tax to be introduced in Australia argue that the Tax Summit of 1985 was a failure, in that it stopped the introduction of the tax. It may have been better to avoid discussion and introduce the tax without a fuss.[20] Avoiding consultation may well mean compromise can be averted, however, this does not always mean the 'best' policy will be introduced, given the occasional fallibility of even the most competent policy analyst. It also means that errors, sometimes very large ones, can be made and not detected. Often the best development of ideas and policy and the 'ironing out' of problems comes though the interchange of different opinions and disagreements, rather than by their avoidance. As well as the reasonably prosaic benefit of avoiding error, this technocratic[21] approach assumes there is one best way of doing something, which, not surprisingly, is not always the case. In economics there is no one settled body of knowledge. Instead, there are competing schools of economics and different ways of organising economies found in various countries, as well as the clashing paradigms and policy prescriptions that exist in other social sciences. In particular policy decisions, there may be a number of perfectly acceptable ways of approaching a problem, with little to choose between them in terms of effectiveness.

A 'technocratic' approach to policy-making also ignores the inherently ideological and political nature of policy-making. Politics is more than just the clash of political parties; it is also a struggle over resources, power, the access (or otherwise) of particular interest groups or classes to influence, and the role of the state, amongst other things. All these are part and parcel of policy formation. At the same time, policy makers are not disinterested 'experts' bringing to bear their superior knowledge in face of the competing self-interested groups. They too bring their own interests, values and ideologies to the policy-making table and to the political processes of policy-making. Nor do policy-making experts apply some 'value-free' science in the determination of 'facts' to settle disputes. No social science, economics included, is value-free, and the core tenets of mainstream economics contain numerous value judgements, implicit or otherwise (Blaug 1996; McLennan 1995, ch. 5; Nelson 1993).[22] Even 'facts' do not exist entirely independently, but empirical work is influenced by theories or paradigms which determine what questions are to be asked, how empirical work is to be conducted and even how evidence is to be interpreted (Hall 1993). Researchers and policy makers working within different paradigms might well interpret the same 'facts' to mean quite different things in policy terms. In any event, as previous chapters have shown, economic policy, especially in New Zealand, has usually been derivative of theoretical strands of economics, often with little empirical basis, and often strongly linked to particular political agendas.

What does the recognition of the political and ideological nature of policy-making mean for the benefits of debate and compromise in policy-making? First, as policy-making is in part an ideological and political process, debate in policy-making can lead to the questioning of assumptions and values that underpin policy advice. By questioning these assumptions and values, their limitations can be exposed. Policy debate is not merely a question of pointing out errors, disputing facts and presenting empirical evidence (although these are vital processes) but of questioning what these facts mean, and what the theories underpinning them mean. It is also a process of putting forward competing values, different ways of looking at the world and the policy issue in question, and presenting different empirical evidence, possibly gathered within dissimilar paradigms and theoretical frameworks. Second, it is often the case that policy makers working within an organisation, such as a Treasury, can become very bound up within a paradigm or a particular world view. Even when policy advice is 'peer reviewed' and checked for error, say by another official within the same organisation, it may be that the similarity of world views between the officials means many of the assumptions, values and core beliefs of that advice go unremarked and possibly unnoticed. Having that advice reviewed and challenged by outsiders might well show up the assumptions and values inherent in its make-up.

Neither is it entirely clear that complex policy-making systems and the involvement of interest groups, with policy made through negotiation and compromise, leads to poor economic performance, poor policy or policy sclerosis, as claimed by some commentators. If the performance of an economy is indeed associated with the quality of economic advice, there is evidence that suggests it is possible to develop good economic policy advice that is not dominated by 'econocrats' or 'technocrats', or one set of experts. If anything, evidence suggests that some complexity in policy-making structures and some sharing of policy influence might well be associated with better economic performance. Notable examples of this include the corporatist arrangements at macro- and meso-levels in a number of highly successful economies such as the Netherlands, Ireland, Germany and Austria (Schmitter and Grote 1997; Casper and Vitols 1997). Corporatist countries have also shown themselves to be particularly adept at facilitating economic restructuring and adjustment (Katzenstein 1985; Ebbinghaus and Hassel 2000). In the United States, another highly successful economy, policy-making is characterised by a high degree of fragmentation and sharing of power (Aberbach 1998). Importantly for this study, in Australia, a complex federal system, a degree of corporatism and the involvement of labour unions in policy formation existed in an economy that has undertaken significant economic restructuring, and, at the same time, has performed significantly better than the New Zealand one.

On the other hand, while institutional structures and the lack of consultation allowed New Zealand policy makers to achieve their aims to a remarkable extent, it is extremely likely that these factors have also contributed to some policy advice and decisions of questionable quality. Debate will continue as to what extent the New Zealand reforms in general have or have not been a success. Apart from this wider debate, however, there are a number of clear examples where a 'crash through' approach has not led to better policy. One example is the flat tax package of December 1988 drawn up in Roger Douglas's office, approved by Cabinet, but later unilaterally abandoned by the Prime Minister David Lange. The package would have had severe detrimental fiscal and distributional effects if it had been introduced. Another example is the superannuation and health changes and charges introduced in the 1991 Budget. Some of these proved to be unworkable, both in a political and practical sense, and were later reversed (Boston 1994).

Conclusion: Implications for economic restructuring in other countries

The public acceptance and success of economic restructuring may be more likely to occur where change is introduced gradually, with some real attempt to explain, to gain support for the changes, and to modify them in the light of resistance and debate. This approach may also generate better policy advice and outcomes. The Australian experience of restructuring during the 1980s and 1990s, known as 'bargained consensus', provides a useful example of this. In Australia's federal system, change was introduced by a government skilful in developing and maintaining support for new policy directions, by incorporating key interest groups into policy formation, and by using the symbols and rhetoric, and sometimes the reality, of consensus. The New Zealand experience of 'crashing through', often touted as an exemplar of economic reform, has not led to better economic outcomes. It also undermined the legitimacy of the political system and led to electoral instability. Criticisms of the New Zealand approach to policy change are not made merely on democratic or constitutional grounds, although these in themselves are serious and important criticisms. The New Zealand experiment can also be criticised on the very grounds for judgement set by the reformers themselves, namely economic performance. Despite the costs of the reform process, the benefits in terms of economic performance are highly debatable and yet to eventuate.

Appendix One
Methods

According to Putnam et al (1993, 12) the 'prudent social scientist, like the wise investor, must rely on diversification [of methods] to magnify the strengths, and to offset the weaknesses, of any single instrument'. As such, this study will rely on a number of methods to understand the structures, processes and patterns of influence in economic policy-making in Australia and New Zealand. First, it draws on the existing literature on economic policy-making in the two countries, as well as newspaper and media accounts, publicly available government documents and files obtained under the Official Information Act in New Zealand. Second, interviews were carried out with institutional elites and nominated influentials (Table 1.4). Eighty-seven interviews (including 17 self-completed questionnaires) were carried out in New Zealand and 93 in Australia (including 25 self-completed questionnaires). These interviews were based on questionnaires with standard questions, but which allowed for examination in depth of a number of economic policy decisions and for discussion of other issues that arose. Length of interviews ranged from a little over half an hour to almost two hours, with the majority around an hour long. Personal interviews were audiotaped and extensive notes were taken. Self-completion questionnaires were similar to those used for the personal interviews and asked the same questions, with space left for additional comments by respondents. Supplementary interviews with initial respondents and others were also carried out in a small number of cases to examine and clarify particular issues. Initial drafts of a journal article that is incorporated into this study were commented on by a number of Australian respondents and the Australian chapters of this study were commented on at length by a former senior member of the Australian cabinet.

The interviews and questionnaires allowed for two main types of data to be collected: first, quantitative data on a variety of questions; and second, qualitative data including 'war stories' and anecdotes. The qualitative and quantitative data were complementary—the 'storytelling' gave context and depth to the quantitative data, and allowed for cross checking of results. The survey of primary and secondary literature also allowed for cross-checking and comparison of results, as did the review of some of the results by respondents. Because data was gathered in a number of ways, some of the limitations of using a single method were compensated for. The rest of this appendix will describe in greater detail how influence in economic policy was established, and examine reservations that might be held about the methods used.

Methods of establishing influence in policy-making

One method used by a number of writers to establish influence is what might be called the 'policy advocacy approach'. Influence is inferred from whether the policies advocated by certain groups, institutions or individuals, bear a resemblance to policies that actually eventuate. It is extremely difficult, however, to establish a causal link between policies advocated and policy decisions. First, there is the problem of overdetermination. In New Zealand, for example, as well as the New Zealand Treasury and the Reserve Bank advocating policies that were very similar to the policies actually enacted by governments after 1984, a number of business groups and the New Zealand policy-orientated public think-tank the New Zealand Planning Council were also advocating some deregulation. In Australia, on such issues as trade liberalisation, financial liberalisation and labour-market liberalisation, there were a variety of groups advocating change. Another problem with the policy advocacy approach is the difficulty of establishing what criteria to use when defining whether policy decisions made reflected policies advocated. This is especially difficult in the context of economic policy in New Zealand, where a large number of groups and individuals were advocating *some* degree of deregulation of the economy, even some who would later be seen as opponents of the economic restructuring (such as some unions, public servants and academics).

A variant of the policy advocacy approach could be to look at whether policies advocated by particular groups were consistently *not* implemented, which would suggest these groups did not exert an important influence on policy formation. Using this method would suggest New Zealand trade unions during this period did not exert an important influence over the general direction of economic policy. According to Ken Douglas, the long-time president of the New Zealand Council of Trade Unions, unions had consistently advocated a broadly corporatist approach to the economy with high-skill, high-wage industry—an approach quite different to the direction economic policy actually took. The policy advocacy approach remains suggestive only when looking at influence in policy formation and should therefore be used in conjunction with other methods.

It may be possible to draw some inference of influence in policy formation through actual participation in the process, such as through formal access to policy machinery, or informal consultation, lobbying, or even through social ties. But again these measures are really only indicative. Formal and informal access of groups to policy-making processes is different to influence in policy-making (Maloney, Jordan and McLaughlin 1994). For example, groups or individuals may be consulted, but their advice ignored. Or alternatively, they may be 'consulted' only to get their agreement for decisions already made (March and Olsen 1983). It is possible that important individuals or represent-atives of groups may be included in formal policy machinery mainly to give the working party or committee status and authority, not for any real attempt to allow these persons to influence policy decisions. Individuals may be important in administration and in seeing that processes are followed without being influential on the direction of policy. On the other hand, that certain institutions or individuals are not formally or informally consulted, or do not explicitly lobby, does not necessarily mean that they are not influential—media commentators and others may not be explicitly or directly involved in the policy formation process, but their views may, nevertheless, be taken into account.

Social and business ties between policy-making figures, such as membership of business or professional associations, interlocking directorships, the movement of individuals between institutional positions (such as from public to private institutions or think-tanks) may not be seen as part of the formal machinery of policy-making but may still be useful indicators of the ways consensus on policy directions might be established (Domhoff 1990; Dye 1990, ch. 9; Marsden and Friedkin 1993). Studies have found significant interlocks of directorships in New Zealand and Australian companies (Murray et al 1995; Alexander 1998; Firth 1987), while a number of respondents had moved between institutional positions (Goldfinch 2000). While much social network analysis has assumed a link between the social ties and the beliefs and actions of individuals, it is difficult to establish empirically how these ties, social or otherwise, might impact on policy decisions. It is also difficult to draw strong conclusions that the existence of social ties indicates influence over policy decisions in a country as small (in population) as New Zealand. The great majority of the respondents worked in the central business district of Wellington within a few minutes walk of each other, and in such a setting it would be virtually impossible *not* to establish some social ties. So while involvement in policy machinery, lobbying and social and professional ties may well be suggestive of influence in policy formation, a more direct measure of influence is needed to supplement them.

Using a combined institutional elite-reputational method

One method that has been widely used to locate influence and power within society, is to see it as residing with institutions and with individuals due to their strategic location within institutions. C. Wright Mills, influenced by Marx as well as the Italian elite theorists Pareto and Mosca, saw power in the United States located in the so-called power elite which he defined 'as those who occupy the command posts' (Mills 1956, 23). Like Mills, Dye sees power as a function of location within key institutions:

> Individuals do not become powerful simply because they have particular qualities, valuable skills, burning ambitions, or sparkling personalities. These assets may be helpful in gaining positions of power, but it is the position itself that gives an individual control over the activities of other individuals . . . Power, then is an attribute of roles in a social system, not an attribute of individuals (Dye 1990, 5).

A number of writers claim that the use of strategic location within institutions as a measure of influence is widely accepted (Burton 1984).

This is disputed, however, by a number of critics. As Dahl (1958) points out in his response to Mill's *Power Elite*, an institutional (or positional) basis of power confuses potential for power with actual power. Accepting Dahl's analysis, an institutional basis of power and influence is used as an *initial* selection for a larger reputational analysis. Respondents in the initial selection were asked to nominate individuals influential in a number of specific economic policy decisions and in the economic policy field generally. This allowed for some snowballing where persons, nominated by respondents, who were not already in the initial selection were contacted for interview. This approach addresses to some extent Polsby's (1980, chs. 3, 8) critique of panel selection methods as a method of nominating 'influentials'; it draws on a strong theoretical and empirical base to justify the initial selection rather than arbitrarily defining a number of persons as 'judges' and then reading too much into their agreement on who constitutes 'top' leaders; and it avoids allowing just one group, such Headey and Muller's (1996) use of the media, to start the initial selection.

Who are the elites?

Which of these institutional elites are potentially influential in economic policy? Dye identified the institutional elites as those occupying 'the top positions in the institutional structure of American society' which he saw as divided into twelve categories.[1] For Higley and Burton, elites are defined very widely and:

> are simply people who are able, through their positions in powerful organizations, to affect national political outcomes individually, regularly and seriously. Elites thus constitute a nation's top leadership in all sectors—political, governmental, business, trade union, military, media, religious, and intellectual—including both 'establishment' and 'counter-elite' factions (Burton and Higley 1987, 296).

Burton et al's and Dye's definition of what constitutes an elite seems so permissive as to question the usefulness of the concept, and raises the question where the dividing line between elite and non-elite can actually be drawn (Cammack 1990). The questionable usefulness of such a broad definition is demonstrated by Higley's own research that shows certain groups seen by him as elites (such as church leaders and media persons) have limited impact on public policy (Higley et al 1991).

Whether some apparent elites are actually (or potentially) important in policy outcomes may be a reflection of historical accident and particularities of the political economy being studied (for example, the inclusion of trade union groups under a social democratic government). To some extent, there may be structural elements to their power such as the privileged place of business in capitalist economies.[2] There may be state-based elites that exert power due to the formal role they have in policy formation and the power the state as a whole exerts in policy initiation and development.[3] For this study, it is also important to note that one area of public policy, that of economic policy-making, is being examined, rather than there being an attempt to establish power and influence across society in general, and that the policy area being studied will be important in determining who might be seen as potentially influential.[4]

Those that might be expected to be influential in economic policy-making include: functional groups; those seen as economic policy makers; politicians; as well as those (such as media and academic economists) who were likely to know the influential institutions and individuals and to exert influence. The initial sample for this study included present and past federal ministers (especially finance ministers and treasurers), senior public servants including past and present chief executives of the top economic policy bodies and main policy departments, ministerial staff, past and present leaders of business associations and business leaders,[5] union officials, senior print media, senior policy and economic academics, and current and past extra-parliamentary party leaders of political parties. There was also a degree to which some respondents moved between institutional positions: public servants became business leaders;[6] union officials became public servants, politicians or party leaders; and union and extra-parliamentary leaders became academics (Goldfinch 2000). This movement of respondents through a number of positions increased the usefulness of the data collected as respondents often had intimate knowledge of a number of policy issues and decisions.

Using a reputational method

The initial selection for interviews was made from among institutional elites thought likely to be influential in economic policy-making. These initial interviewees were then asked to nominate individuals influential in select economic policy decisions and in economic policy generally, allowing for some snowballing. This reputational approach has been widely used (Headey and Muller 1996) and widely critiqued (Polsby 1980). Polsby criticised Hunter's use of the reputational method for not explicitly defining influence in terms of specific policy issues. He maintained that as Hunter asked who were the most influential people across the system as a whole, this gave a bias towards elitism as it assumed influence ranged across all policy fields. As an attempt to counter this criticism, and drawing on the vast policy network literature which strongly suggests influence in one policy decision or issue does not necessarily mean influence in another decision or issue (Atkinson and Coleman 1992), a number of key economic policy decisions were selected for this study and respondents asked to name individuals particularly influential in those decisions.[7] Since the initial writings of the pluralist and elitist writers of the 1950s and 1960s, there has also been considerable debate over the meaning and the structure of power. It is argued that concentrating on the actual decisions made does not include a close examination of second dimensional agenda setting or questions of the so-called third or fourth faces of power (Digeser 1992; Headey and Muller 1996; Lukes 1974). However, the main purpose of this study is to discover who was influential in making those economic policy decisions. In such a situation, a first dimensional study of power (supplemented by the study of the role of ideas and paradigm making, and by an examination of streams of policy advice in primary and secondary sources) serves well to this end.

Another criticism that Polsby directed to the reputational method was that nominators may not know who the influential people were. As noted, the initial selection was based on those directly involved in economic policy-making, such as central agency officials, and those one would expect to be knowledgeable of the economic policy area. For example, the chief executives of government departments usually have a good idea of what is going on in other departments through their regular meetings with other heads of departments. A considerable number had previous experience in the central agencies. Others outside the official bureaucratic economic policy machinery, such as union officials, business and business association leaders, often had involvement in policy-making through such things as their incorporation into consultative machinery and through their movement through a number of institutional positions. In this study, respondents were not encouraged to nominate 'influentials' if they did not have knowledge of the policy decision in question. Most importantly, the snowballing in this survey, where persons nominated as 'influential' were interviewed, lead to responses from persons specially knowledgeable about certain policy decisions and the persons influential in those policy decisions.[8]

Polsby has also criticised some reputational studies for arbitrarily limiting the number of influentials (Polsby 1980, chs. 3, 8). This study makes no assumptions regarding the number of 'influentials' in a policy decision. Instead, as tables in this study show, a system of 'votes' has been used. Influentials are listed according to the number of times they have been nominated, down to two votes in the case of economic policy decisions and three votes in the case of influence in economic policy generally.

Polsby (1980, 144) points out the different understandings some social science practitioners and laypersons may have of such terms as 'influence' and 'power' and that this could cause confusion when conducting interviews. In this survey respondents were told that influence is taken to include at least one of the following: a major role in initiating the policy; or a major role in formulating and developing the policy; or exercising an ability to significantly modify the policy, including vetoing aspects of it. This is similar to Polsby's own definition of 'rule' as 'initiate, modify, veto, or in some visible manner to act as to change outcomes of selected community decisions' (Polsby 1980, 95).

Other limitations to the methods

There are a number of other objections that can be raised to the institutional elite–reputational method used in this study. First, it relies on the memory of respondents, asking them to recall incidents and individuals, sometimes from events occurring years before the interviews were carried out. Memory is a fragile thing, able to be created and recreated, reinterpreted, manipulated and destroyed. Some reliance on memory, however, is unavoidable in a survey-based study. This study does, however, provide some cross-checking of individual respondents' memories. While it is possible that a large number of people all share the same incorrect memory, this seems unlikely, and the considerable number of persons interviewed provides some check on the memories of individual respondents. Documentary evidence and existing accounts provide a further check. It is also the case that some respondents had kept notes of the events being studied and were able to rely on these, in addition to their own memories.

Second, there is some danger in a reputational study that there may be bias towards naming well-known individuals or politicians as influential in particular decisions, because they may be the public and memorable face given to the policy. There seems some evidence for this effect in those nominated as influential in Accord I. While Paul Keating was nominated as influential by a number of respondents, a number of other highly important individuals saw him as having an extremely limited role in the decision. It may be that a number of respondents mistook Keating's undoubted importance in later Accords for influence in Accord I. There is also evidence, however, that this bias towards naming well-known figures has not been great in other decisions. One of the key findings of this study has been that public servants have often been nominated as important by more respondents than even prime ministers and important extra-parliamentary figures. Once again, the importance of a combination of methods in studying influence is highlighted. By checking reputational results against the qualitative interview and documentary data, the limitations of that method can be exposed and compensated. At the same time, the reputational method has exposed the names of 'faceless' influential individuals often missed by existing accounts or in primary documentary sources.

Third, the decisions selected and the individuals interviewed (or not interviewed) may mean the results could be biased. It could be that if different decisions were selected, or different individuals interviewed, different patterns of influence would arise. I will address these issues in turn. First, as noted in previous chapters and in this appendix, this study does not attempt to find patterns of influence across society as a whole, but seeks to find who was influential in key decisions of economic policy. The rationale for the selection of the decisions is explained at length in previous chapters. Choosing other areas of policy or particular decisions may well have shown different individuals and institutions as important, but would not have served the purpose of this study. Second, it is possible that if some people not interviewed had been able to comment, a slightly different group of individuals would have been nominated. However, given the extremely good response to the New Zealand survey (see below), the acceptable response to the Australian survey and the snowballing employed in both, it is likely that the response would not have been greatly different. And as already noted a number of times, the use of supporting methods has compensated for some of the failings that may arise from the institutional elite–reputational method.

Finally, the social sciences lack the precision found in the physical sciences and no method or combination of methods will be entirely without flaw. All knowledge is provisional and as such should be treated with some caution. Given these concerns, by using the methods outlined here is it hoped that a convincing account of economic liberalisation and policy change, and those institutions and individuals influential in that process, can be provided.

Survey response rates

Response rates for the initial selection in New Zealand were very good (over 75 percent). The response rate of the second selection was less impressive. Even with a follow up letter, the rate was just below 50 percent (including two direct interviews organised from this second mail out). Nearly all business association leaders who were approached agreed to be interviewed, as did all but one of the then (1996) current chief executives of government departments, all but three current and ex-ministers approached, and all but two union officials. Importantly, all treasury secretaries from 1984 to 1996 and all ministers of finance from 1984 to 1996 granted interviews. All Labour Party presidents from 1984 to 1996 were interviewed, and one past National Party president. Of those names generated during the interview process, those who were directly contacted during the five weeks I was in Wellington and Auckland were, on the whole, willing to grant an interview if they were able (there was only one direct refusal), while the rest were contacted by mail-out questionnaire. Some individuals from the initial survey who were unable to grant an interview while I was in New Zealand (because, for example, they were out of the country) but had not directly refused, were also sent questionnaires. In all, 70 direct interviews were carried out (three of these by telephone) and 17 completed questionnaires were received, making a total of 87 responses.

The response rate was considerably poorer in Australia than in New Zealand. The response rate to the first selection was around 40 percent, while a similar level of response was received to the second selection. Responses were good from current and former public servants with a considerable number of interviews carried out with current and former departmental chief executives, including a number of Treasury, Finance and DPMC secretaries and all the governors of the Reserve Bank from 1982 to 1996, as well as other senior Reserve Bank officials. Responses were also good from business association leaders. While responses from politicians were not as good as in New Zealand, a number of treasurers, a minister of finance, a deputy prime minister and other senior cabinet ministers during the Labor government agreed to be interviewed. Personal interviews were preferred and I carried these out over a number of months during 1997 in Melbourne, Sydney and Canberra. Questionnaires were sent to those who could not be interviewed directly and two interviews were conducted over the telephone. In all, 93 interviews were conducted, including 25 self-completed questionnaires.

Appendix Two
Neoclassical Economics, Public Choice and New Institutional Economics

The term neoclassical economics originally described what was orthodox economics from the time of the so-called marginalist revolution of the late nineteenth century, until its supplementation to some extent by Keynesianism macroeconomics during the 1930s and 1940s.[1] Present neoclassicism is largely the term applied, often by non-economists, to what is in some ways a revival and expansion of this tradition in the face of the apparent discrediting of Keynesian economics due to its inability to deal with the stagflation of the 1970s.[2] Certain schools of orthodox neoclassical thought have largely rejected the innovations of Keynes and Keynesian thinkers, and have attempted to rehabilitate (sometimes slightly modifying and extending) the theorems that were held by the pre-war neoclassicists. The term neoclassical is complicated by the overlap between economists who accept some element of Keynesian macroeconomics and others who may not hold totally orthodox positions. Others would argue that Keynesian macroeconomics left the existing neoclassical microeconomic largely untouched.[3] Some Keynesian economists also accept some of the supply-side liberalisation arguments of neoclassical economics and have been called Market Keynesians (Bertram 1997).

This discussion of schools of economics should be seen in the light of the so-called 'Washington Consensus'. Since the end of the golden age of Keynesian-influenced economic policy during the 1970s, there has arisen a set of beliefs, held especially by government and intergovernmental agency economists, that has been termed the 'Washington Consensus'. This consensus is broadly neoclassical in outlook and is drawn in part from the models and theories outlined below. Its prescriptions are, however, broad enough to allow some variation in policy. According to Williamson (1994a, 26–8), this consensus consists of the following prescriptions: fiscal discipline; public expenditure reform to redirect expenditure from politically sensitive areas to economically efficient ones; tax reform to broaden the tax base; financial liberalisation; exchange rates set at a competitive level; trade liberalisation; removal of barriers to foreign investment; privatisation; deregulation; and protection of property rights.

This discussion of schools of economics is in some ways a historical survey. In some cases, key components of the schools of economics discussed below (for example some aspects of New Classical economics and the targeting of monetary aggregates recommended by Chicago School monetarism)[4] have fallen out of favour somewhat in the academic and (sometimes) the policy community, while some commentators claim Keynesian economics has to some extent undergone a revival in the academe.[5] It should also be noted that this appendix attempts to give a broad picture of the general policy paradigm or mindset of policy makers in the 1980s and 1990s and the way economic ideas might have impacted on their thinking and their approach to policy. It does not attempt to present a survey of what now might be considered state-of-the-art economics taught to graduate students in university economics departments. The policy prescriptions of policy makers and advisers may often disregard the qualifications and reservations held by some of the more detached and cautious academic economists. It is also the case that particular economic theories that have fallen out of favour in academia can still maintain a hold amongst public servants, policy makers and media commentators: theoretical ideas can be seen as 'common sense' long after they have become unfashionable in the academic world from which they originated.

Some of the schools examined here, such as Public Choice and New Institutional economics, are not in fact strictly part of neoclassical economics, but instead present a challenge to some of its tenets. To some extent, however, these schools are developments or extensions of neoclassical economics. They use the assumption of the instrumentally rational individual and the deductive methods used by neoclassical economics, and apply these to areas otherwise neglected by mainstream neoclassical economics. And while academic economists may be aware that different theories contain disagreements on what are correct policy directions, these gradations and disputes can be skimmed over and largely lost in the less rarefied and highly politically charged atmosphere of policy-making. Instead, as chapter two shows, rather than providing competing and irreconcilable views on 'correct' economic policy, these variants of neoclassical and related schools of economics provided different but supportive components of a more-or-less coherent policy paradigm, especially in New Zealand. The view of the economy as a self-regulating mechanism peopled by optimising individuals underpins the general approach to economic policy, including microeconomic reform and the scepticism of the value of activist macroeconomic policy. Public Choice and New Institutional economics provided the underpinnings for the changes to the public sector, again, especially in New Zealand. At the same time, the policy prescriptions of Public Choice sought to isolate policy instruments and policy-making from rent-seeking interest groups and opportunist politicians, while at the same time also viewing government provision of services as inherently less efficient than market provision. The New Institutional economics provided some direction in institutional design, such as the contractual arrangements of the New Zealand Reserve Bank Act, that could be used to deliver particular and often theoretically derived policy directions. These contractual arrangements provided some shielding from opportunistic politicians and 'vested' interest groups.

This appendix will outline the key components of neoclassical economics, before examining some policy prescriptions of various schools of economics.

A self-regulating economy

Neoclassical economics is essentially a deductive discipline, closer to mathematics than to more empirically based disciplines such as biology or a social science such as experimental psychology (Bergmann 1989; Peters 1987; Rosenberg 1992). It sees the economy largely as a self-regulating mechanism following something approaching 'laws', similar to those found in the physical sciences (Dugger 1989; Hosseini 1990).

These 'laws', to a large extent, reflect the history and development of economics from the late eighteenth century on, when they were first adopted and adapted (Katouzian 1980, ch. 2). These 'laws' are assumed to apply in different historical and cultural contexts. Critics of neoclassical economics note the continuing influence of the core assumptions of neoclassical analysis, despite the lack of empirical verification and even in the face of apparent empirical falsification (Bergmann 1989; Redman 1991; Rosenberg 1992).

What does constitute the core assumptions of neoclassical economics is open to some dispute. Hausman (1992, 272) sees neoclassical economics as the 'articulation, elaboration, and the application of equilibrium theory'. Equilibrium theory 'consists of consumer choice, the theory of the firm, and the thesis that equilibrium attains'.[6] Hahn states: that neoclassical economics attempts 'to locate explanations in the actions of individual agents' (that is, methodological individualism); that in 'theorising about the agent [it looks] for some axioms of rationality'; and that it holds 'that some notion of equilibrium is required and that the study of equilibrium states is useful' (Hahn 1984, 1–2).[7] I will use Hahn's threefold division as a framework to examine neoclassical economics in more detail.

Methodological individualism, rationality and equilibrium

Neoclassical economics bases its study on the unit of the individual and the firm (treated as an individual). (The individual is often equated with the household; with the household seen as having unitary wants and interests, and with little account being taken of division or conflict within the household.) Society (so-called) and the economy are merely the aggregate of these individuals and firms; that is, the sum of their individual actions, wants and needs. Society and economy are not stratified by class or by legitimate interest groups. Such groupings have no independent existence; instead, they are just collections of discrete individuals following their own interest.

Rationality in neoclassical economics takes an instrumental form which assumes that the individual (the agent) will act selfishly to satisfy the preferences held by that agent, and choose the best means of satisfying those preferences (Heap 1989, 3–4). The agent has set preferences, which are generally stable over time (Wolfson 1994). These subjective preferences are largely evidenced through the choices made and are assumed to exhibit an internal coherence. Economics does not concern itself with how these preferences are formed, this being the concern of sociology, psychology, history or some other social science. Instead, the agent is assumed to be a largely asocial and ahistorical being. Nor does the instrumental rationality assumption mean that preferences need be 'good' for the agent. For example, an agent may prefer to eat foods that are more likely to cause heart disease rather than healthier foods.

The rational optimising individual provides the building block for one of the key beliefs of neoclassical economics—that the optimising actions of individuals and firms leads to the tendency of the self-regulating economy to move towards 'equilibrium' and an optimal outcome. Equilibrium is seen as a state of rest or order, where the supply of goods and services is equated with the demand for those goods and services—that is, where markets are seen to clear. This equilibrium is an outcome where optimising individuals and firms have voluntarily traded their goods, services or labour to achieve the greatest benefit for themselves. Through their individual selfish actions, however, the greatest sum of welfare is generated overall.[8]

Some equilibrium analysis focuses on the equilibrium reached in a single or few markets and is known as 'partial equilibrium' analysis. In 'general equilibrium' theory, analysis focuses on the inter-relationships across all markets, including those for goods and labour.[9] Drawing on a number of heroic assumptions, general equilibrium theory sees a set of prices being simultaneously determined in each market that allows *all* markets to clear; 'everything depends on everything else'. This outcome is seen as Pareto optimal, which means that none can be made better off, without someone else being made worse off (Blaug 1996).[10] For some economists, equilibrium analysis functions more as a metaphor than a description of some sort of reality and there is some scepticism as to its usefulness in its mostly highly mathematical general equilibrium forms. Despite the reservation held by many, general equilibrium analysis, or some belief in the equilibrating tendencies of the economy, seems to underpin much neoclassical and other economic analysis. This is seen in the often strongly held belief that the economy tends towards full employment general equilibrium where all markets are cleared and all resources (including labour) are employed (Clark 1989; Rosenberg 1992, ch. 7). This is the case of course, unless the economy is prevented from moving to such an equilibrium by 'market distortions' such as the stickiness of prices and wages or the interventions of government. For example, the downward rigidity of wages is often seen as the primary cause of unemployment.[11]

Applications of schools of economics to economic policy

Market liberalisation

The model of perfect competition (where firms are assumed to be small, numerous and powerless price takers, with perfect information) underpins the larger part of neoclassical analysis and is a key assumption of equilibrium theory (Munkirs 1989). The assumptions needed to deliver perfect competition, however, are so rigid as to make its attainment extremely difficult, or even impossible, in normal life, and this means that neoclassical economists are not of necessity inherently pro-market in all situations. Instead, as markets seemingly do not function as theory would allow, there may be a role for government in the market place to correct 'market failures' (see Wallis and Dollery 1999). This has, in the past, been recognised by several neoclassical economists.[12] In general, however, there is an assumption in neoclassical and related schools of economics that markets are superior to alternative provisions in terms of efficiency of outcomes, the greater sum of welfare they generate, and the freedom they effect. In such a vein, policy prescriptions of many economists focus on freeing up markets to allow the achievement of these optimum conditions.

This belief in the benefits of markets can be held to a lesser or greater degree depending on the school of economics in question. In the Chicago School, for example, prices that agents transact in the market are generally assumed to be prices that clear the market (that is, that equilibrium attains) and optimising prices for agents contracting in the market (Reder 1982). Markets behave *as if* they are perfectly competitive (Griffin 1988/89; Reder 1982). In contrast, a non-individually optimising government can only be ineffective or will cause outcomes that are less than optimal (Reder 1982). Because of the assumption that market prices are optimal prices and will allocate resources of agents most efficiently, Chicago School policy prescriptions focus on allowing markets to achieve these 'correct prices' (Griffin 1988/

89; Rayack 1987, 54). The Chicago School therefore recommends a broad programme of market liberalisation, including introducing markets where they have been replaced by other forms of allocation or where they have not previously existed. This includes: the elimination of trade barriers, subsidies and exchange controls; a reduction of consumer, labour and environmental regulation; the deregulation of the financial sector; the curtailment of the influence of trade unions; and the privatisation of state enterprises and state services (Friedman and Friedman 1980).

Contestability theory claims the threat of *potential* competitors can discipline market-dominant and potentially monopolistically behaving firms and so encourage them to price competitively. Traditional economic theory held that regulatory intervention might be appropriate where a market with many buyers was dominated by a few (or one) firms, so allowing monopolistic behaviour. In contrast, contestability theory holds that:

> when the number of incumbents in a market is few or even when only one firm is present, sufficiently low barriers to entry [for potential competitors] may make antitrust and regulatory attention unnecessary. Indeed, their costs and inefficiencies they cause may then offer little or no offsetting benefit (Baumol and Willig 1986, 22).

Contestability theory gives support for a light-handed approach to regulation of markets, even in the face of apparent market domination by one or few firms.

There has also been, since the 1970s, a greater focus in mainstream economics on the role of the supply-side[13] in economics in fostering economic growth, and the role of market liberalisation in fostering this growth. The supply-side, where 'production is organised, factors of production are hired, and prices are set' (Bertram 1997, 49) had been somewhat neglected in mainstream neoclassical and Keynesian economics that was largely static in its analysis and focused on the 'demand side' of the economy. Supply-side measures include: reform of the tax system to increase investment and work effort, the removal of restrictive regulations and practices in labour and other markets, and the reduction in welfare disincentives to work seeking and effort. The focus on free markets in promoting growth has also included increasing attention being paid to the role of free trade in encouraging growth (Bertram 1997; World Bank

1987). This approach provides further support for the liberalisation of markets.

Hayek and the Austrian school, not strictly part of neoclassical economics, reject static perfect competition and general equilibrium models, and are sceptical of the optimising, rational model of the individual found in rational expectations models and neoclassical economics. Instead, in their influential formulation, Austrian economists see the importance of the market residing in the scope it provides for innovation and learning. The market is seen as a discovery procedure, a learning process bringing together the widely dispersed knowledge of many individuals where this information can be simplified and coordinated by the price system. Central planning by government agencies could not hope to acquire the broad and changing knowledge carried by these individuals because of their special skills, tacit and private knowledge, and factors of time and place. Government planning will therefore be less efficient than the private market (Hayek 1982; O'Driscoll and Rizzo 1996).

Monetary and fiscal policy

In contrast to Keynesian economics, which saw a role for government in activist monetary and fiscal policy, neoclassical economics is sceptical about how effective government can be in promoting better economic outcomes.[14] In the Chicago version, and in its descendent New Classical economics, it is argued that macroeconomic policy should focus solely on controlling inflation.

Milton Friedman and the Chicago School reinvigorated the quantity theory of money held by the prewar neoclassicists. Chicago School theorists believe money is neutral; that is, in the long run changes in the supply of money have no impact on 'real' variables such as income and output but may impact on prices. The increase in the money supply, then, is the substantial reason for inflation and inflation is, in the long run, 'always and everywhere a monetary phenomenon' (Friedman and Friedman 1980, 254). Some New Classicals see money as super neutral; even in the short run increases in the money supply have no effect on real economic variables (Dornbush 1990; Hoover 1988, 214–6).

Milton Friedman, in a speech to the American Economics Association in 1967 argued there was a 'natural rate of unemployment' and that monetary expansions eventually led to inflation without changing this natural rate (Blaug 1996).[15] The so-called Phillips Curve had argued that there was a stable relationship between unemployment and inflation, and policy makers could trade off reduced inflation for increased unemployment, and vice versa. This relationship seemed to be breaking down by the late 1960s, however, as policy makers faced both rising unemployment and inflation. In what became known as the expectations-augmented Phillips Curve, Friedman argued that the government can, at least in the short run, trade off increased inflation for employment through such measures as monetary and fiscal expansions. As the demand for goods and services increases because of these expansions, this extra demand bids up both product and labour prices. However, product prices are assumed to rise more quickly than labour prices, and as real wages fall relative to product prices, employers hire more labour. As workers assume prices are stable, they mistake the rising nominal wages as a rise in their *real* wages, and so are willing to supply more labour. Eventually, however, workers react to the fall in their real wages and withdraw their labour. The economy then returns to its natural rate of unemployment at a higher rate of inflation (Blaug 1996, 678–81).[16] As each successive monetary or fiscal expansion ultimately fails to reduce the natural rate of unemployment, inflation continues to rise. Keynesian-type policies are therefore ineffective, and monetary and fiscal policy should focus solely on controlling inflation.

The New Classical school holds that monetary and fiscal expansions have no effect on real economic outcomes, even in the short run, so that government macroeconomic policy is essentially impotent. The expectations-augmented Phillips Curve outlined above saw individuals temporarily 'fooled' by surprise inflation into expanding their supply of labour. Instead, New Classical economics assumes that individuals hold what are called 'rational expectations', and so are not mistaken even in the short run. Rather than basing their perceptions of economic outcomes (such as inflation) on what has gone before, individuals are assumed to have access to all relevant economic information, and can predict what policy outcomes will be based on current policy settings and on economic theory. That is, individuals can effectively model the economy. These expectations are held without systemic error; that is, they are assumed to be correct on average. Given these rational expectations, agents anticipate intended policy results and so react to any government policy, negating its impact on 'real' economic activity (Dornbush 1990; Hoover 1988).[17]

One outcome of the rational expectations assumption, was to focus attention on the 'creditability' of monetary policy. As agents are assumed to know that governments can manipulate monetary policy to produce short run increases in employment, and may be tempted to do so for electoral advantage, they factor this into their behaviour, such as in wage and interest contracting. Therefore, government announcements regarding price stability lack creditability, and agents maintain their inflationary expectations and consequent behaviour. To be effective, then, governments must convince agents that they genuinely intend to reduce inflation. They may do this through institutional measures, such as an independent central banker and/or removing employment and output from policy makers' objectives (Dalziel 1993).

Chicago and New Classical policy prescriptions then are similar. Activist policy should be abandoned and monetary policy should focus on inflation, with fiscal policy in a supporting role aiming at balanced budgets or even fiscal surpluses. The value of activist macroeconomic policy is further limited, because as the Chicago and some other economists would argue, government spending and investment crowds out private investment (which is assumed to be more efficient) and informational limitations of government and time lags in implementation of policy mean that activist policy has unpredictable and destabilising effects (Griffin 1988/89; McCann 1988). It is argued that any shocks to the economy caused by controlling inflation will be quickly overcome by the self-regulating economy, so that targeting inflation through the money supply will not have detrimental long run effects on employment or outcome (Whitwell 1992).

Public Choice and New Institutional economics

While not necessarily part of neoclassical economics, Public Choice and the New Institutional economics extend some of the methods and assumptions of neoclassical economics to the study of government and private sector institutions, and to contractual arrangements. They often provide further arguments against the government provision of services (especially in the case of Public Choice), argue for the insulation of policy from the influence of 'vested' interest groups and opportunist politicians, and give directions on institutional design, including to some extent on how this policy insulation is to be achieved.

Public Choice applies the rational optimising individual of neoclassical economics and its deductive methods to the study of politics, politicians and public servants. Notions that individuals may be motivated by such things as 'public good' or 'duty' are rejected and they are assumed to consistently follow their own interests (Buchanan and Tullock 1984; Niskanen 1971). In this way, public servants seek better pay and conditions and attempt to increase their power and influence by expanding the resources and size of their departments. They identify with the interest groups they deal with, acting in support of their wishes against the greater good of society. They also have little motivation to use resources efficiently, because there is no market to discipline inefficiencies. Politicians offer public goods in return for votes, sacrificing the greater good for their short-term gain, while voters seek to advance their own interests through the electoral system. Interest groups are seen as largely illegitimate interests pursuing regulatory and other government interventions, the benefits of which accrue to the interest groups, but whose costs are widely diffused throughout the population. At the same time, the policy demands of the clashing interest groups lead to policy 'gridlock' or sclerosis (Olsen 1982). Followers of Public Choice claim market failure has been overemphasised and the possibility of government failure all but ignored, so that even in the case of so-called market failure government intervention may be inappropriate (see, for example Wallis and Dollery 1999). In sum, government provision of services is 'inherently inferior to the market' (Buchanan and Tullock, 1984: 81).

Agency theory looks at how contracts are to be designed by one party (the principal) with another party (the agent) to achieve the optimum outcome for the principal (Althaus 1997; Boston et al 1996). This includes designing the appropriate incentive structure for the (assumed) instrumentally rational agents in the face of incomplete and asymmetrical information, and problems of agent selection, uncertainty, potential opportunism and moral hazard. Agency theory was originally designed for owner–manager separation problems, but came to be applied to a range of contractual instances including employer– employee relationships. Contracts are defined very widely and include traditional written contracts, implied contracts and so-called 'relational contracting'.

Transaction Cost analysis looks at how exchange is best governed and how organisations are best designed to govern this exchange. This entails the instrumentally rational individual (or organisation) selecting the type of exchange and governance structure that will minimise aggregate production and transaction costs. The classic distinction is that made between transactions within a firm or organisation (a hierarchy) or outside the firm (the market) (Coase 1937; Williamson 1975; 1985). Exchanges which are simple, discrete and non-repetitive are likely to be carried out in the market, while transactions that include uncertainty, recur frequently and involve 'transaction specific investments' are more likely to be carried out in the hierarchically organised firm. Internalising transactions is seen to avoid unexpected contractual difficulties and opportunism by actors outside the firm. Transaction costs can be *ex ante*— that is, costs entailed to avoid transaction failure such as drafting and negotiating a contract—and *post hoc* costs—those entailed to deal with contractual difficulties and governance structures needed to maintain the transactions (Boston et al 1996, 22).

Summary and conclusion

Neoclassical economics focuses on the actions of (assumed) highly atomised, rational and selfish individuals and firms. These are the building-blocks that go to make up the model of the economy held by many neoclassical and mainstream economists: that of a self-regulating mechanism tending towards a state, where all resources, including labour, are employed. As this appendix has noted, some of the assumptions and methods of neoclassical economics have been extended to apply to the design of institutions and to politics and the public sector. These different components provided a more-or-less coherent policy paradigm when approaching economic policy, especially in New Zealand. This view of the economy has certain implications for the views held by many neoclassical or mainstream economists and policy makers on what is appropriate economic policy.

First, it implies a strong belief in the efficacy of the market in delivering the greater sum of welfare and efficiency, and hence a scepticism of attempts to regulate or replace it by government or other types of provision.

Second, it implies doubt regarding the effectiveness of the government in macroeconomic policy, which shows itself in the avoidance of activist macroeconomic policy, including such measures as rule-based monetary policy focused only on inflation and legislative limits on fiscal spending. In some versions of neoclassical economics, especially its related New Right strands, the ideal state is seen as a minimal one, existing only to provide a legislative and coercive framework for the continuing operation of the free economy.

Third, focus on the optimising individuals within organisations and the public sphere sees management structures developed to focus on financial incentive driven performance (within the public service) and on limits on bureaucratic and political 'opportunism' and interest group rent-seeking, such as in rule-based macroeconomic policy and contractual arrangements. The characterisation of interest groups in Public Choice as illegitimate vested interests also gives cause to exclude them from policy formation.

Appendix Three
Australian, New Zealand and OECD Economic Performance Compared

This appendix presents data gathered from mainly OECD statistical sources, focusing on the period 1978–99, depending on the availability of statistics. It shows that despite the many claims to the contrary, and what Dalziel (1999b, 27) calls the 'sense of complacency among the

Figure A.1 GDP per capita, in US dollars, in Australia, New Zealand and OECD 1970–97[1]

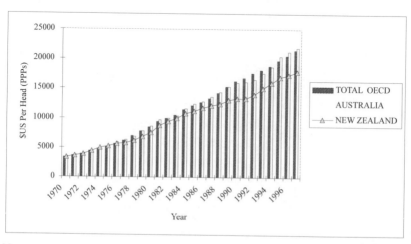

Notes

1. In US dollars current prices and current PPPs. Sources OECD (1999d), series 0097, 5497, 5997.

Figure A.2 Standardised unemployment rates in Australia, New Zealand, G7 and OECD, 1978–98 [1]

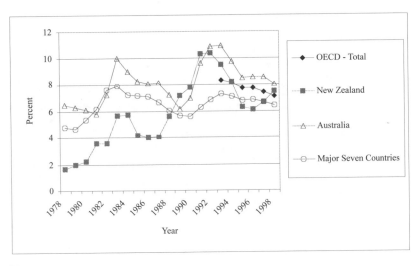

Notes
1. Sources OECD 1999d, Series 002505DSA, 592505DSA, 542505DSA, and 072505DSA.

economics profession about the overall outcome' of New Zealand's reforms, New Zealand has generally not performed well when measured by a number of commonly used economic indicators, compared to Australia and the OECD. New Zealand has performed particularly badly in terms of economic growth, with its relative decline compared to Australia and OECD continuing.

Economic growth

Figure A.1 shows the real GDP growth per capita in New Zealand and Australia since 1970, measured in current prices and current Purchasing Power Parities (PPPs).[1] As this graph and Figure 1.1 in chapter one show, New Zealand has performed significantly worse than Australia and the OECD in generating economic growth. If GDP is measured by PPPs as in Figure A.1, this divergence has been particularly marked since the mid-to-late 1980s. This relative decline has continued, with New Zealand entering a recession in 1998 with the economy contracting by 0.7 percent of real GDP, while the Australian economy and the OECD expanded by 5.1 and 2.4 percent of real GDP, respectively (OECD 1999b).

Figure A.3 Employment growth in Australia, New Zealand and OECD, 1982–98[1]

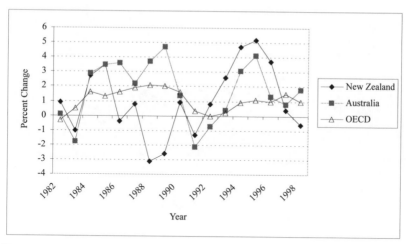

Notes
1.   Sources OECD 1999b. Annex Table 20.

Figure A.4 Labour productivity growth in Australia and New Zealand, 1978–98[1]

Notes
1.   Source Dalziel 1999b.

Labour-market

Figure A.2 shows standardised rates of unemployment in Australia, New Zealand, the OECD, and the G7 countries (United States, Japan, Germany, France, Italy, the United Kingdom and Canada). As the graph shows, New Zealand moved from a level of unemployment well below that of Australia and the OECD before the reforms, to a level of unemployment similar to that of Australia and the OECD. Australia has been considerably more successful at creating employment over the reform period as Figure A.3 shows, although New Zealand has performed well over the same period compared to the OECD average over 1984–98. Figure A.4 shows that labour productivity growth in New Zealand has *slowed* since 1992, compared to Australia. This is despite New Zealand sharing a similar rate of productivity growth with Australia for the fourteen years prior to 1992, and in the face of repeated claims for the success of the Employment Contracts Act 1991.

Price stability

Both Australia and New Zealand have been successful at constraining consumer price inflation, at least since the early 1990s, to levels similar to those faced by their major trading partners (Figure A.5). As the

Figure A.5 Consumer price inflation—Percentage change from previous period in Australia, New Zealand, G7 and EU15, 1978–98[1]

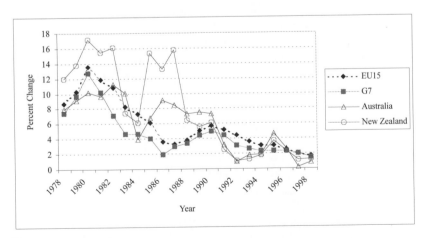

Notes
1. Sources OECD 1999c. Series 025241K, 075241K, 545241K and 595241K.

aggregate OECD data includes such high inflation countries as Mexico, Hungary and Greece, I have compared New Zealand and Australia to the European Union countries and the G7 countries.

Balance on the current account

Both Australia and New Zealand face severe current account deficits, with New Zealand performing particularly badly (Figure A.6). Deficits in both countries are at levels that should cause serious concerns for policy makers.

Government financial balances

Both New Zealand and Australia have performed slightly better than the OECD on central government financial balances, with Australia performing well during the late 1980s and New Zealand performing well in the mid-to late-1990s (Figure A.7). New Zealand slid into fiscal deficit by 1999, while Australia has maintained the fiscal surplus first reached in 1998.

Figure A.6 Current account balance as percentage of GDP in Australia, New Zealand and OECD[1] 1978–99[2]

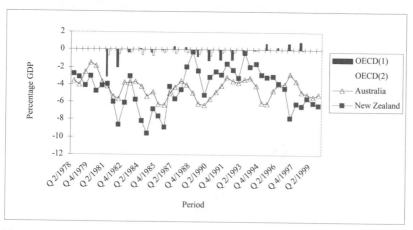

Notes
1. OECD(1) is small countries, OECD(2) is OECD total.
2. OECD1999d. Series 54 CBGDPR and 59 CBGDPR. OECD 1999b Annex Table 52; OECD(1) and OECD (2) totals are annual, 1981–98.

Figure A.7 Government financial balances as percentage of nominal GDP in Australia, New Zealand and OECD, 1982–98[1]

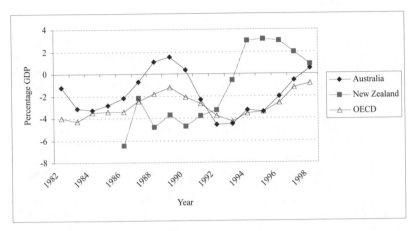

Notes
1.   Source OECD 1999b. Annex Table 30.

Notes

Chapter 1

1 The average tariff rates fell from 11.2 percent in Australia and 10.6 percent in New Zealand in 1988/9, to 4.4 and 5.1 percent in 1996, respectively. This is compared to an increase in the United States in the same period from 4.4 to 5.2 percent, while the European Union decreased slightly to 7.7 percent. Norway increased from 5.3 to 22.3 percent, while Canada increased from 8.7 to 12.1 percent. In 1996, non-tariff barriers in Australia and New Zealand were considerably lower than many of their trade barriers at 0.6 and 0.2 percent respectively, compared to 7.7 percent in the United States, 6.7 percent in the European Union and 7.4 percent in Japan (OECD 1999b, 27).

2 For accounts of New Zealand's economic history see, for example, Easton 1997a; Gould 1982; Hawke 1985; 1992. For Australia see, for example, Boehm 1993; Kelly 1994; White 1992.

3 Both countries were characterised by the early dominance of Britain as an export market and as a source of capital and imports. This had lessened by the 1970s, especially in Australia.

4 Both developed welfare states, although to differing extents. New Zealand's was a comparatively comprehensive welfare state developed under the Liberals from 1891 to 1911, then the Labour government from 1935 to 1949. New Zealand ceased being a welfare leader in the 1950s, although there was rapid growth after 1972 (Rudd 1993; 1997). Australia's welfare state was considerably less developed, relying more on the 'wage earners' welfare state' where income was delivered through regulatory intervention in the wages system (as to some extent was New Zealand's) (Bryson 1994; Castles 1985).

5 New Zealand had essentially no unemployment (less than 0.5 percent) until 1974, when it began to grow steadily. From 1947 to 1955 the monthly average of registered unemployed was less than 100 (in a workforce of 750 thousand) (Gould 1982, 55).

6 Measured at current prices and using purchasing power parities (US dollars, benchmark year 1990). In 1997 New Zealand was ranked nineteenth, and Australia tenth.

7 The reduction in the top income tax bracket from 66 cents to 60 cents in the dollar made in the 1982 Budget, without a concurrent reduction in expenditure, contributed to this worsening fiscal situation.

8 According to one former Labour President:

> It is my view that we had a vacuum where our economic policy should have been prior to 1984. That vacuum was what Douglas jumped into. It was custom and practice that economic policy had not been our forte, that we were really good on social policy, and the economic policies were there to service the social policies, but . . . not in a way that substantially addressed the international economic changes. [This lack of a prepared economic policy] was traditionally part of our make-up [i.e. it wasn't just a function of the snap election.]

9 In 1999 the Heritage Foundation, another conservative American think-tank, placed New Zealand third behind Hong Kong and Singapore. Australia was placed eighth. France was placed 38th (Economist 1999).

10 Changes in economic policy in both countries were shadowed by a number of other significant policy reforms. These included: major restructuring of the pub-

lic sector; significant changes to the welfare state, including the increased use of targeting of services and benefits and significant cuts under the New Zealand National Government; and environmental regulation changes, among other things (Castles, Gerritsen and Vowles 1996; Evans et al 1996; Mathews and Grewel 1997).

11 The terms of trade are now below their level in the mid-1960s.

12 For a critique of some of these claims, empirical and otherwise, see Easton 1997a.

13 The CER (Closer Economic Relations) treaty was signed between the two countries in 1983. This has resulted in free trade in goods achieved five years ahead of schedule in 1990, the establishment of a joint food authority, the mutual recognition of good standards and registered occupations by May 1998, and considerable effort devoted to harmonising commercial law (Dunbar 1998; Le Heron and Pawson 1996, 43–8).

14 The possible exception being the currency trading changes and the devaluation in face of the currency crisis in 1984.

15 All quotes in this study are taken from interviews with the author, unless stated otherwise.

16 As noted above, however, Hawke's government stage-managed the Economic Summit to obtain broad support for its policy directions.

17 It should also be noted that governments in New Zealand and Australia intentionally tied themselves further into the world economy early in the reform process by such things as by lifting exchange controls, floating their respective dollars and allowing foreign banks to trade (RBA 1996). Whether the float was an inevitable response to changing economic conditions is another question (see Garnaut 1994b). Trade liberalisation further cemented ties to the world economy.

18 The Swedish recovery after 1992 shows that while the market pressures for change can be extreme, these pressures can be adopted to achieve political aims and over time skilful policy makers can defend elements of the welfare state once the immediate crisis has past (Hinnfors and Pierre 1998).

19 As such it is possible the present system may not last forever.

20 While the Asian economic crisis of 1997–8 may have cast some doubt on aspects of the Asian economic success, this does not discredit the overall achievements of their economic management. As World Bank Chief Economist George Stiglitz (1999, 8) notes:

> The East Asian crisis of 1997–8 . . . does not unravel the overall development success of the region. Even if these countries were to endure a few years of zero or negative growth . . . their success would remain largely untarnished. Their per capita GDP . . . will still be a multiple and poverty rates will be a fraction of what they were a half-century ago, literacy will remain near-universal, and health standards will remain high.

By 1999/2000 most Asian economies, with the exception of Indonesia, were showing high rates of economic growth.

21 The Dutch and German systems have been successful in redistributing income and avoiding poverty over a ten-year period, the American system less so.

22 'Federal' politicians refers to Australia only. As New Zealand is a unitary state, this separation of state and commonwealth politicians is not an issue.

Chapter 2

1 The term 'New Right' refers to a broad neo-liberal policy oriented agenda that received most prominence under Thatcher and Reagan during the late 1970s and early 1980s. Certain influential schools of economic thought (in terms of impact on economic policy) such as the Chicago School, Public Choice and the New Classicals are normally seen as part of the New Right movement; most are also reasonably orthodox in the neoclassical tradition.

2   However, as chapter six argues, this was largely driven by the desires of certain unions to push for wage rises.

3   Pusey does little to establish the causal link between the 'economic rationalist' views held by members of the central agency elites and the changes in economic policy.

4   Corporatism has been defined by Katzenstein as:

> an ideology of social partnerships expressed at the national level; a relatively centralized and concentrated system of interest groups; and voluntary and informal coordination of conflicting objectives through continuous political bargaining between interest groups, state bureaucracies, and political parties (cited Capling and Galligan 1992, 13).

Matthews (1994) has described the Accord as an example of corporatism without business, while Singleton has described it as an example of 'labourism' which is the 'product of the interdependence of the political and industrial wings of the Australian labour movement . . . It has its basis in the long-standing tradition . . . that the capitalist state can be managed to the advantage of the working people by a combination of a strong trade union movement and a parliamentary labour party' (cited Capling and Galligan 1992, 49). While I am not going to enter into this debate, it is worth noting that the Labor Government self-consciously appropriated some of its ideas from corporatist European countries. It may be that existing traditions of labourism facilitated the adoption of corporatist ideas. Capling and Galligan (1992) have seen the industry plans as examples of meso- or sectoral-corporatism.

5   Only 4 percent did not see a common set of ideas underpinning the reforms.

6   Phelps was one of the originators of the natural rate of unemployment hypothesis.

7   It is notable that many of these theories are highly contested both at a theoretical and empirical level. See, for example: Ormerod (1994) for a critique of neoclassical economics in general; Self (1993) on Public Choice; Hoover (1988) on New Classical economics; and Wallis and Dollery (1999) on Agency theory and New Institutional economics.

8   This chief executive went on to say 'It was straight out of [Hayek]. It was basically unquoted quotes . . . *Road to Serfdom* . . . in another form.' This view is rejected by another public sector chief executive, who said 'this idea that there is a sort of Chicago School or Hayek or something . . . I didn't read Hayek until about a couple of years ago.' Possibly, there may be some Hayekian or neo-liberal influence on policy in New Zealand, if sometimes in a filtered or second-hand way. The Treasury's treatment of the market in some of its briefing papers seems at times to owe something to Hayek and Austrian economics, while Business Roundtable employee Penelope Brook's book , which influenced the Employment Contracts Act, quotes Hayek at length, as well as other neo-liberal thinkers such as Chicago School lawyer Richard Epstein; see Brook (1990).

9   I am using this distinction between empirical and theoretical economics partly as a heuristic device. Empirical work will always be informed and influenced by theoretical beliefs and frameworks.

10 A number of those mentioned became departmental chief executives, with Graham Scott becoming Secretary to the Treasury, Roderick Deane the State Services Commissioner, while, as noted, Roger Kerr became the head of the Business Roundtable.

11 The commonly held view that the Treasury was shut out of policy-making during the Muldoon era should not be overstated. As former Treasury Secretary Henry Lange notes:

> He wasn't too bad as long as you stood up to him. He was a bully of the first order but he always, in my time, listened to advice, he read all the reports. He disregarded some of them but that

was his prerogative. He was always formal and polite, the only trouble was when you stood up to him you would have some fairly major fights. He won most but by no means all the fights (Russell 1996, 29).

12 Bryce Wilkinson was a former head of Economics I, which looked at macroeconomic policy, including monetary policy.

13 The National Government continued in the direction set by the Labour Government, radically extending the liberalisation of the labour-market and making large cuts to the welfare state.

14 Douglas's influence of the direction of economic policy is suggested by the name often given to the reforms: Rogernomics.

15 A number of respondents also pointed out that he was a reluctant reader of ministerial briefs, preferring to be verbally briefed.

16 However, while New Zealand academics are seen to have little influence on policy debate, a number of visiting academics and commentators, some brought over by the Business Roundtable, have been important in adding to the chorus of approval, as discussed above.

17 The *National Business Review* has also attacked Professor Jane Kelsey and other academics who have had the temerity to express opinions on public sector issues. Roger Kerr of the Business Roundtable has also attempted to intimidate academic critics (Kelsey 1998).

18 One senior Treasury official and future departmental secretary was seconded to the OECD. He considered this partly as a banishment as he was sceptical regarding some of the policy changes.

19 The ACTU's most important self-conscious 'think piece' was *Australia Reconstructed* (ACTU/TDC 1987). This did not have as much impact on industry policy as they might have hoped (Anthony 1993).

20 Respondents were asked to nominate the *most* important influence. A number

noted that while one was most important, others were also important. As one respondent said after he nominated practical experience, writers and view of colleagues: 'Of these, I would put 'practical experience' first, but all are important'. A number of respondents nominated more than one, without ranking, especially in the questionnaires sent to New Zealand respondents, which partly accounts for the high rate of missing cases in the New Zealand data.

21 It is notable that Roger Douglas and Ruth Richardson (Minister of Finance from 1990–93) in New Zealand and Paul Keating in Australia have not received formal training in economics.

Chapter 3

1 According to a former director of the New Zealand Planning Council:

I have always thought of the NZPC as the last expression of some of the good things of the postwar consensus. People like [academic] Frank Holmes and [Treasury Secretary] Henry Lang had a strongly held view that if citizens were provided with information and the arguments were dispassionately laid out, they were capable of assisting the politicians to take the tough and right decisions needed if New Zealand were to break out of the malaise of the late 1960s to mid-1970s. There was therefore a need for an apolitical body concerned with the 'longer term': the three-year electoral cycle and 'politics' generally being essentially 'short term'. There is an element of corporatism too.

2 In carrying out this function the council could:
(i) assist and advise the Government in the process of consultative planning
(ii) foster discussion among Government and private planning agencies
(iii) prepare reports and submit them to the Minister, as it sees fit
(iv) encourage public understanding and discussion by publishing documents and reports on planning topics.

3 The Planning Council had a special body known as the Economic Monitoring Group to monitor economic development and publish reports when it saw fit.

4 For a discussion of Robert Muldoon's Government and his decline, especially in his last term, see Russell 1996 and Templeton 1995.

5 Since the introduction of the proportional representation system, Mixed Member Proportional (MMP), in 1996, coalition governments are more likely to arise, and it is likely that this executive dominance has been reduced somewhat. The two party system has also been modified, partly in the response to MMP.

6 Robert Muldoon, Prime Minister from 1975 to 1984, was probably unique in New Zealand's history for the power he wielded both within his Cabinet and his party.

7 The Department of Commerce has been involved in some microeconomic issues.

8 In 1994–5 $50 million was appropriated to Treasury to provide policy advice. This was around one sixth of the total appropriated to policy advice and more than twice that received by any other department (Boston et al 1996, 126–7).

9 While Robert Muldoon was conscientious about seeking Treasury advice, he was possibly less likely to follow it than Douglas or Richardson.

10 Ruth Richardson, the National Government's Finance Minister from 1990 to 1993 noted the influence of Rennie on Prime Minister Jim Bolger:

Rennie would do an outstanding job on helping to educate Jim, and steadying him at crucial times. Jim even became considerably attached to Iain who, when we took office, for a time went into the Prime Minister's Department. Those of a paranoid disposition, who believe Treasury has its tentacles everywhere and secretly runs the country, would have had their theories further reinforced had they observed Iain Rennie's influence on Jim (Richardson 1995, 56).

11 In 1985, the functions of the Reserve Bank as outlined in the Reserve Bank of New Zealand Act 1964 were listed by the *Reserve Bank Bulletin* as:

To act as the central bank for New Zealand.

To ensure that the availability and conditions of credit provided by financial institutions are not inconsistent with the sovereign right of the Crown to control money and credit in the public interest.

To advise the Government on matters relating to monetary policy, banking and overseas exchange.

Within the limits of its powers, to give effect to the monetary policy of the Government as communicated in writing to the Bank (by the Minister of Finance) and to any resolution of Parliament in relation to that monetary policy (RBNZ 1985b, 512).

12 The inflation target was broadened out in December 1996 as part of the new coalition agreement between the National Party and New Zealand First. Price stability was now defined as annual average price increases between 0 and 3 percent (RBNZ 1997).

13 However, it may be difficult to do this in the highly charged environment of a political office.

14 The Prime Minister's Department, headed by future Treasury Secretary Bernie Galvin and containing one-time Reserve Bank economist L. C. Bayliss, was closely involved in economic policy formation during the early years of the Muldoon Government.

15 See Sheppard (1999) for a discussion of Lange's inability or unwillingness to argue cases and muster support for policy directions. However, Lange did 'draw the line in the sand' in the flat tax debate of 1987–8, which he unilaterally aborted despite it receiving prior Cabinet approval. It should also be noted that Lange was strongly supportive of policy innovations, at least until 1986.

16 According to a minister quoted by McLeay (1995, 98), the Expenditure Review Committee involved:

pretty detailed work that required a lot of negotiation with Ministers and Ministries over what and where their expenditure's going, whether they want to divert funds inside their existing votes, or applications for existing money, and there's quite a lot of negotiation that goes on in trying to finally set what the Crown will accept as additional funding pressures, or what it will allow to be diverted from where originally it intended it to be in the Budget when it brought down the Appropriation Bill.

17 The Prime Minister David Lange could have required the papers to be deferred in accordance with cabinet rules, but chose not to do so (Henderson 1997).

18 Roger Douglas was especially skilled at getting his way in Cabinet, partly as he was one of the more experienced in a Cabinet that was generally new to the processes of Government. According to one Cabinet colleague:

> There were four that had been in the Kirk Government 1972–5; Douglas and Moyle and Tizard and Colman. I do not myself believe that Douglas would have achieved anything like as much had he not been. He knew the ropes and he was that much more advanced than the rest of us. He was not a shouter in Cabinet, he was a very quite operator. He spoke less, in the lower quartile of the Cabinet in terms of actual talking. He had done his talking before. He had seen people. He had corralled them, he talked to departments. A master of . . . back stairs intrigue. What he did was . . . work out who it was he wanted onside, what it was he wanted done. We were politicians, nothing unusual about that at all. It doesn't matter what you want. If you don't do that [marshal support] . . . you come a cropper.

19 This was with the exception of Cabinet Minister Winston Peters, who was expelled from the National Government Cabinet in 1991, expelled from the Cau-

cus in 1992 and formed the political party New Zealand First in 1993. New Zealand First formed a coalition government with the National Party after the 1996 election. For a detailed discussion of factionalism in the Labour Government after 1986 see Sheppard 1999.

20 In the Act, responsible fiscal management is defined as the following: debt should be reduced to prudent levels; operating expenses should not exceed operating revenues over a reasonable period (i.e. budget deficits should not be maintained); Crown net worth should be maintained at sufficient levels to counter adverse events; the fiscal risks facing the Government should be managed prudently; and fiscal policies should be consistent with predictable stable tax rates.

21 During the Coalition, according to a former National cabinet minister, Winston Peters was the Treasurer but the Minister of Finance, Bill Birch, did all the work. Michael Cullen signalled, before the 1999 election, that the two positions would be amalgamated into a single Minister of Finance, as has subsequently occurred. However, Deputy Prime Minister and Alliance leader Jim Anderton, holds the position of Minister of Economic Development and the Ministry of Commerce was renamed the Ministry of Economic Development in February 2000. It was unclear at the time of writing what these developments meant in economic policy terms.

22 The Treasury was the most influential department within the triple-tiered committee system that existed before 1984 for a number of reasons, including the fact that the permanent head chaired the officials' committee and Treasury also supplied the chair and secretary for the working parties, as well as having a permanent presence on the Cabinet Economic Committee (Galvin 1985; Galvin 1991, 16; Moriarty 1956). After 1952, the economic policy machinery consisted of the Cabinet Committee on Economic Policy, Officials

Committee on Economic Policy, and various working parties of officials (Moriarty 1956).

23 The Officials' Economic Committee was replaced by the Officials' Coordination Committee during the Labour Government.

24 According to one former high-ranking SSC official:

> We had a fundamental argument at the beginning [on public sector reform]. Once that was resolved we didn't go back to it . . . that was why the State Service Commission was almost eliminated, and we must have come pretty close, in the minds of the politicians anyway. The Treasury was very keen . . . their whole purpose in the State Sector Act was to get rid of us. That was the second attempt, the first attempt, would have been in 1984 [when] they saw us as a hindrance . . . in 1988, they wanted to get rid of us because they no longer saw us as necessary.

25 This process could be very secretive. In the early stage of the corporatisation process, for example, secret meetings were held between ministers and officials at Douglas's house.

26 An important one being the Officials Committee on Expenditure Control formed by the National Government to shadow the Cabinet Expenditure Control Committee.

27 Cronin (1997) argues that after 1991 the NZBR's influence declined in the face of opposition from manufacturers and primary producers.

28 Members of the NZBR account for 64 percent of market capitalisation in 1986 (Murray, Bierling and Alexander 1995), and '10 percent of all goods and services [and] 200,000 members of the workforce' in 1995 (Cullinane 1995).

29 According to Boston, Martin, Pallot and Walsh (1996, 126) there are few think-tanks in New Zealand and they have not played the important role in policy formation found in other countries. For this reason, I have not examined them in any

detail in this or the following chapters. The close ties and overlapping membership that existed between the Centre for Independent Studies and NZBR should, however, be noted.

30 The Manufacturers' Federation reconciled itself to the new policy directions after the economic recovery post-1992–3.

31 As one senior union official noted, the unions 'had been involved in negotiations specifically prior to the election. But once the devaluation process had occurred then that whole programme of expectations . . . that we had negotiated were thrown out the window. The union movement to a large extent was from then on the 'back foot.'

32 The NZCTU was also criticised by those on the left, including some within the union movement, for not resisting the Act with enough vigour, such as through a general strike (Bramble and Heal 1997). This perceived lack of action was a reason for the formation of the Trade Union Federation.

33 The publicly owned National Radio, that one print journalist described as 'relatively even handed' was probably the highest quality news source. During the 1980s and 1990s, New Zealand had two free-to-air publicly owned television stations, but these were indistinguishable from the commercial broadcasters.

34 The lack of debate over policy in the media was seen in part, according to the one print journalist, because:

> journalists are under-educated and not intellectually equipped to help carry out such a debate. [One of] the hazards of a small society is that the academics are unwilling to put their heads above the parapets and say something different. There are a few 'usual suspect' types who always will. You can predict in advance what they are going to say.

35 One respondent, a former office holder in the Labour Party, describes the process thus:

> The Labour Party had a bit of rebellion [against GST]. A decision

brokered by Margaret Wilson (then the Party President) was that there should be a series of debates at the regional conferences of the Labour Party—Harris—Federation of Labour (FOL) executive—go to three, Campbell—also FOL executive—go to another three and at each one, one of the Finance Minsters would go. Both sides would present it and have a debate. All sorts of trickery was involved. Some of the Labour Party unions were unwilling to vote the Government down, so they got out of Douglas a guarantee that [they would approve] GST if the fate of lower-middle income earners [was improved]. Douglas gave this assurance to get key voters. The Family Support Package was the way this assurance was put into effect.

Whether the Government would have gone ahead with the GST without party approval is a moot point. One former party president, at least, thought they would have.

36 In the 1998–9 financial year, the Treasury spent $61.5 million on consultants (Brockett 1999). In 1992–3 departments spent about $48.5 million on consultant advice, almost a sixth of the total spent on policy advice. Three departments, including the Treasury, accounted for over half this total. The Labour Government elected in 1999 signalled that it intended to stamp out the use of consultants in the public sector.

37 According to one print journalist:

Treasury trains its acolytes who go out and convert [the private sector] and also provide the chorus of approval for government policy. This is very important, because if you are the media, [these former officials] are those people you go to for comment. In a small country they are going to be bank economists, they're going to be in the major insurance institutions, the major investment groups.

Bryce Wilkinson and Rob Cameron, both important in preparing Economic Management, are two prime examples.

38 The Enterprise Council became 'inactive' after the election of the Labour Government in 1999.

Chapter 4

1 Rhodes (1997, 29) sees networks as a 'meso-level concept which provides a link between the micro-level of analysis, dealing with the role of interests and government in particular policy decisions, and the macro-level of analysis, which focuses on the broader questions about the distribution of power within modern society.' In contrast, others, such as Wilks and Wright, also use the policy networks approach to examine micro-level or subsectoral policy-making and interpersonal relationships, as do some social and business studies of networks (Wilks and Wright 1987).

2 As the decisions selected were all major economic policy decisions, it would in any event be hard to argue that they did not fit within Polsby's criteria of importance.

3 The deregulation of the financial markets could be seen as not one decision but a number of them, spread over a number of years. However, for the sake of this study, financial deregulation can be seen as a programme; once the decision to deregulate the markets was made, then the programme was put into place and modified in light of experience.

4 Ideally, the study would have also included the State Sector Act 1988, the Public Finance Act 1989 and the Fiscal Responsibility Act 1994. However, the difficulty that arose was one of limiting the number of decisions that could adequately be studied in a period when a phenomenal number of radical changes in policy were being made, and these three decisions were excluded for the following reasons. First, it was decided to study almost a decade from the 1984 election to the 1993 election, when the policy activism of the National Government largely abated. This meant the Fiscal Responsibility Act 1994 fell outside

this, admittedly arbitrary, period. Second, two of the three acts were mainly concerned with machinery of government issues rather than economic policy that more directly and obviously affected the public. Arguably, they were not highly controversial in terms of exciting public opposition, except possibly from within parts of the public service. This makes them less interesting in terms of studying how decisions can still be made in the face of controversy. Third, while it is hard to imagine Rogernomics without some key decisions, such as the financial liberalisation or the 1984 Budget, it seems possible that it could be imagined without changes to machinery of government. Finally, existing literature already suggests these decisions were driven either from within the public service (particularly the Public Finance Act) or by Ruth Richardson and the public service, in the case of the Fiscal Responsibility Act (Goldfinch 1998).

5   This run on the currency led to a vast amount of overseas borrowing. According to Roderick Deane:

> People didn't realise how enormously serious it was. People didn't know that the Treasury and the Reserve Bank borrowed $1.7 billion in four weeks in order to prop up the currency and the country (Russell 1996, 56).

6   One Chief Executive of a bank described banks as having 'bugger all' influence on bank deregulation.

7   Two senior Reserve Bank officials had also travelled to Australia to consult with the Australian Reserve Bank as Australia had floated in 1983.

8   Under a clean floating regime, speculative gains and losses would accrue to private market participants only.

9   According to O'Shaughnessy (1997, 103–4) Douglas saw the float as means to facilitate liquidity management:

> Douglas talked of the currency float as being essential due to the exchange and liquidity management problems of late 1984 as capital flowed into New Zealand as an indirect expres-

sion of support for the Government's burgeoning deregulation programme and as a direct result of the high interest rates stemming from the Government's adoption of a tight monetary policy. The net result was a 'vicious circle' whereby the capital inflows swelled the monetary base setting off, in turn, a further round of interest rate increases and capital inflows.

10   This story has been corroborated a number of times. In other versions, however, Prebble is said to have used rather stronger language, as he was known to do.

11   The decision to float was released only to a number of officials due to the demands of secrecy. When the dollar was actually floated, a number of people (such as senior union officials, who up until that time had expected to be consulted on major policy decisions) were notified after the event, leading to some of the first signs of a breakdown in the relationship between the Government and unions.

12   Douglas himself saw the economic policy changes as 'pretty conventional' and instead characterised the previous economic framework as 'radical' in that it departed from what was standard economic policy in other countries. Radical in this paper is used in the sense that there was significant and rapid departure from previous policies.

13   Notably excluded were representatives from the extra-parliamentary Labour Party, such as President Margaret Wilson.

14   Oliver notes the rapid development of Douglas's thinking away from some policies contained in his 1980 book *There's Got to be a Better Way!* (that would have been considered anti-Rogernomics after 1984) to a position more in line with that of the Treasury. These ideas developed to some extent through his interaction with Andrews and Swier, and with business friends.

15   In retrospect, one senior Treasury offi-

cial saw Douglas as following the right path because 'when GST was finally introduced, because of the enormous length of time that went into selling it and explaining it, Douglas had to give away significant [fiscal benefits]. In the circumstances Douglas's idea would have been better.'

16 She did not receive a large number of nominations as an influential figure, however.

17 A Green Paper is a document outlining various positions for discussion. Submissions are then received on the Green Paper.

18 This issue-by-issue struggle between the proponents and opponents of market deregulation was described by one Labour Party president as follows:

[On one side] Treasury and Cabinet, the opposition was led by me, on behalf of the Party and the unions. It was a constant source of negotiation: to get the process established whereby there could be Party and union input. So I devoted my time and energy on saying there should be more than one point of view. I think for a while Fran Wilde was very instrumental.

I just kept arranging lots of meetings. It was a real stand-up knock-'em-up negotiation clause by clause really. It was the only period I can recall [this sort of process] on the major policy issues. That's because there was a great deal of commitment to it. It dealt with organisational issues [and] with the party as well. It was both ideological, organisational, and there was an institutional base and also we had some experience by then about how it all worked.

The unions by that stage weren't prepared to start negotiating, because don't forget, prior to that they were incredibly divided about what their strategy should be. But I think they had suddenly realised what was happening. And Ken Douglas by then had replaced Jim Knox. [Although

they were ambivalent] about wanting to be part of the process.

19 Although one lawyer, who presented submissions on the bill and had ties to the Employers' Federation, and was later heavily involved in the development of the Employment Contracts Act, saw it as:

real progress . . . from the 1973 Act, because it removed compulsory arbitration and conciliation to voluntary agreements. It still had the nasty trappings of the old system, because it had compulsory awards and compulsory unions but it made real progress in that the arbitrarial function of the Arbitration Court was removed. There were provisions in the Labour Relations Act that weren't used, such as compulsory conferences . . . the state funding of the process was removed.

Chapter 5

1 Petrocorp issued shares to the public following the English model of privatisation. According to one respondent, the Government had been faced with a need to recapitalise Petrocorp but were reluctant to do so themselves and, looking to the British model, saw the market as one way of doing this. According to a former chair of Petrocorp, at the time the float 'was extremely successful'. However Treasury were not in agreement because they thought the share float had been undervalued, because the shares went up significantly from the share price at float. Treasury were also, according to the same person, reluctant to lose control of the privatisation process. Following the Petrocorp float, Treasury advised that assets should usually be sold by tender to single buyers or consortiums.

2 A former cabinet minister holding a number of different portfolios during the Labour Government noted:

Various assurances . . . particularly the Prime Minister [with regard to the privatisation of Telecom] were given. Assurances that turned out to be embarrassing. That was an off-the-cuff comment. [It] certainly hadn't been cleared with the Cabinet Policy Committee that was really deciding these things.

3   One former party president describes a meeting with Government ministers on the privatisation of Telecom:

At an executive level of the party we debated the issue vigorously with the Cabinet Ministers. I remember flying to Wellington for a three-hour meeting . . . on why they shouldn't [privatise] Telecom and coming home the next day and hearing the enabling legislation being introduced to the House. It was absolutely a waste of time. We had access to a lot of information, but we had no influence.

4   The current owners of Telecom would also now consider themselves to have achieved an extremely good price.

5   As a former state services commissioner (and therefore titular head of the public service) at the time says:

I can remember one stormy meeting with Ministers one night when they wanted to introduce the State Owned Enterprise Act on the 1st April 1986, and I made it clear that I couldn't do it that quickly. And I'm sure Roger Douglas saw me as trying to frustrate that process, although all I was trying to say was we'll do what we can, but you can't do it, because you don't have enough time. There aren't enough sitting days in the house.

6   According to Moore (who later supported many of the asset sales) 'there were some people who were prepared to do it anyway [that is, proceed with asset sales] and didn't share that with their Caucus and Cabinet colleagues'.

7   Lange, not necessarily a friend of Roger Douglas, agrees that while Douglas 'had an ultimate agenda, he didn't have it before the [1984] election; people are most unfair to Roger.'

8   This is something believed by Roger Douglas, amongst others.

9   According to David Caygill:

The problem with debating privatisation as if it was a sort of formal programme was that [it was] not how we decided the matter. There never was [a decision to privatise everything]. There was a decision that we faced, a problem of public debt . . . a decision was made to look at a number of individual enterprises. Some were sold, some were looked at and not sold and [some] were added in as time went by.

10 This was followed by a letter to SOE heads, written jointly by Prebble and Douglas, on 17 February outlining specific actions they were to take to facilitate the asset sales.

11 As a Treasury (1986) paper to Douglas says:

the Government's net worth is not substantially altered through the lowering of a deficit by asset sales or off-budget borrowing, although these moves may still be highly desirable for efficiency reasons. In the case of financing the deficit through asset sales the Government may reduce its borrowing requirements and consequent debt-servicing payments but it also loses, if it exists, the future income stream from the asset it sells.

Douglas says in *Unfinished Business* that 'Ministers were fully aware of and motivated by the question of efficiency, but it did not suit Labour Party philosophy to give it priority in the government's public rationale' (Douglas 1993, 186). The National Government was more explicit about privatisation being driven by reasons of efficiency (Richardson 1991, 45–52).

12 According to one Cabinet Minister:

Possibly, the single most unpopular thing we did, was to sell Telecom. Roger wasn't even in the Cabinet then. We were facing an election only a few months later that year . . . we debated it and we came to the conclusion [that we should sell it]. We assumed it would be unpopular, we were not under any illusion that people were going to support it. We believed it was right.

By the time of the Telecom sale, Prebble had returned to Cabinet as Minister of SOEs.

13 As already noted, this target was later extended to 0–3 percent.

14 The Reserve Bank would respond by saying:

> monetary policy is generally regarded as the major determinant of inflation but it is not considered to have a significant sustainable effect on real sector variables such as output and employment, although it may have a short-term effect on such variables. In the longer term, therefore, the best that monetary policy can do is achieve price stability. This in turn will contribute to '. . . promoting the highest level of production and trade and full employment . . .', the ultimate objectives which were previously included as statutory objectives for monetary policy (RBNZ 1990c, 30).

15 This specified that registered banks were required to have 'capital equal to 7.25 percent of risk weighted assets by the end of 1990 and 8 percent by the end of 1992' (RBNZ 1990d, 15).

16 According to a number of respondents, this was a phrase used by Douglas to describe the aim of the Bill. Whether this was actually the case is hard to document. As one Reserve Bank official suggested, as regards the phrase 'Muldoon proof':

> aspects [of it were] in common usage long before the autonomy proposals started to be developed. Hence, I suspect the use of the phrase in terms of any discussions between Douglas and RBNZ staff may have grown from folklore.

17 According to a former member of the Reserve Bank Board:

> Treasury wanted to privatise [the bank]. Then we had this debate about privatisation, we spent hours. It was like a very high-level graduate seminar, it was quite interesting, as long as you didn't realise these people were serious. I don't think there was any danger. A group was [pushing for it],

but you are never sure in Treasury because they were almost autonomous. They would set up contestable positions like a think-tank environment, contested all the way [but working] within the same paradigm. So you are talking about an extreme or moderate position within that paradigm.

18 Although as Table 5.3 shows, Holmes, Goodhart, Wilson and Elworthy were not nominated as influential in the Act.

19 Some intended loosening of monetary policy had been signalled by the National Party before the 1990 election. Instead of the negotiated inflation target with the Reserve Bank being below two percent by 1992, the target year would be extended out to 1993, as subsequently happened (Boston 1991b).

20 There is some concern regarding the small number of persons nominated as influential in the 1991 Budget. The results may be explained as follows: first, the sample, especially amongst politicians, contained a larger number of former Labour cabinet ministers than National ones, due in part to the greater ease with which I was able to obtain interviews and completed questionnaires from former Labour ministers. This may have limited the number of individuals nominated as influential. Second, the greater length of time that had passed with earlier decisions also meant in some cases it was easier to obtain interviews with retired public servants, rather than ones still serving the government. This again possibly limited the range of people nominated as influential. Third, the 1991 Budget was possibly driven to a greater extent by Cabinet Ministers than some previous decisions studied, as examined in the text. Therefore, respondents focused largely on the influence of Cabinet Ministers when nominating those who had been influential.

21 Like Douglas, Ruth Richardson liked to present a broad package of reforms. As she says, 'the decisions we took in six weeks set the scene for the next six years.

Which was part of the strategy.'

22 As a former secretary to the Treasury says: 'With the speed of this thing ministers clearly played a very dominant role. You don't change somebody's mind in two minutes if they have been in opposition for six years.'

23 Richardson was largely successful in this endeavour, as she says:

Basically, the whole Cabinet took a major stake in that document. Clearly, the critical player was the Prime Minister. He chaired the cabinet committee that looked at all the social policy redesign. He had to have the courage to sign up. He is not a radical conservative by nature. He was the key person to recruit and keep recruiting . . . [The spending ministers, Upton, Shipley, Smith] were . . . absolutely committed to the reforms. That made my tenure very different to Roger Douglas's. He was never once able to recruit and have the support of his spending ministers.

Richardson may have overstated the degree of dissent within the Labour Cabinet—at least until 1986–7—when there was a large amount of agreement on policy directions.

24 As one departmental chief executive says: [During the budget] they did make a major effort to talk to officials (outside Treasury), unlike the Labour Government. [But] it was a paradox—on one hand the National Government did want to talk to officials more and gave that appearance, but there was some key things [they didn't]. There was a failure to consult widely enough [and] they got the implementation things wrong. In the things that had gone wrong in health and some of the social areas, as opposed to things that had gone right, there was a very great difference. There was a significant gap between those involved [in] policy and those involved in implementation. The orthodoxy is to separate policy and operations, but what it showed was that

it is the opposite. The people you expected to operate this huge new reform at a critical point didn't know why this thing had been done and how it had been done. You were asking them to do the impossible.

25 According to an Employers' Federation official there had been some discussion of individual contracting going back to the 1970s.

26 Which is not to say it did not spell out the main concepts of what would be the Act.

27 According to a senior NZCTU official, there was an attempt at some further deregulation of the labour market:

We wanted to exit from the occupation-based awards to either industry or enterprise depending . . . on what was appropriate to the workers concerned. We were in negotiation with Stan Rodger . . . but he wouldn't act unless the Employers' [Federation] agreed . . . so they changed the law [anyway] to allow this exiting to industry and enterprise based agreements [the 1990 amendment to the Act]. The Employers' Federation boycotted it because they didn't want it to work because they were holding out for their . . . full agenda [as Labour was clearly going to lose the next election].

28 Kiely also presented 21 submissions on the Bill for a number of clients.

29 Kerr downplays his and the Roundtable's role in the process and claimed it was a normal policy formation process. This is contradicted by some active members of the Business Roundtable who claim the organisation did produce some sort of draft legislation or drafting instructions.

Chapter 6

1 The members of the federal lower house, the House of Representatives, are elected by preferential voting and the winning party provides the federal government. However, election to the Senate is by proportional representation and this will often deny the government an absolute

majority in the Senate. This gives the Senate a significant role as a check on the power on the government and as a house of review. The main differences in power between the two houses are that the Senate cannot initiate or amend money bills. However, it can refuse to pass them, or to pass them unless amendments are made, as Prime Minister Whitlam found in 1975.

2 During Whitlam's Labor Government (1972–5) Caucus was more important and the convention of cabinet collective responsibility was not strongly held. Caucus could and did contest ministerial decisions, with the caucus committee on economic policy being important. During the Fraser Government, the Labor opposition reaffirmed cabinet collective responsibility and supremacy over the caucus.

3 Junior ministers that exist outside cabinet face slightly relaxed rules of collective responsibility and can oppose cabinet decisions in the party room (but not in public) (Davis 1997).

4 There has been a considerable recruitment of economists in other departments during the 1980s and 1990s, however, and this may have redressed the balance towards other departments somewhat.

5 According to Langmore (1988), Fraser's relationship with the Treasury reached a low point after an alleged leak by Treasury about the 1976 devaluation. Fraser's split of Treasury in 1976 was widely seen as an attempt to lessen Treasury's power.

6 The Financial Management Improvement Program (FMIP) required

departments to move from 'line item budgets' setting out expenses, towards program budget statements which list what a program has achieved, and the costs involved in delivering that service. Such budgets rely in turn on sophisticated information systems to track activity, and on corporate plans with performance indicators and evaluation cycles (Davis 1997, 97).

7 In 1998, the natural resources policy function was combined with economic and industry policy to form Economic, Industry and Resources Policy (DPMC (Australia) 1998).

8 Don Russell was appointed as the Ambassador to the United States.

9 One former cabinet minister noted the appointment of Dr Meredith Edwards into the public sector bureaucracy (in this case the DPMC) as serving such a role.

10 According to one chief executive, in the early years there was considerable cooperation between the three central agencies on budget strategies as 'early in the budget process in February the three departments would sit down and work out high level strategies—what are we trying to achieve in this budget, and this would be put to the treasurer.' This cooperation dissipated somewhat after 1986.

11 With Bob Hawke as Prime Minister, according to John Button:

Hawke would decide what he wanted to do and he would call around various ministers, including me and try and persuade them about what was the desirable course before it went to Cabinet. Then when it came to Cabinet there were never any furious debates.

Ralph Willis makes a similar comment regarding Hawke's style:

which was very much an approach of talking issues through and to not impose a view on controversial issues. But that wasn't universally the case . . . he was quite clearly strongly in favour [of financial deregulation]. But his style was more generally to let discussion run. Sometimes he hadn't made up his own mind. [Discussion] could sometimes run and run, to the point where it was almost excruciating. He would sum up what the majority position was. It wasn't always what I would have thought the majority position was.

12 Hawke's chairmanship of the ERC also gave him some control over the budget

processes rather than leaving them purely in the hands of Treasurer Keating. This influence did not always extend to other areas such as monetary policy, which often tended to be made by the Treasurer and his officials, although there was some discussion between the offices of Keating and Hawke (Edwards 1996, 250–51). Hawke was also considerably stronger on driving the direction of economic policy in the early years of his Government as Keating was finding his feet as Treasurer. Keating and Hawke would often form common positions before taking them to Cabinet or the ERC, with any disagreement smoothed out beforehand.

13 The Coalition Government's Charter of Budget Honesty Act 1998 introduced a regime of scrutiny of fiscal objective and performance, similar in some ways to New Zealand's Fiscal Responsibility Act 1994 (see chapter three). The Act provides for enunciation of the government's fiscal objectives, consistent with principles of 'sound fiscal management' as laid down in the Act. Budget papers since 1997–8 have provided more information on the government's fiscal agenda than previously and further information is provided in the Mid-year Economic and Fiscal Outlook. The Act requires the publication of a Pre-election Economic and Fiscal Outlook report within ten days of the issue of writs for a general election. Formal arrangements allow for the costing of government and opposition election commitments by the Treasury and Finance and Administration (Treasury (Australia) 1998).

14 The Reserve Bank Act 1959 requires the bank to exercise its monetary and banking policy 'in such a manner as, in the opinion of the Board, will best contribute to "the stability of the currency", "the maintenance of full employment in Australia" and "the economic prosperity and welfare of the people of Australia"' (s.10(2)). Section 11(1) of the same Act requires the board of the bank, 'from time to time, to inform the Government

of the monetary policy and Banking policy of the Bank.'

15 This tended to upset other senior officials in the Bank somewhat, because as one respondent said, 'we weren't quite sure what the Governor was up to'.

16 Hawke's relationship with the union movement (beyond his relationship just with Kelty) was always deeper and wider than Keating's.

17 The machinery of government underwent considerable reorganisation under the Labor Government, most notably with the consolidation of 26 commonwealth departments into 16 super departments in 1987, and departments suffered a number of name changes through the period (Wiltshire 1990). For example, the Department of Industry, Technology and Commerce later became Industry, Technology and Regional Development, and then Industry, Science and Technology. The Department of Trade amalgamated with the Foreign Affairs to become Department of Foreign Affairs and Trade in 1987 and the Department of Employment and Industrial Relations became Department of Industrial Relations in 1987. Primary Industries became Primary Industries and Energy in 1987.

18 Absorbed administratively in 1996, then officially under the Productivity Commission Act 1998, into the Productivity Commission.

19 Formed from the merger of the Bureau of Agricultural Economics and the Bureau of Resource Economics in 1987.

20 According to one former member of the Commission:

Small business and the professions ostensibly had access to the government through EPAC. Their submissions weren't taken very seriously by the government—partly because they were not systematic or well articulated or well backed up. Their spokespersons weren't particularly persuasive or powerful. So they didn't produce what had increasingly become the norm in policy-making, which is not that research and analysis determines an outcome but that it is essential [to] legitimating an outcome.

21 It was intended that with a 'broadened character, new guidelines and reporting requirements . . . the Commission [would] play a central role in the ongoing processes of structural reform to improve productivity' (Industry Commission 1990, 1).

22 There have, however, been times where business groups have formed coalitions and worked towards common aims, including forming ad hoc committees and groups around policy aims. This was especially the case in the late 1980s. This has included 'a considerable new commitment to extended cross-association dialogue, networking and ad hoc forums and meetings' and special issue forums including the Business Forum on Consumer Affairs (Bell 1994). In 1992, the Confederation of Australian Industry merged with the Australian Chamber of Commerce to form the Australian Chamber of Commerce and Industry. The Metal Trades Industry Association and the Australian Chamber of Manufactures amalgamated to form the Australian Industry Group in 1998.

23 John Dawkins would respond to this by saying:

> While much has been made of the so-called outflanking of business by the Government and the ACTU at the 1983 Economic Summit, I have never been able to ascertain on what issues business was defeated.
>
> Essentially, the whole agenda was pro-business in the sense that policies which reduced costs and particularly wage costs, reduced inflation, increased competition and economic growth were likely to benefit those businesses capable of rising to the new challenges (Dawkins 1994, 3).

McEachern (1991) makes similar claims; that although business was at times divided amongst itself and critical of the Labor Government, by and large the policies followed by the Labor Government were supportive of business. This is a common argument in neo-pluralist and neo-Marxist literature (Lindblom 1977).

24 According to respondents from the former Labor Government and the BCA, the initial good relationship ended when the Government introduced a compulsory 3 percent superannuation levy in Accord II without consulting business.

25 According to a former minister the 'ideas weren't coming from [the media]—they were selling and reinforcing them.' Politicians also used the media to test the reaction to policies and to seek reassurance that they were heading in the right direction. According to the same former Labor cabinet minister there was a hierarchy of newspapers in this testing, with the *Financial Review* and the *Australian* on the top and then 'a long way after that' the *Sydney Morning Herald* and the *Age*. At the other extreme were the tabloids as 'no one wants a bad headline in the *Herald Sun*'.

26 The Industrial Relations Act 1996 re-amalgamated the Industrial Court and the Industrial Relations Commission (Industrial Relations Commission 1996).

27 Marsh has claimed, without saying how this influence was measured, that:

> The impact of the 'neo-liberal' group of organisations has been very substantial—quite as significant as that of the issue movements and major interest groups. These 'think-tanks' have pioneered the agenda concerned with responses to the changed world economy now championed in greater or lesser extent by both major parties in the discourse of public servants and media commentators (1991, 30).

28 An important example being Access Economics, founded in 1988 and including a number of ex-Treasury officials and other government officials. Access has carried out work for various government departments and interest groups and provided the major external advice for

the Federal Opposition's taxation proposals in the 'Fightback!' package of 1991.

Chapter 7

1 The deregulation of the financial markets could be seen as not one decision but a number of them, spread over a number of years. However, for the sake of this study financial deregulation can be seen as a programme; once the decision to deregulate the markets was made, then the programme was put into place and modified in light of experience.

2 Ralph Willis, for example, had been a research officer at the ACTU and Bob Hawke had been an ACTU president.

3 It was only in the later Accords such as Accord VII and VIII that the bureaucracy became important beyond implementation.

4 The Australian Labor Party Advisory Council is the formal body for 'co-operation, consultation and consensus' between the peak union councils and the Australian Labor Party (Singleton 1990, 102).

5 According to Willis:

There was trust there [between the unions and the Labor Government]. And Hawke was onside. In terms of day-to-day working of it [he was not so important] but very onside. Very onside when he was in parliament, he wasn't quite so on the outside. But this was not a conceptual problem for him, but it got caught up with the rivalry with Hayden. Hayden wasn't sure about the Accord mainly because he mistrusted Hawke. Hawke was disinclined to be too supportive of the Accord 'cos it might assist Hayden. [Hawke] was quite important in seeing that it came together. If he had been against it would probably never have happened.

6 As an assistant secretary in the ACTU in 1997 said:

Everyone realised it was a very major step everybody was taking to commit the Government and to make that commitment with an institution out-

side the government area, [and] for the ACTU to make commitments regarding wage outcomes and the way we would [establish] a better wages environment. There was dissent from the radical left of the union movement who felt it was giving up too much in the way of independent action . . . and they weren't prepared to accept it. They wanted Government to make commitments regarding wages without any offsetting commitments from ourselves in terms of our general approach to economic policy, level of wage outcome, etc. It was more particular people within unions [rather than whole unions]. The Food Preservers Union was one . . . that was very outspoken . . . but they were very much the exceptions. Bearing in mind . . . things were looking pretty bloody awful . . . we needed a circuit breaker and the Accord was hopefully going to do that.

7 Scepticism again grew about the usefulness of the Accords. According to a one-time Treasury deputy secretary, the Accord 'was a valuable idea . . . of overcoming the potential for wage explosion [and to] get out of the freeze . . . [but] it outlived its usefulness in two or three years.'

8 According to one Keating staffer (who was arguing for the Accord and for consensual policy-making in general), Keating's scepticism was because he 'had very few links in the ACTU. It was the Melbourne end of the union movement that was running things. [And he had] experience of the Sydney union movement.'

9 While Keating is named by a number of respondents as influential on Accord I, other respondents and sources claim that he was opposed to the first Accord but came to support the process when it delivered early results. It may be that some respondents have confused Keating's support for later Accord agreements with the first Accord.

10 The other member of the group was D. J. Cleary.

11 One chief executive of a major bank does not think banks were important in financial deregulation, although they were strongly in favour of it. 'I don't think it was a matter of influence [but] of inevitability.'

12 John Kerin, a future treasurer who was at the time the Minister of Primary Industry, says he raised the matter of the float early in the life of the government:

> I was on the monetary committee of Cabinet through 1983 and we used to look at the exchange rate quite regularly. About June of that year I made a mistake politically by putting into that committee a paper by the Bureau of Agricultural Economics . . . it didn't say float the currency, but did say by the [pegged regime] we are rewarding raiders on our currency [and] we are too small to resist. This was rejected wholeheartedly by Treasury and Finance and as I recall Keating was particularly nonplussed by this paper. And Stone was very much against floating the dollar at this stage. That was a mistake as I was really challenging what Treasury saw as its prerogative. I got so intimidated by that experience that I didn't put any more papers in.

13 Previously the dollar was set by 'A little group of wise men—the Secretary of the Treasury, Governor of the Reserve Bank, nominally at least the Secretary of the Prime Minister's Department. They were to formulate advice to the government', as one chief executive, then a senior Treasury official terms it.

14 Some respondents thought Keating had not made up his mind to float even as late as the final meeting on the Friday before the float. This, according to a member of Keating's office at the time, was not that Keating did not support a float, but that it was because:

> . . . one of the techniques to get a decision is to not come in hard. And both sides would be deliberately playing coy as a way of testing the other. [Keating was strong on the float] I

know he was. He would often be strong on something, but it is not necessarily the best tactic when you are dealing with an issue to show you are strong on something. If you want to persuade people, you have to show you are sensitive to their concerns and that you haven't pre-empted them.

15 Professor Barry Hughes, in Keating's office at the time, agrees:

> What had happened is that Hawke and Keating are claiming credit. There is a bit of Indian arm-wrestling over who did what. [But] it was not the politicians. It doesn't mean that either politician was not significant, but that the entire thrust of advice, with the exception of the official Treasury [and] Stone position, was to float, and if you want to pick out who was pre-eminent in power in all that lot, I would have thought the Reserve Bank.

16 A dirty float is one in which the central bank will intervene from time to time in the market to influence the value of the currency. A clean float is where the central bank leaves the currency entirely up to the market. The New Zealand float has largely been a clean one, while the Australian Reserve Bank has seen the need to intervene occasionally.

17 The forward rate is 'the exchange rate today for settlement later, and reflects the difference between the interest rates paid on deposits in the currencies over the period' (Edwards 1996, 222).

18 As Edwards (1996, 220–21) documents, Stone argued that the real problem was the fiscal deficit, that the float would lead to a more volatile exchange rate, that policy change should be made on the basis of written evidence (of which there was little) and that an evolutionary approach to policy change should be taken (not a revolutionary approach).

19 Hawke says he was tipped off late in the election campaign to expect a budget blowout (Hawke 1994, 147).

20 The minute said:

> The magnitude of the fiscal imbal-

ance is unprecedented in Australia during peace times, as is the level of Government spending. The budget deficit is projected to deteriorate from near zero to more than six percent of GDP in a two-year period. The speed and magnitude of that deterioration is almost without precedent among the major OECD countries in the post-war period (cited Hawke 1994, 148).

21 According to one departmental chief executive:

[D]PMC was very influential in that budget. I seem to recall it was being driven out of [D]PMC. Treasury of course were the prime movers on the macroeconomic problems of the day, but in terms of individual proposals I know the [D]PMC were very prominent in that. In matters relating, for example, to the Medicare changes and the levy that was brought in at the time.

22 The nine point plan consisted of the following: first, no increase in the overall tax burden as a percentage of GDP; second, reform must continue with the tax cuts already begun; third, a concentration on tax avoidance and evasion; fourth, a simplification of the tax system; fifth, development of a fairer progressive system; sixth, tax reform must not disadvantage welfare beneficiaries; seventh, indirect taxes must be acceptable to community groups; eighth, reform must be conducive to investment, employment and growth; and ninth, the package must have widespread community support developed though a tax summit.

Chapter 8

1 This department went through a number of name changes during the period.

2 The Motor Vehicle Plan was designed, according to Button, in his office because his department was opposed. When David Charles took over as Secretary, the Industry Department became an advocate of trade liberalisation.

3 As Capling and Galligan (1992, 150) point out, a depreciated dollar raised the cost of imports, lessening the impact of the tariff cuts.

4 A number of respondents did not see Keating as a major player in tariff or in microeconomic reform. He seems to have come to push for these changes later, once the agenda had largely been set. One former departmental head says 'Keating has claimed much more credit for that than is his due.'

5 The introduction of the two-tier wage bargaining system in Accord III, in 1987, led to centralised wage indexation being abandoned. To some extent the two-tiered system allowed for some enterprise bargaining; it is the case, however, that Accord VI was the first to be *explicit* about the move to enterprise bargaining.

6 The reasons it gave for this decision were:
the necessity to follow up the process set in place in 1987 with reference to the 'efficiency and restructuring' and 'structural efficiency' principles;
the high rate of unemployment minimising the possibility of any increase in wages;
the fact that Enterprise Bargaining [EB] in the Australian context normally meant over award payments;
the serious challenge with insufficient argument to the long-established principle that the benefits of productivity should be distributed on a national rather than industry or enterprise basis;
reservations about the ability of the market to prevent wage breakouts;
that EB places at a relative disadvantage those sections of the labour force where women predominate;
that employers and employees at large had not reached a level of maturity to handle a decentralised wage system (Thompson 1992, 53).

7 Enterprise bargaining was not supported by all business groups. It was resisted in the metal trade industry where were strong and united unions.

8   As a Cabinet colleague says:
      Kelty by that time was extraordinar-
      ily influential because Hawke and
      Keating were competing for his fa-
      vours. Keating [won]. By 1990,
      Keating is saying there is no other
      Treasurer in the world as influential
      with the trade union movement and
      in reality that is total bullshit. He got
      himself very close to Kelty and in his
      mind the two were the same thing and
      I don't think that was ever true, but he
      was immensely influential on Kelty. I
      would say Kelty was leading Keating.
   However as the respondent continues:
      Curiously enough enterprise bargain-
      ing was [finally] introduced in a re-
      cession when our bargaining power
      was not as strong as it had been . . .
      although there were certain parts of
      the economy where bargaining power
      is high. And that's why the unions like
      my own . . . Textiles . . . were so re-
      sistant. In boom times we could've
      possibly achieved more, but for us
      centralised wage fixation was the way.
   Occasionally during Accord negotiations, this meeting would be for a considerable length of time, as each union
   tried to get special references to themselves placed in the Accord documents,
   without altering the core initiatives of
   the document.

11 According to the same official:
      it wasn't really until VII and VIII and
      also once Paul Keating was no longer
      Treasurer [that] we became more cen-
      tral in the actual process. We had
      someone from the department, some-
      one from out of the Minister's office
      and someone from the ACTU drafted
      both VII and VIII. Obviously with
      instructions.

12 According to the statement, the changes
    in the tax scales were:
      to reduce the marginal tax rate facing
      the majority of the full-time
      workforce, including those on median
      and average wages, from 38 percent
      to 30 percent;
      to reduce the marginal tax rate for

those earning up to $50,000 per year,
including, for example, those who
derive such income through overtime
of shift loading, from 46 percent to
40 percent (Keating 1992, 43).

13 Button had a public falling out with
    Keating when Button mentioned in a
    television interview in May 1990 that
    Australia was in a downturn of some se-
    verity. He was forced to tell the Senate
    that although he believed there was a
    downturn, this was somehow different
    from a recession (Tingle 1994, 85).

14 John Dawkins released revised economic
    forecasts in the first week of January
    1992. Prepared by the Joint Economic
    Forecasting Group, these predicted zero
    growth for the year and a fall in employ-
    ment of 0.5 percent during the year (Tin-
    gle 1994, 159).

15 According to Edwards (1986, 457) ele-
    ments of the bureaucracy, such as Tony
    Cole and Rod Sims, were less opposed
    to some fiscal stimulus by the time
    Keating took over as leader. According
    to Tingle (1994, 160–61) by the time
    Keating had taken over, the Treasury had
    gone through a 'road to Damascus ex-
    perience' and changed its stance on the
    fiscal stimulus and was recommending
    one of three billion. Tingle's claim doesn't
    seem to accord with the recollections of
    some respondents in my interviews.

16 This ran into implementation problems.
    According to Tony Cole, the group was
    told by the Railways that the Railway
    Links Project was already designed and
    could be got off the ground within three
    weeks. It in fact took three years.

17 Despite the relatively early announce-
    ment of the sale of the Australia National
    Line, there was a long delay in its actual
    sale due to a number of management and
    other problems (Wettenhall 1997).

18 In 1988 the Government introduced a
    series of reforms to improve the com-
    mercial performance of Government
    Business Enterprises (GBEs). This in-
    cluded requiring GBEs to operate on a
    strictly commercial basis and return a
    dividend to the government, as well as

increase productivity, efficiency, price and service quality. In 1993 the Department of Finance prepared a new set of guidelines. The GBEs were also scrutinised by external sources such as the Steering Committee on National Performance Measurement of Government Trading Enterprises (Beckett 1994).

19 After the statements by Hawke in 1987 and his 1991 'Building a Competitive Australia', which called for a 'national framework of competition policy and law', competition policy reached its most comprehensive form in the 1995 agreements between the state and federal governments on building a National Compassion Policy. This had been preceded by the Hilmer report of 1993 (Harman 1996; S. King 1997). The National Competition Agreements removed trading advantages from GBEs.

20 Peter McLaughlin, then the BCA's Executive Director said in a speech to the Institute of Directors in 1988 that 30 out of 100 efficiency improvements would be delivered by private ownership (cited Kelly 1994, 394). According to another former BCA chief executive, while the BCA was generally in favour of privatisation, the ownership of the asset was less important in terms of efficiency aspects than the fact that the GBEs had to operate in a competitive environment.

21 Hogg saw support in Cabinet being of two types:

You had those . . . that wanted the Commonwealth to get out of any service activity or infrastructure activity coupled with those who wanted to free up their budget choices by having a return on the sale.

22 The fiscal benefits of privatisation are highly contested (Quiggan 1995; King 1997).

23 Once partly privatised, the Government found that, although it was the largest shareholder, it did not have as much say in the running of the Bank as it would have expected, as the Board would often expect the interests of other shareholders to be taken into account. As the influence was less than imagined, a number of advisers suggested selling off a second tranche of the Bank. However there were some difficulties with this. According to one senior Treasury official:

Keating had made a commitment he would not privatise any more [of the Bank]. So we had to go and convince a number of people that we weren't really breaching the promise, that we would maintain the majority ownership so we were still really in charge. We didn't let on to people that we didn't think we were in charge even with 75 percent. I can only remember one occasion when we had to tell the Board that if they did something we would exercise our majority vote . . . over directors' payments.

24 Conditions of the original agreement were that the government would maintain majority ownership in perpetuity and that non-government equity would be limited to 30 percent.

25 Before the sale of Aussat, Telecom's 25 percent stake was purchased by the Government, restrictions on which services it could provide were removed (so making it a potential competitor in telecommunications) and it was recapitalised by the Government (Beckett 1994).

26 Earlier there had been considerable debate between Beazley and Keating over the direction telecommunications reform should take, with Beazley winning out. Keating had wanted a fully competitive model; Beazley (supported by Hawke) wanted the duopoly that was eventually decided upon (Kelly 1994, 617). The fully competitive model was adopted by 1997.

27 The commitment to an open aviation market between Australia and New Zealand was later abandoned by the Australian Government.

Chapter 9

1 Easton talks of a 'blitzkreig' approach to policy formation (Easton and Gerritson

1996). I have used the more common and internationally accepted term.

2 The comparison of New Zealand and Australia, two countries with similar majority cultures and histories of economic development, shows the importance of institutional structures and federalism in explaining differences in policy-making.

3 Rodger fell out with the Public Service Association after the lack of consultation involved in the State Sector Act 1988.

4 Keating makes much of his working class roots (see Edwards 1996).

5 This was possibly true of the National Government from 1990–93. After the near defeat in the 1993 election and Richardson's removal as finance minister, the National Party returned to its traditional gradualist and pragmatic methods of making policy. However, in the year before their loss in the 1999 election, the minority National Government did increase the speed of policy change.

6 Lost votes in the overwhelmingly Labour constituencies could be traded for the professional and affluent votes gained in marginal constituencies (Nagel 1998).

7 Academics are not held in high regard in New Zealand, and were not always seen as having a legitimate role in policy formation such as interest groups would have had prior to 1984.

8 In the 1993 election the Alliance gained 18.1 percent of the vote and two seats, while New Zealand First also gained two seats and polled 8.4 percent. In the 1996 election, the first under MMP, the Alliance won 13 seats, ACT 8, New Zealand First 17, the Labour Party 37 and the National Party 44. National later formed a coalition Government with New Zealand First, which collapsed in 1998.

9 Warhurst (1996) disputes Maddox's and others' claims that the 1983–96 Labor Government betrayed Labor tradition.

10 An argument can be made that the New Zealand economy at times performed poorly *despite* favourable external conditions. The extended recession of the late 1980s was in the face of favourable terms of trade and a booming world economy. As Dalziel (1999b, 27) points out, Australia faced worse terms of trade during the same period.

11 The sequencing issue is discussed at length in a number of publications (see, for example, Evans et al 1996; Nagel 1998). As Murrell (1995) points out, there is a normative and theoretical basis to much of the sequencing literature, and its empirical verisimilitude is fragile, at least as it is applied to the liberalisation of Eastern Europe. Drawing on Murrell, according to Evans et al the New Zealand programme strongly resembles what Fisher calls the:

> standard reform prescription for an ex-socialised country [which] is to proceed as fast as possible on macroeconomic stabilisation, the liberalization of domestic trade and process, current account convertibility, privatization and the creation of a social safety net (cited Murrell 1995, 164).

Despite this, Evans et al (1996, 1871) claim that the New Zealand 'evidence, combined with theoretical insights, suggests that, abstracting from political concerns and time constraints, the chosen sequence was suboptimal'. However, they go on to say that political factors have to be taken into account and that traditional sequencing literature need not dominate the practicable option of proceeding rapidly on all fronts. Consideration needs to be given to the dynamics of the reform process. New Zealand's reform efforts began in the financial sector in response to a financial crisis. Success here allowed the program to move forward into more controversial areas (Evans et al 1996, 1894).

12 See Dalziel (1999a; 1999b), Philpott (1999) and other contributors to Chatterjee et al (1999) for a discussion of the reasons for New Zealand's poor performance.

13 It is also by no means clear that those economies most deregulated are always the best performed.

14 This underlines the fallaciousness of the belief that the process itself can be separated from the end product. The 'crash through' approach allowed these highly theoretically based policies to be introduced. A more considered and negotiated process would have possibly led to different, or at least modified, policies.

15 In an interesting display of ad hocism, Ormsby (1998, 358) claims:

> A further objective has been to distinguish criticisms which identify weakness in the theory from criticisms which are external to the theory. Inevitably, this approach raises the question of whether the reforms have always been implemented in accordance with the theory. An ineffective or maladroit reform does not falsify the theory if the reform has not been carried out in accordance with that theory.

As it is often used in New Zealand, this approach means that if policies do not achieve the results claimed for them, their proponents can say this is not the theory's fault, but instead that of policy development and implementation—'reform has not gone far enough' (for example, see Myers 1998). Such an approach, in Popperian terms, is potentially unfalsifiable and so unscientific. It is rather akin to the argument made by a millenarist when the saviour does not appear on the mountain as predicted—'you did not have enough faith'. In any event, the laboratory type conditions prevalent in New Zealand during 1984–96, that allowed largely unmodified policies to be introduced, make such an approach difficult to maintain.

16 Using Australia as a counterfactual to New Zealand in terms of economic performance can be justified by the following reasons. First, there are strong institutional, cultural, legal and political similarities, including developed systems of business and property law. Second, there are similar structures to the economy in the sense that both are dependent on primary exports, although Australia is advantaged by possessing significant mineral resources. Third, there are some similarities in policy settings before 1983–4—with both countries following a programme of 'domestic defence' with industry having significant trade protection, government involvement in labour-markets, and significant regulation of financial, capital and other markets (Castles 1985). Fourth, Dalziel (1990b) argues that Australia had a similar enough GDP growth trajectory before 1984 to act as a 'reasonable counterfactual'.

17 Low income households are those in the bottom 40 percent of income distribution.

18 Some commentators have argued that current account deficits are not a problem as 'they reflect the willingness of overseas investors to lend to Australia, [and] that it is the result of micro decisions on lending to and investment by Australian companies and government' (Gleber 1998, 16). Gleber sees this as a naive belief in markets and, rather than financing new investment, the current account deficit is 'effectively capitalising interest and maintaining consumption levels' (1998, 20). It is also the case that current account deficit and debt are criteria used by credit rating agencies.

19 GDP per head index using current Purchasing Power Parties (OECD = 100).

20 This view might of course be disputed by opponents of the goods and services tax.

21 Technocratic in this sense refers to the belief that policy-making should be left to the 'experts.'

22 This view of economics as value laden is held by a number of respectable mainstream economists (for example, Blyth 1987). As the economist Blaug (1996) notes, many of the tenets of welfare economics, and even such concepts as efficiency, while they may be accepted by most mainstream economists, still contain value judgements. I would also argue that neoclassical economics functions as a political ideology, or is often used as such. Its core assumptions are

held despite their doubtful empirical verisimilitude, and in some of its variants it makes assumptions regarding human nature, the role of the state and the market, how social order is to be determined, as well as discussing race, gender and social issues in a particular way.

Appendix One

1 These are (1) industrial corporations, (2) utilities, transportation and communications, (3) banking, (4) insurance, (5) investments, (6) mass media, (7) law, (8) education, (9) foundations, (10) civic and cultural organisations, (11) government, and (12) the military (Dye 1990, 10).

2 It can also be argued that locating influence within strategic locations may miss hidden bases of power such as class. However I do not see the two as mutually exclusive; it may be that institutional power is merely at a lower level of abstraction. There may indeed be a structural basis for the power of some institutions, such as large business corporations in capitalist economies.

3 Borrowing from the state autonomists such as Skocpol (1979), it is accepted that the state can be an independent actor in policy development. However, the approach I am using highlights the divisions within the state itself, rather than seeing the state as a monolithic unity. Borrowing from the network approach also highlights the relationships that can form between state and non-state actors.

4 For example, if one was studying environmental policy or health policy it may be sensible to include some of the leading environmental groups or include groups representing medical practitioners.

5 In New Zealand, current and some former chief executives of the top thirty companies and top five banks were approached for interviews, as well as leaders of the main business associations. In Australia, I decided to concentrate on business association leaders for the following reasons. First, chief executives in New Zealand had considerably less information regarding policy processes than did business association leaders. Second, there was a wide variety of business associations in Australia compared to the five major ones in New Zealand, giving a large number of potential subjects. Third, I believed it would be difficult to arrange interviews with Australian chief executives. This was confirmed when I tried unsuccessfully to arrange interviews with chief executives that had been nominated as influential in Australia. In New Zealand, only those chief executives or chairs of companies based in Wellington or Auckland were approached for a direct interview. The four companies of this top thirty that were outside these main centres were sent questionnaires, none of which were returned.

6 Notably Rod Deane who had been deputy governor at the Reserve Bank, chairman of the State Services Commission and chief executive of ECNZ, and recently resigned as the chief executive of Telecom.

7 Due to research design and the difficulties of cross-country research, there was some cross-country difference in those contacted for interview after being nominated by the snowball approach. The extremely high response to the first sample in New Zealand meant questionnaires were normally sent or interviews conducted with persons nominated by two or more respondents, but this was not strictly adhered to, however, and many respondents were contacted after only one nomination, especially if this course was recommended by another respondent. In Australia, the two person nomination was abandoned because of the less favourable response to the initial and second sample and because I was able to interview a number of people over a longer time period and a larger geographic spread.

8 As noted in earlier chapters, New Zealand respondents were initially asked to

nominate 'about five or six' individuals 'particularly influential in formulating this policy?' While in Australia respondents were asked, 'Are there a group of individuals particularly influential in [this policy]. Can you name them?' This change was made in light of experience gained through interviewing. New Zealand respondents were prompted, after the initial question, to name any other individuals they thought influential. As a result, numbers ranged from well below five or six to well over five or six. It seemed easier to streamline the question for the Australian interviews and just ask the respondent to name influential individuals. This may be problematic for a cross-country comparison. First, it is possible that asking for a particular number may have influenced the number of individuals named. However, it is difficult to tell which direction this influence may have been. It is possible that it may have encouraged respondents to name 'only' that number; it is also possible that asking for 'five or six' may have encouraged respondents to name *more* than they would have initially. The further prompting may overcome the difficulties involved in initially asking for 'five or six'. In any event, there does not seem to be much difference in the number of individuals nominated between the two countries. For the question regarding influential individuals on economic policy generally (rather than in particular decisions), no suggested number was given in either study.

Appendix Two

1   Keynesianism, as it was practised in the postwar years (as opposed to what might be seen as a necessarily theoretically consistent approach), can be seen as having the following characteristics:

i   A view that the economy is not inherently stable or self-regulating and does not tend always towards full employment equilibrium but 'seems capable of remaining in a chronic condition of subnormal activity [with high unemployment] for a considerable period without any marked tendency towards either complete recovery or complete collapse' (cited Whitwell 1986, 39).

ii   A positive role for government in addressing unemployment and smoothing out business cycles by intervening in the economy and using activist demand management policies. This may take the form of fiscal policy (for example, adjusting taxation, running fiscal deficits during recession, and providing automatic stabilisers such as welfare payments) and monetary policy. These polices are seen to have real effects; that is, they affect the real (rather than nominal) output of an economy to some extent in the long term. (Bertram 1993; Blaug, 1985, 654–78; Whitwell 1986, 26–52; 1994)

iii   A system of exchange rate and capital controls set up after the Second World War by the Bretton Woods agreement under the patronage of Keynes, with the belief that fiscal monetary and incomes policy should be conducted in such a way to allow for acceptable balance of payments, within the borders of fixed exchange rates (Bertram 1993; White 1992, 226–7).

iv   A largely macroeconomic focus. While it bred a scepticism to the clearing abilities of some markets, the so-called neoclassical synthesis reintegrated its macroeconomic focus with the already existing neoclassical microeconomics (unsuccessfully, according to some critics such as Post-Keynesians and Marxists) (Bertram 1993).

According to some commentators, Keynesianism has seen something of a revival since the early 1990s (Bertram 1997; Blaug, 1996, ch. 16.)

2   One commentator on this appendix noted that stagflation did not discredit Keynesians or Post-Keynesians as such, but more the 'bastard' Keynesians, who were enamoured of the Phillips Curve.

3   An argument that would not be accepted by Post-Keynesians, who argued that

Keynes had partially discredited the existing neoclassical microeconomics, and who have to some extent developed a competing microeconomics of their own.

4 Although not, it seems, its main focus on inflation. The Chicago School argument, that central banking influences aggregate demand only in the short run, became accepted by many mainstream economists in the 1970s.

5 It is also worth noting that nearly all aspects of neoclassical economics and its offshoots are highly contested on theoretical and empirical grounds, at least in the academic world (Ormerod 1994). The so-called Washington Consensus is also coming under increasing critical scrutiny, even from members of organisations formerly seen as its leading advocates, such as in the case of World Bank Chief Economist, Joseph Stiglitz (Stiglitz 1999).

6 See Hausman 1992, chapters 1–3, or any introductory economics text book, for an explanation of these concepts.

7 Hausman would probably accept all three of these axioms. They form the building blocks of his characterisation of equilibrium theory; 'removing rational greed and the possibility of equilibrium from their central places' in equilibrium theory is largely forbidden (1992, 272). As such, even for him, they form a 'pseudo hard core'.

8 Or as Adam Smith puts it, in his much quoted passage in Book IV of *The Wealth of Nations*:

> Every individual necessarily labours to render the annual revenue of the society as great as he can. He generally, indeed, neither intends to promote the public interest, nor knows how much he is promoting it. He intends only his own gain, and he is in this, as in many other cases, made by an invisible hand to promote an end which was not part of his intention.

9 Hausman sees equlibrium theory as the fundamental theory of neoclassical economics and general equilibrium as a particular application of this fundamental theory (Hausman 1992).

10 For the many critiques of general equilibrium theory and welfare economics see, for example, Blaug (1996) and Feldman (1987).

11 Equilibrium analysis also functions as a system of social order for some economists; society as well as the economy reaches a harmonious state of order through the operation of self-interested individuals (Clark 1989; Rosenberg, 1992, 215–21). While individuals following their own interest will lead to this order, the pleading of interest groups, and the actions of government, tend to lead to its subversion (Hayek 1979, 90–97).

12 Recent research in economics, such as New Institutional economics surveyed here, has also questioned the traditional neoclassical theory of the firm (Borland and Garvey 1994).

13 This focus on the 'supply-side' should be distinguished from the 'supply-sider' economists associated with the early days of the Reagan regime. These supply-siders focused on the effect of monetary incentives—high tax rates and welfare payments are seen to discourage savings, investment and work (seeking and effort) (Goldfinch 1997). While supply-sider economics is inherent to some extent in neoclassical economics, the more extreme claims of the supply-siders—such as that cutting taxes will lead to greater government revenue—are sometimes disavowed by mainstream economists. Supply-sider economics puts far greater emphasis on the speed and extent of adjustment (in terms of savings and fiscal outcomes, and effects on outcome) to lower marginal tax rates and to a smaller government sector (Fieldstein 1986).

14 Fiscal policy is concerned with government revenue and spending, while monetary policy focuses on the control of the money supply, including such things as the availability and price of credit.

15 Friedman sees the natural rate of employment as the

> rate of employment which is consist-

ent with the existing real conditions in the labor market. It can be lowered by removing obstacles in the labor market, by reducing friction (cited Ekelund and Hebert 1990, 548).

16 This assumes that there are voluntary unemployed who refuse to work if wages fall too far (that is, there are not involuntary unemployed who are willing to work at the going wage rate but are unable to find a job) and that the economy is in long run equilibrium.

17 Hoover (1988, 13–14) defines New Classical economics thus:

First, agents' real economic decisions—for example, about savings, consumption or investment—are based solely on real, not nominal or monetary, factors. Second, agents are, to the limits of their information, consistent and successful optimizers, that is, they are continuously in equilibrium. Third, agents make no systematic errors in evaluating the economic environment, that is, they hold rational expectations.

New Classical economics is now largely seen as highly empirically challenged, if not discredited (Bertram 1997; Blaug 1996; Peters 1987).

Appendix Three

1 Purchasing Power Parities (PPPs) are the rate of currency conversion, which removes the differences in price levels across countries. PPPs are obtained by comparing the costs of a basket of goods and services between countries for components of GDP.

Bibliography

Aberbach, Joel D. 1998. 'Sharing Isn't Easy: When Separate Institutions Clash.' *Governance* 11(2):137–152.

ACTU/TDC. 1987. *Australia Reconstructed. ACTU/TDC Mission to Western Europe. A Report by the Mission Members to the ACTU and the TDC.* Canberra: Australian Government Publishing Service.

Alexander, Malcolm. 1994. 'Business Power in Australia: The Concentration of Company Directorship Holding Among the Top 250 Corporates.' *Australian Journal of Political Science* 29: 40–61.

———. 1998. 'Big business and directorships networks: the centralisation of economic power in Australia.' *Journal of Sociology* 34(2): 107–22.

Althaus, Catherine. 1997. 'The Application of Agency Theory to Public Sector Management.' In *The New Contractualism?*, eds. Glyn Davis, et al. South Melbourne: McMillan Education.

Anthony, Stephen. 1993. 'Industry Policy and the ACTU: Divisions Between Theory, Formal Policy and Practise.' *The Journal of Australian Political Economy* July (31): 41–56.

Armitage, Catherine. 1996. 'ANU and Government.' *The Australian* 31 July: 18–9.

Atkinson, Michale, and William Coleman. 1992. 'Policy Networks, Policy Communities and the Problems of Governance.' *Governance* 5(2): 154–180.

Australian, The. 1984. *The Australian* 15 November: 2.

Australian Council of Trade Unions (ACTU). 1997. 'ACTU National Voice: Australian Trade Unions—Background Paper.' At web site: http//www.actu.asn.au/national/about/history/.

Balfour, James. 1993. 'Partial privatisation of the Commonwealth Bank.' In *Privatisation: The Financial Implications*, eds. Kevin Davis and Ian Harper. St Leonards: Allen & Unwin.

Bascand, A., and N. Humphries. 1988. 'The Post-Crash Economic Outlook.' *Reserve Bank Bulletin* 51(1): 5–10.

Baumol, W. J., and W. D. Willig. 1986. 'Contestability: Developments since the Book.' *Strategic Behaviour and Industrial Competition (Oxford Economic Papers)*. Oxford: Clarendon Press.

Beckett, Ian 1994. 'Microeconomic Reform and the Transport Communications Portfolio.' In *From Hawke to Keating. Australian Commonwealth Administration 1990–93*, ed. Jenny Stewart. Canberra: Centre for Research in Public Sector Management, University of Canberra & Royal Institute of Public Administration Australia.

Bell, Stephen. 1993. 'Weak on the State: Economic Rationalism in Canberra.' *Australian and New Zealand Journal of Sociology* 29(3): 389-401.

———. 1995. 'The Collective Capitalism of Northeast Asia and the Limits of Orthodox Economics.' *Australian Journal of Political Science* 30(2): 64–87.

———. 1997. 'Globalisation, Neoliberalism and the Transformation of the Australian State.' *Australian Journal of Political Science* 32(3): 345–68.

Bergmann, B. 1989. 'Why Do Economists Know So Little about the Economy?' In *Unconventional Wisdom: essays on economics in honour of John Kenneth Galbraith*, eds. Samuel Bowles, Richard Edwards and William G. Shepherd. Boston: Houghton Mifflin.

Bertram, Geoff. 1993. 'Keynesianism, Neoclassicism and the State.' In *State and Economy in New Zealand*, eds. B. Roper and C. Rudd. Auckland: Oxford University Press.

———. 1997. 'Macroeconomic Debate and Economic Growth in Post-War New Zealand.' In *The Political Economy of New Zealand*, eds. C. Rudd and B.

Roper. Auckland: Oxford University Press.

Blaug, M. 1985. *Economic Theory in Retrospect.* Fourth Edition. Cambridge: Cambridge University Press.

_____. 1996. *Economic Theory in Retrospect.* Fifth Edition. Cambridge: Cambridge University Press.

Blyth, Conrad. 1987. 'The Economist's Perspective of Economic Liberalisation.' In *Economic Liberalisation in New Zealand,* eds. A. Bollard and R. Buckle. Wellington: Allen & Unwin and Port Nicholson Press.

Boehm, E. A. 1993. *Twentieth Century Economic Development in Australia.* Third Edition. Melbourne: Longman Chesire.

Boix, Carles. 1998. *Political Parties, Growth and Equality.* Cambridge: Cambridge University Press.

Bolger, J., R. Richardson. and W. Birch. 1990. *Economic and Social Initiative—December 1990.* Wellington: New Zealand Government.

Bollard, Alan, ed. 1988. *The Influence of United States Economics on New Zealand.* Wellington: NZ–US Educational Foundation and NZIER.

Bollard, Allan. 1994. 'New Zealand.' In *The Political Economy of Policy Reform,* ed. John Williamson. Washington DC: Institute for International Economics.

Bollard, Allan, and Robert Buckle, eds. 1987. *Economic Liberalisation in New Zealand.* Wellington and Sydney: Allen & Unwin and Port Nicholson Press.

Bollard, Allan, R. Lattimore, and B. Silverstone. 1996. Introduction to *A Study of Economic Reform: The Case of New Zealand.* Amsterdam: Elsvier.

Bollard, Allan, and David Mayes. 1993. 'Corporatization and Privatization in New Zealand.' In *The Political Economy of Privatization,* eds. Thomas Clarke and Christos Pitelis. London and New York: Routledge.

Borland, Jeff, and Gerald Garvey. 1994. 'Recent Developments in the Theory of the Firm.' *The Australian Economic Review* 1st Quarter: 60–82.

Boston, J. 1989. 'The Treasury and the Organization of Economic Advice: Some International Comparisons.' In *The Making of Rogernomics,* ed. B. Easton. Auckland: Auckland University Press.

_____. 1990. 'The Cabinet and Policy Making under the Fourth Labour Government.' In *The Fourth Labour Government.* Second Edition. eds. M. Holland and J. Boston. Auckland: Oxford University Press.

_____. 1991a. 'Reorganizing the Machinery of Government in New Zealand: Objectives and Outcomes.' In *Reshaping the State: New Zealand's Bureaucratic Revolution,* eds. J. Boston, et al. Auckland: Oxford University Press.

_____. 1991b. 'Economic Strategies.' In *The 1990 General Election: Perspectives on Political Change in New Zealand. Occasional Publication No 3.* Wellington: Department of Politics, Victoria University of Wellington.

_____. 1993. 'Decision-Making and the Budgetary Process in New Zealand.' In *Decision Making in New Zealand Government,* eds. J. R. Nethercote, et al. Canberra: Federalism Research Centre.

_____. 1994. 'Grand Designs and Unpleasant Realities: the Fate of the National Government's Proposals for the Integrated Targeting of Social Assistance.' *Political Science* 46(1): 1–21.

Boston, J., and F. Cooper. 1989. 'The Treasury: Advice, Coordination and Control.' In *New Zealand Politics in Perspective.* Second Edition. Ed. H. Gold. Auckland: Longman Paul.

Boston, J., John Martin, June Pallot, and Pat Walsh. 1996. *Public Management: the New Zealand Model.* Auckland: Oxford University Press.

Botsman, Peter. 1988. 'The Capital Funding of Public Enterprises. A Summary of the Evatt Report.' *Canberra Bulletin of Public Administration* 55(June): 125–8.

Bramble, Tom and Sarah Heal. 1997. 'Trade Unions.' In *The Political Economy of New Zealand,* eds. C. Rudd and B. Roper. Auckland: Oxford University Press.

Brash, D. 1989. '1989 Annual Report—Governor's Statement.' *Reserve Bank Bulletin* 52(3): 188.

Brockett, Matthew. 1999. '$61m goes to consultants.' *The Press,* 6 October: 6.

Brook, Penelope. 1989. ' Reform of the Labour Market.' In *Rogernomics: Reshaping New Zealand's Economy,* ed. Simon Walker. Wellington: New Zealand Centre for Independent Studies.

———. 1990. *Freedom at Work.* Auckland: Oxford University Press.

Bryson, Lois. 1994. 'The welfare state and economic adjustment.' In *State, Economy and Public Policy in Australia,* eds. S. Bell and B. Head. Melbourne: Oxford University Press.

Buchanan, J., and G. Tullock. 1984. 'An American Perspective: From "Markets Work" to "Public Choice".' In *The Emerging Consensus.* Second Edition. Ed. A. Seldon. London: Macmillan.

Burton, Michael. 1984. 'Elites and Collective Protest.' *The Sociological Quarterly* 25 (Winter): 45–66.

———. and John Higley. 1987. 'Elite Settlements.' *American Sociological Review* 52 (June): 295–307.

Business Council of Australia. 1987. 'Towards an Enterprise Based Industrial Relations System.' *Business Council Bulletin* March 32: 6–10.

Cabinet Office (NZ). 1991. *Cabinet Office Manual.* Wellington: Cabinet Office.

Cammack, Paul. 1990. 'A Critical Assessment of the New Elite Paradigm.' *American Sociological Review* 55(June): 415–20.

Campbell, S. J., Colin and John Halligan. 1992. *Political Leadership in an Age of Constraint: Bureaucratic Politics under Hawke and Keating.* St Leonards, NSW: Allen & Unwin.

Capling, Ann, and Brian Galligan. 1992. *Beyond the Protective State.* Melbourne: Cambridge University Press.

Casper, Steven, and Sigurt Vitols. 1997. 'Special Issue: The German Model in the 1990s.' *Industry and Innovation* 4(1): 1–115.

Castles, Francis. 1985. *The Working Class and Welfare.* Sydney: Allen & Unwin.

Castles, Francis, R. Gerritsen, and J. Vowles, eds. 1996. *The Great Experiment: Labour Parties and Public Policy Transformation in Australia and New Zealand.* Auckland: Allen & Unwin.

Chapman, Bruce. 1996. 'The Study of Economics and Direct Involvement in Policy: The Case of the Higher Education Contribution Scheme.' Paper delivered to the Eighth Annual PhD Economics Conference, Canberra, ACT.

Chatterjee, Srikanta, Peter Conway, Paul Dalziel, Chris Eichaum, Peter Harris, Bryan Philpott, and Richard Shaw. 1999. *The New Politics: a Third Way for New Zealand.* Palmerston North: Dunmore Press.

Choat, D. 1993. 'Where Do They Get Their Ideas? Treasury, the Reserve Bank and the International Economics Community.' Paper presented to the Annual Conference of the New Zealand Political Science Association, Christchurch, August.

Clark, C. 1989. 'Equilibrium for What? Reflections on Social Order in Economics.' *Journal of Economic Issues* 23(2): 597–606.

Coase, R. H. 1937. 'The Nature of the Firm.' *Economica* 4: 386–405.

Codd, Michael. 1990. 'Cabinet Operations of the Australian Government.' In *The Cabinet & Budget Processes,* eds. Brian Galligan, et al. Canberra: Centre for Research on Federal Financial Relations.

Committee of Inquiry into the Australian Financial System. 1981. *Final Report of the Committee of Inquiry.* Canberra: Australian Government Publishing Service.

Commonwealth of Australia. 1983. *Cabinet Handbook.* Canberra: Australian Government Publishing Service.

———. 1986a. *Commonwealth Government Directory. FOI Statements. Treasurer's Portfolio.* Vol. 2. Canberra: Australian Government Publishing Service.

———. 1986b. *Commonwealth Government Directory. FOI Statements. Finance Portfolio.* Vol. 2. Canberra: Australian Government Publishing Service.

_____. 1991. *Cabinet Handbook*. Canberra: Australian Government Publishing Service.

_____. 1993. *Commonwealth Government Directory*. Canberra: Commonwealth of Australia.

_____. 1994. *Commonwealth Government Directory. March–May*. Canberra: Commonwealth of Australia.

Commonwealth-State Relations Secretariat. 1998. 'Commonwealth-State Relations Secretariat.' At web site: http://www.dpmc.gov.au/cover.html.

Compact Working Party. 1989. 'Report of the Compact Working Party on Consultative Mechanisms for Economic and Social Policy.' 18 September.

Cronin, Bruce. 1997. 'The Decline of the Business Roundtable'. Paper presented to the NZPSA Annual Conference, University of Waikato, June.

Cullinane, Tim. 1995. 'The Business Roundtable in 1995.' Speech to the Spectrum Club, Rotorua, 12 June.

Dabscheck, Braham. 1990. 'The BCA's Plan to Americanise Australian Industrial Relations.' *Journal of Australian Political Economy* 27: 1–14.

Dahl, R. 1958. 'A Critique of the Ruling Elite Model.' *American Political Science Review* 52 (June): 463–9.

Dalziel, Paul. 1989. ' The Economic Summit: What People Were Thinking.' In *The Making of Rogernomics*, ed. B. Easton. Auckland: Auckland University Press.

_____. 1993. 'The Reserve Bank Act.' In *State and Economy in New Zealand*, eds. B. Roper and C. Rudd. Auckland: Oxford University Press.

_____. 1994. 'A Decade of Radical Economic Reform in New Zealand.' *British Review of New Zealand Studies* 7: 49–72.

_____. 1999a. ' Third Way': What Might This Mean in New Zealand? In *The New Politics: A Third Way for New Zealand* eds S. Chatterjee, et al. Palmerston North: Dunmore Press.

_____. 1999b. 'Evaluating New Zealand's Economic Reforms: an Economist's Per-

spective.' Paper delivered to the Department of Political Science Seminar Series, University of Canterbury, 8 September.

Davis, G. 1997. 'The core executive.' In *New Developments in Australian Politics*, eds. Brian Galligan, Ian McAllister and John Ravenhill. South Melbourne: Macmillan.

Davis, G., J. Wanna, J. Warhurst, and P. Weller. 1993. *Public Policy in Australia*. St Leonards: Allen & Unwin.

Dawkins, John. 1994. *Corporate Public Affairs Oration. Business-Government Relations: a decade of economic reform and the role of business*. Melbourne: The Centre for Corporate Public Affairs.

Deane, R. 1986. 'Financial Sector Policy Reform.' In *Financial Policy Reform*, ed. Reserve Bank of New Zealand. Wellington: Reserve Bank of New Zealand.

_____. 1989. 'Reforming the Public Sector.' In *Rogernomics Reshaping New Zealand's Economy*, ed. Simon Walker. Wellington: New Zealand Centre for Independent Studies.

_____. 1994. 'People, Power and Politics: The Dynamics of Economic Change.' Address upon the Inaugural Award of the NZIER/Qantas Economic Award.

Deane, R, P. Nicholl and R. Smith. 1983. *Monetary Policy and the New Zealand Financial System*. Wellington: Reserve Bank Of New Zealand.

Deeks, J., J. Parker and R. Ryan. 1994. *Labour and Employment Relations in New Zealand* Second Edition. Auckland: Longman Paul.

Department of Prime Minister and Cabinet (DPMC (Australia)). 1990. *Annual Report 1989–90*. Canberra: Department of Prime Minister and Cabinet.

_____. 1998. *Annual Report 1997–98*. Canberra: Australian Government Publishing Service.

Department of Prime Minister and Cabinet (DPMC (NZ)). 1998. 'Introduction to the department.' At web site: http://www.dpmc.govt.nz/intro/index.html.

Derry, Stephen, David Plowman and Janet Walsh. 1995. *Industrial Relations: A Contemporary Analysis*. Sydney: McGraw-Hill.

Digeser, Peter. 1992. 'The Fourth Face of Power.' *Journal of Politics* 54(4): 977–1007.

Domhoff, G. William. 1990. *The Power Elite and the State: How Policy is made in America*. New York: Aldine De Gruyter.

Dornbush, R. 1990. 'The New Classical Macroeconomics and Stabilization Policy.' *American Economic Review* 80(2): 143–7.

Douglas, Roger. 1984. *Budget 1984 Part I: Speech and Annex*. Wellington: Government Printer.

_____. 1990. 'The Politics of Successful Structural Reform.' *Policy* Autumn: 2–6.

_____. 1993. *Unfinished Business*. Auckland: Random House.

Dugger, W. 1989. 'Instituted Process and Enabling Myth: The Two Faces of the Market.' *Journal of Economic Issues* XXIII(2): 607–15.

Dunbar, Jane. 1998. 'Trans-tasman trade's core in apple-pie order.' *The Australian* April 22.

Dye, Thomas. 1990. *Who's Running America? The Bush Era*. Englewood Cliffs, New Jersey: Prentice Hall.

Easton, Brian. 1989a. 'From Run to Float: The Making of the Rogernomics Exchange Rate Policy.' In *The Making of Rogernomics*, ed. B. Easton. Auckland: Auckland University Press.

_____. 1989b. 'The Commercialisation of the New Zealand Economy: From Think Big to Privatization.' In *The Making of Rogernomics*, ed. B. Easton. Auckland: Auckland University Press.

_____. 1994. 'Royal Commissions as Policy Creators: The New Zealand Experience.' In *Royal Commissions and the Making of Public Policy*, ed. Patrick Weller. Brisbane: Macmillan.

_____. 1996. 'Income Distribution.' In *A Study of Economic Reform: The Case of New Zealand*, eds. Brian Silverstone et al. Amsterdam: Elsvier.

_____. 1997a. *In Stormy Seas*. Dunedin: University Otago Press.

_____. 1997b. *The Commercialisation of New Zealand*. Auckland: Auckland University Press.

Easton, Brian, and R. Gerritson. 1996. 'Economic Reform: Parallels and Divergences.' In *The Great Experiment: Labour Parties and Public Policy Transformation in Australia and New Zealand*, eds. F. Castles, et al. Auckland: Allen and Unwin and Auckland University Press.

Ebbinghaus, Bernhard, and Anke Hassel. 2000. 'Striking deals: concertation in the reform of continental European welfare states.' *Journal of European Public Policy* 7(1): 44–62.

Economic Monitoring Group to the New Zealand Planning Council (EMG). 1979. *New Zealand's Economic Trends and Policies. Report No 2*. Wellington: New Zealand Planning Council.

_____. 1981. *New Zealand's Economic Trends and Policies. Report No 4*. Wellington: New Zealand Planning Council.

_____. 1982. *New Zealand's Economic Trends and Policies. Report No 5*. Wellington: New Zealand Planning Council.

Economist, The. 1996. 'Economic Freedom.' *The Economist* (13 January): 19–21.

_____. 1999. 'Business This Week.' *The Economist* (4 December): 25.

Edwards, John. 1996. *Keating: The Inside Story*. Ringwood, Victoria: Penguin Books.

Egeberg, M. 1995. 'Bureaucrats as Public Policy Makers and their Self-Interest.' *Theoretical Politics* 7(2): 157–67.

Ekelund, Robert B., and Robert F. Hebert 1990. *A History of Economic Theory and Method*. Third Edition. New York: McGraw-Hill.

Ellercamp, Paul. 1984a. 'Peacock uses gains tax as ALP bludgeon.' *The Australian* October 16: 1.

_____. 1984b. 'Tax summit move to kill capital gains as issue.' *The Weekend Australian* October 20-21: 1.

_____. 1984c. 'PM sets the scene for unfettered tax review.' *The Australian* November 1: 3.

Employer Relations Study Commission. 1989. *Enterprise-based Bargaining Units: A Better Way of Working*. Melbourne: Business Council of Australia.

EPAC/Cooper&Lybrand. 1994. 'External Review of EPAC Reports.'

Evans, Lewis, Arthur Grimes, Bryce Wilkinson, with David Teece. 1996. 'Economic Reform in New Zealand 1984–95: The Pursuit of Efficiency.' *Journal of Economic Literature* XXXIV(December): 1856–902.

Federated Farmers. 1984. 'Agriculture—The Anchor of the Economy.' Federated Farmers: Wellington.

Feldman, Alan. 1987. 'Welfare Economics.' In *The New Palgrave. A Dictionary of Economics*, eds. J. Eatwell, M. Milgate and P. Newman. London and Basingstoke: MacMillan Press.

Firth, M. 1987. 'Multiple Directorships and Corporate Interlocks in New Zealand.' *Australian and New Zealand Journal of Sociology* 23(2): 274–81.

Fox, Carol B., William Howard and Marilyn J. Pittard. 1995. *Industrial Relations in Australia: Development, Law and Operation.* Melbourne: Longman.

Fraser, B. 1993. 'Some Aspects of Monetary Policy.' *Reserve Bank of Australia Bulletin* April: 32–7.

_____. 1994. 'The Art of Monetary Policy.' *Reserve Bank of Australia Bulletin* October: 17–25.

Freedman, Craig, and Robin Stonecash. 1997. 'A Survey of Manufacturing Industry Policy: From the Tariff Board to the Productivity Commission.' *The Economic Record* 73(221): 169–83.

Friedman, M., and R. Friedman 1980. *Free To Choose.* London: Secker and Warburg.

Galligan, B. 1995. *A Federal Republic: Australia's Constitutional System of Government.* Cambridge and Melbourne: Cambridge University Press.

Galvin, B. 1985. ' Some Reflections on the Operation of the Executive.' In *New Zealand Politics in Perspective.* First Edition. Ed. H. Gold. Auckland: Longman Paul.

_____. 1991. *Policy Co-ordination, Public Sector and Government.* Wellington: Institute of Policy Studies.

Gardner, W. J. 1992. ' A Colonial Economy.' In *The Oxford History of New Zealand*, ed. G. W. Rice. Auckland: Oxford University Press.

Garnaut, Ross. 1994a. ' Australia.' In *The Political Economy of Policy Reform*, ed. John Williamson. Washington DC: Institute for International Economics.

_____. 1994b. 'The Floating Dollar and the Australian Structural Transition: Some Asia Pacific Context.' *The Economic Record* 70(208): 80–96.

Gerritsen, Rolf, and Gwynneth Singleton. 1991. 'Evaluating the Hawke Government's Industry Agenda: Democratic Economic Planning Versus Economic Rationalism?' In *Business and Government Under Labor*, eds. Brian Galligan and Gwynneth Singleton. Melbourne: Longman Chesire.

Gittins, Ross. 1995. 'The Role of the Media in the Formulation of Economic Policy.' *The Australian Economic Review* 4th Quarter: 5–14.

Gleber, Frank. 1998. 'Tackling the Current Account Deficit.' In *Manufacturing Prosperity*, eds. Rodin Genoff and Roy Green. Annandale: Federation Press.

Goldfinch, Shaun. 1997. 'Treasury and Public Policy Formation.' In *The Political Economy of New Zealand*, eds. B. Roper and C. Rudd. Auckland: Oxford University Press.

_____. 1998. 'Evaluating Public Sector Reform in New Zealand: Have the Benefits Been Oversold?' *Asian Journal of Public Administration* 20(2): 203–32.

_____. 2000. 'The Old Boys' Network? Social Ties and Policy Consensus amongst Australian and New Zealand Policy Elites.' Paper delivered to the Public Policy Network Conference, Griffith University, Brisbane, February.

Goldfinch, Shaun, and M. Perry. 1997. 'Promoting Business Networks.' *New Zealand Geographer* 53(1): 41–6.

Goodin, Robert E., Bruce Headey, Ruud Muffels and Henk-Jan Dirven. 1999. *The Real Worlds of Welfare Capitalism.* Cambridge: Cambridge University Press.

Gould, J. 1982. *The Rake's Progress? The New Zealand Economy Since 1945.* Auckland: Hodder and Stoughton.

Grace, Gerald. 1990. 'Labour and Education: The Crisis and Settlements of Education Policy.' In *The Fourth Labour Government*. Second Edition. Eds. M. Holland and J. Boston. Auckland: Oxford University Press.

Green, D. 1987. *The New Right: The Counter Revolution in Political, Economic and Social Thought*. Sussex: Wheatsheaf Books.

Griffin, K. 1988/89. 'Monetarism.' *JBA* 18(1/2): 67–109.

Gruen, Fred, and Michelle Grattan. 1993. *Managing Government. Labor's Achievements & Failures*. Melbourne: Longman Chesire.

Hahn, F. 1984. *Equilibrium and Macroeconomics*. Oxford: Basil Blackwell.

Hall, Peter. 1993. 'Policy Paradigms, Social Learning and the State.' *Comparative Politics* 25(3): 275–96.

Harcourt, Tim. 1994. 'All You Wanted to Know About the ACTU But Were Afraid to Ask.' Speech to International Students. Victorian University of Technology, Thursday 2 June.

Harding, Ann. 1997. 'The Suffering Middle: Trends in Income Equality in Australia: 1982 to 1994.' *The Australian Economic Review* 30(4): 341–58.

Harman, Elizabeth. 1996. 'The National Competition Policy: A Study of the Policy Process and Network.' *Australian Journal of Political Science* 31(2): 205–23.

Harris, Paul. 1995. '"Intimacy" in New Zealand Politics: A Sceptical Analysis.' *Political Science* 47(1): 1–33.

Hausman, Daniel. 1992. *The inexact and separate science of economics*. Cambridge and New York: Cambridge University Press.

Hawke, Bob. 1984. *National Reconciliation: the Speeches of Bob Hawke*. Sydney: Fontana.

———. 1994. *The Hawke Memoirs*. Port Melbourne: William Heinemann.

Hawke, Gary. 1985. *The Making of New Zealand: An Economic History*. Cambridge: Cambridge University Press.

———. 1988. *Report of the Working Group on Post Compulsory Education and Training, 1988.* Wellington: Office of the Associate Minister of Education.

———. 1992. 'Economic Trends and Economic Policy, 1938–92'. In *The Oxford History of New Zealand*. Second Edition. Ed. G. W. Rice. Auckland: Oxford University Press.

Hayek, F. 1979. *Law, Legislation and Liberty*. Volume 3. *The Political Order of a Free People*. London and Henley: Routledge and Kegan Paul.

———. 1982. 'The Use of Knowledge in Society.' In *The Libertarian Reader*, ed. T. Machan. New Jersey: Rowman and Littlefield.

Hazledine, Tim. 1993. 'New Zealand Trade Patterns and Policy.' *The Australian Economic Review* 4th Quarter: 23–7.

———. 1998. *Taking New Zealand Seriously*. Auckland: Harper Collins.

Headey, Bruce, and Denis Muller. 1996. 'Policy agendas of the Poor, the Public and Elites: A Test of Bachrach and Baratz.' *Australian Journal of Political Science* 31(3): 347–67.

Heap, S. 1989. *Rationality in Economics*. Oxford: Basil Blackwell.

Henderson, David. 1995. 'The Revival of Economic Liberalism: Australia in an International Perspective.' *The Australian Economic Review* 1st Quarter: 59–85.

Henderson, John. 1997. ' The Prime Minister.' In *New Zealand Politics in Transition*, ed. Raymond Miller. Auckland: Oxford University Press.

Higgins, Christopher, and David Borthwick. 1990. 'The Role of Central Agencies.' In *The Cabinet & Budget Processes*, eds. Brian Galligan, et al. Canberra: Centre for Research on Federal Financial Relations.

Higley, John, Ursula Hoffman-Lange, Charles Kadushin, and Gwen Moore. 1991. 'Elite integration in stable democracies: a reconsideration.' *European Sociological Review* 7(1): 35–53.

Hilmer, F., P. McLaughlin, D. Macfarlane, and J. Rose. 1991. *Avoiding Industrial Action: A Better Way of Working*. Melbourne: Allen & Unwin and the Business Council of Australia.

Hinnfors, Jonas, and Jon Pierre. 1998. 'The Politics of Currency Choice: Policy Choice in a Globablised Economy.' *West European Politics* 21(3): 103–19.

Hirst, Paul, and Grahame Thompson. 1996. *Globalization in Question.* Cambridge: Polity Press.

Hoover, Kevin. 1988. *The New Classical Macroeconomics: A Sceptical Inquiry.* Oxford: Basil Blackwell.

Horn, Murray J. 1995. *The Political Economy of Public Administration.* Cambridge and New York: Cambridge University Press.

Hosseini, H. 1990. 'The Archaic, the Obselete and the Mythical in Neoclassical Economics: Problems with Rationality and Optimizing Assumptions of the Jevons-Marshallian System.' *American Journal of Economics and Sociology* 49(1): 81–92.

Hubbard, A. 1992. 'The Players.' *New Zealand Listener* 5: 14–6.

Industrial Relations Commission. 1996. 'Industrial Relations Commission.' At web site: http://www.agd.nsw.gov.au/industri.html.

Industry Commission. 1990. *Annual Report 1989–90.* Canberra: Australian Government Publishing Service.

Jaensch, Dean. 1994. *Power Politics. Australia's Party System.* St Leonards, NSW: Allen & Unwin.

Jesson, Bruce. 1999. *Only their Purpose is Mad.* Palmerston North: Dunmore Press.

Johnston, R. A. 1989. 'The Reserve Bank's Role in Economic Management.' *Reserve Bank of Australia Bulletin* May: 14–6.

Katouzian, H. 1980. *Ideology and Method in Economics.* New York and London: New York University Press.

Katzenstein, P. 1985. *Small States in World Markets.* Ithaca: Cornell University Press.

Keating, Michael. 1994. 'The Role of Government Economists.' *Canberra Bulletin of Public Administration* December(77): 1–7.

Keating, Michael, and G. Dixon. 1989. *Making Economic Policy in Australia 1983–1988.* Melbourne: Longman Chesire.

Keating, Paul. 1983. *Budget Speech '1983–84'.* Canberra: Australian Government Publishing Service.

_____. 1985. *Budget Speech '1985–86'.* Canberra: Australian Government Publishing Service.

_____. 1992. *One Nation.* Canberra: Australian Government Publishing Service.

Kelly, Paul. 1994. *The End of Certainty.* St Leonards: Allen and Unwin.

Kelsey, Jane. 1995. *Economic Fundamentalism.* London: Pluto Press.

Kerr, Roger. 1994. 'Looking Back Together.' Address to Tasman Institute. Melbourne, November.

Kilroy, Simon. 1991. 'Enterprise Council to balance Treasury advice—Bolger.' *The Dominion* November 12: 2.

King, P. 1997. 'Privatization in Australia: the good, the bad, and the awful.' Paper delivered to Australia–Japan Comparative Economic and Public Sector Restructuring Conference. Centre for Public Policy, University of Melbourne.

King, Stephen P. 1997. 'National Competition Policy.' *The Economic Record* 73(222): 270–84.

Klinkum, Grant. 1999. 'The New Zealand Parliamentary Library: A Case Study of an Emerging but Underdeveloped Research Provider for the Legislature.' Paper Delivered to New Zealand Political Studies Association, Annual Conference, Wellington, 1–3 December.

Langmore, John. 1988. 'Treasury and the Hawke Government.' *Journal of Australian Political Economy* 22: 69–72.

_____. 1991. ' The Labor Government in a De-Regulatory Era.' In *Business and Government Under Labor*, eds. Brian Galligan and Gwynneth Singleton. Melbourne: Longman Chesire.

Le Heron, Richard, and Eric Pawson, eds. 1996. *Changing Places. New Zealand in the Nineties.* Auckland: Longman Paul.

Lim, G. C. 1984. 'The Martin Report.' *The Australian Economic Review* 2nd Quarter: 26–34.

Lindblom, C. 1977. *Politics and Markets.* New York: Basic Books.

Lissington, P. 1987. 'The 1984 Devaluation

and Inquiry.' New Zealand Treasury: Unpublished report prepared for the New Zealand Treasury.

Low, A. 1970. 'Indicative Planning—The New Zealand Experience.' in *Proceedings of the Conference of Australian and New Zealand Economists*, Part 2, May.

Lukes, Steven. 1974. *Power: A Radical View.* London and Basingstoke: MacMillan.

Lutz, Susanne. 1998. 'The revival of the nation-state? Stock exchange regulation in an era of globalized financial markets.' *Journal of European Public Policy* 5(1): 153–68.

McCann, E. 1988. 'US Theories of Monetary and Fiscal Policy.' In *The Influence of United States Economics on New Zealand*, ed. Alan Bollard. Wellington: NZ–US Educational Foundation, New Zealand Institute of Economic Research.

McCarthy, Gregory, and David Taylor. 1995. 'The Politics of the Float: Paul Keating and the Deregulation of the Australian Exchange Rate.' *Australian Journal of Politics and History* 41(2): 219–38.

McEachern, Doug. 1991. 'Taking Care of Business: The Hawke Government and the Political Management of Business.' In *Business and Government Under Labor*, eds. Brian Galligan and Gwynneth Singleton. Melbourne: Longman Chesire.

Macfarlane, I. J. 1996. 'Making Monetary Policy: Perceptions and Reality.' *Reserve Bank of Australia Bulletin* October: 32–7.

_____. 1997. 'Monetary Policy Regimes: Past and Future.' *Reserve Bank of Australia Bulletin* October: 32–7.

McLaughlin, P. A. 1991. 'How Business Relates to the Hawke Government: The Captains of Industry.' In *Business and Government Under Labor*, eds. Brian Galligan and Gwynneth Singleton. Melbourne: Longman Chesire.

McLeay, Elizabeth. 1995. *The Cabinet & Political Power in New Zealand.* Auckland: Oxford University Press.

McLennan, Gregor. 1995. *Pluralism.* Buckingham: Open University Press.

McQueen, H. 1991. *The Ninth Floor.* Auckland: Penguin.

Maddox, Graham. 1989. *The Hawke Gov-*

ernment and Labor Tradition. Ringwood, Victoria: Penguin.

Maloney, William, Grant Jordan and Andrew McLaughlin. 1994. 'Interest Groups and Public Policy: the Insider/Outsider Model Revisited.' *Journal of Public Policy* 14(1): 17–38.

March, James, and Johan Olsen. 1983. 'The New Institutionalism: Organizational Factors in Political Life.' *American Political Science Review* 78: 734–49.

Marsden, Peter, and Noah Friedkin. 1993. 'Network Studies of Social Influence.' *Sociological Method & Research* 22(1): 127–51.

Marsh, I. 1991. *Globalisation and Australian Think Tanks.* Committee for Economic Development of Australia.

Marshall, John. 1983. *Memoirs. Volume 1. 1912 to 1960.* Auckland: Collins.

Mathews, Russell, and Bhajan Grewel. 1997. *The Public Sector in Jeopardy.* Melbourne: Centre for Strategic Economic Studies, Victoria University.

Matthews, Trevor. 1994. ' Employers' Associations, Corporatism and the Accord: The Politics of industrial relations.' In *State, Economy and Public Policy in Australia*, eds. S. Bell and B. Head. Melbourne: Oxford University Press.

Mills, C. Wright. 1956. *The Power Elite.* New York: Oxford University Press.

Moriarty, M. 1945. 'Administering the Policy of Economic Stabilization.' *New Zealand Journal of Public Administration* 7(2): 27–37.

_____. 1956. 'Making Economic Policy in New Zealand.' *The Economic Record* 7(2): 224–38.

Mulgan, Richard. 1992. ' The Elective Dictatorship in New Zealand.' In *New Zealand Politics in Perspective.* Third Edition. Ed. H. Gold. Auckland: Longman Paul.

_____. 1996. 'The Australian Senate as a House of Review.' *Australian Journal of Political Science* 31(2): 191–204.

_____. 1997a. 'Restructuring—the New Zealand Experience.' *Discussion Papers in Economics and Business.* Faculty of Economics and Osaka School of International Public Policy (Discussion Paper 97–10).

_____. 1997b. 'State and Democracy in New Zealand.' In *The Political Economy of New Zealand*, eds. C. Rudd and B. Roper. Auckland: Oxford University Press.

Munkirs, J. R. 1989. 'Economic Power: A Micro-Macro Nexus.' *Journal of Economic Issues* XXIII(2): 617–23.

Murray, Georgina, Jacques Bierling and Malcom Alexander. 1995. 'The Rich Countries: Australia, New Zealand and Japan.' *Current Sociology* 43(1): 1–10.

Murrell, Peter. 1995. 'The Transition According to Cambridge, Mass.' *Journal of Economic Literature* 33(1): 164–78.

Myers, Doug. 1998. 'New Zealand is Dangerously Close to the Rocks Again.' *The Press* December 16: 9.

Nagel, Jack H. 1998. 'Social Choice in a Pluralitarian Democracy: The Politics of Market Liberalization in New Zealand.' *The British Journal of Political Science* 28(2): 223–67.

National Party. 1990. *National's Economic Vision*. Wellington: New Zealand National Party.

Nelson, J. 1993. 'Value-Free or Valueless? Notes on the Pursuit of Detachment in Economics.' *History of Political Economy* 25 (1): 121–45.

New Zealand Council of Trade Unions (NZCTU). 1998. 'About the NZCTU.' At web site: http://www.union.org.nz/about.html.

NZ Government. 1985a. *Industrial Relations: A Framework for Review*. Vol. 1. Wellington: Government Printer.

_____. 1985b. *Industrial Relations: A Framework for Review*. Vol. 2. Wellington: Government Printer.

_____. 1986a. *Industrial Relations A Framework for Review—Summary of Submissions*. Wellington: Government Printer.

_____. 1986b. *Government Policy Statement on Labour Relations*. Wellington: Government Printer.

NZ Planning Council (NZPC). 1989. *The Economy in Transition: Restructuring to 1989*. Wellington: New Zealand Planning Council.

Niskanen, William. 1971. *Representative Government and Bureaucracy*. Chicago: Aldine.

O'Driscoll, Gerald, and Mario Rizzo. 1996. *The Economics of Time and Ignorance*. London and New York: Routledge.

OECD. 1993. *OECD Economic Surveys 1992–1993: New Zealand*. Paris: OECD.

_____. 1994a. *OECD Economic Surveys 1993–1994: Australia*. Paris: OECD.

_____. 1994b. *OECD Economic Surveys 1993–1994: New Zealand*. Paris: OECD.

_____. 1996. *OECD Economic Surveys 1995–1996: New Zealand*. Paris: OECD

_____. 1997a. *OECD Economic Surveys 1996–1997: Australia*. Paris: OECD.

_____. 1997b. *OECD Economic Outlook* 62: (December). Paris: OECD.

_____. 1997c. *Historical Statistics 1960–95*. Paris: OECD.

_____. 1998. *OECD Economic Outlook* 63 (June). Paris: OECD.

_____. 1999a. *OECD Economic Outlook* 65 (June). Paris: OECD.

_____. 1999b. *OECD Economic Outlook* 66 (December) Paris: OECD.

_____. 1999c. 'Puma Statistical Window Index.' At web site: http://www.oecd.org/puma/stats/window.

_____. 1999d. *OECD Statistical Compendium* (CD Rom. Number 2). Paris: OECD

Oliver, W. 1989. 'The Labour Caucus and Economic Policy Formation, 1981–1984.' In *The Making of Rogernomics*, ed. B. Easton. Auckland: Auckland University Press.

Olson, Mancur. 1982. *The Rise and Decline of Nations*. New Haven, CT: Yale University Press.

_____. 1984. 'Australia in the Perspective of the Rise and Decline of Nations.' *The Australian Economic Review* 3rd Quarter: 7–17.

Ormerod, P. 1994. *The Death of Economics*. London and Boston: Faber and Faber.

Ormsby, Maurice J. 1998. 'Country Report. The Purchaser/Provider Split: A Report from New Zealand.' *Governance* 11(3): 357–87.

O'Shaughnessy, Eamonn Paul. 1997. 'Financial Deregulation in New Zealand 1984–90'. A thesis submitted in fulfilment of the degree of Master of Commerce and Administration in Economic History. Victoria University of Wellington: Wellington.

Painter, Martin. 1995. 'Economic Policy, Market Liberalism and the "End of Australian Politics".' *Australian Journal of Political Science* 31(3): 287–99.

Patterson, Ross H. 1996. 'How the Chicago School Hijacked Competition Law and Policy.' *New Zealand Universities Law Review* 17(December): 160–92.

Perry, M. and S. Goldfinch. 1998. ' Developing Business through Networks.' In *Manufacturing Prosperity*, eds. Rodin Genoff and Roy Green. Annandale: Federation Press.

Peters, M. 1987. 'A Dismal Science: An Essay on New Classical Economics.' *De Economist* 135(4): 442–86.

Philpott, Byran. 1999. 'New Zealand Structural Policies: Outcomes for the Last Fifteen Years and New Directions for the Next.' In *The New Politics: A Third Way for New Zealand*, eds. S. Chatterjee et al. Palmerston North: Dunmore Press.

Polsby, Nelson. 1980. *Community Power & Political Theory.* New Haven and London: Yale University Press.

Pontusson, Jonas. 1995. 'From Comparative Public Policy to Political Economy: Putting Political Institutions in Their Place and Taking Interests Seriously.' *Comparative Political Studies* 28(1): 117–47.

Prasser, Scott, and Simon Paton. 1994. 'Advising Government.' In *From Hawke to Keating*, ed. Jenny Stewart. Canberra: Centre for Research in Public Sector Management, University of Canberra & Royal Institute of Public Administration Australia.

Probert, Belinda. 1994. ' Globalisation, Economic Restructuring and the State.' In *State, Economy and Public Policy in Australia*, eds. Stephen Bell and Brian Head. Melbourne: Oxford University Press.

Pusey, Michael. 1991. *Economic Rationalism in Canberra: A Nation Building State Changes its Mind.* Melbourne: Cambridge University Press.

Putnam, Robert, Robert Leonardi and Raffaella Y. Nanetti. 1993. *Making Democracy Work: Civic Traditions in Modern Italy.* Princeton, New Jersey: Princeton University Press.

Quiggan, John. 1995. 'Does Privatisation Pay?' *The Australian Economic Review* 2nd Quarter: 23–42.

Rafferty, Michael. 1997. 'Union Amalgamation: the Enduring Legacy of Australia Reconstructed?' *Journal of Australian Political Economy* June (3): 99–105.

Ravenhill, John. 1994. ' Australia and the Global Economy.' In *State, Economy and Public Policy in Australia*, eds. Stephen Bell and Brian Head. Melbourne: Oxford University Press.

Rayack, E. 1987. *Not so Free to Choose.* New York: Praeger Publishers.

Reder, M. 1982. 'Chicago Economics: Permanence and Change.' *Journal of Economic Literature* 20(1): 1–38.

Redman, A. 1991. *Economics and the Philosophy of Science.* Oxford and New York: Oxford University Press.

Reserve Bank of Australia (RBA). 1985. 'The Reserve Bank's Domestic Market Operations.' *Reserve Bank of Australia Bulletin* June: 1–7.

_____. 1986. 'The Role of the Central Bank.' *Reserve Bank of Australia Bulletin* February: 1–7.

_____. 1987. *Reserve Bank of Australia. Functions and Operations.* Sydney: Reserve Bank of Australia.

_____. 1996. 'Statement on the Conduct of Monetary Policy.' At web site: http://www.rba.gov.au/about/ab_scmp.html.

_____. 1997. 'Privatisation in Australia.' *Reserve Bank of Australia Bulletin* December: 7–16.

Reserve Bank of New Zealand (RBNZ). 1960. 'Central Banking Practise in New Zealand.' *Reserve Bank Bulletin* 23(3): 39–44.

_____. 1983. 'Reserve Bank Annual Report.' *Reserve Bank Bulletin* August: 336–42.

———. 1984a. 'Reserve Bank Annual Report.' *Reserve Bank Bulletin* August: 354–60.

———. 1984b. 'The New Zealand Economy: Six Monthly Review.' *Reserve Bank Bulletin* 47(10): 533.

———. 1984c. *Annual Report*. Wellington: Reserve Bank of New Zealand.

———. 1985a. 'Monetary Policy in New Zealand.' *Reserve Bank Bulletin* 48(6): 293–300.

———. 1985b. 'The Functions of the Reserve Bank.' *Reserve Bank Bulletin* 48(9): 512–8

———. 1985c. 'The Challenge of Change.' *Reserve Bank Bulletin* 48(1): 3–4.

———. 1985d. 'Reserve Bank Annual Report.' *Reserve Bank Bulletin* 48(8): 447–54.

———. 1986. 'Reserve Bank Annual Report.' *Reserve Bank Bulletin* 49(8): 385–92.

———. 1990a. 'Monetary Policy: the New Zealand Experience 1985–1990.' *Reserve Bank Bulletin* 53(3): 252–69.

———. 1990b. 'Reserve Bank of New Zealand Act 1989.' *Reserve Bank Bulletin* 53(1): 29–36.

———. 1990c. 'Reserve Bank of New Zealand Policy Targets Agreement.' *Reserve Bank Bulletin* 53(1): 26–8.

———. 1990d *Annual Report*. Wellington: Reserve Bank of New Zealand.

———. 1992a. 'The New Zealand approach to Central Bank Autonomy.' *Reserve Bank Bulletin* 55(3): 203–20.

———. 1992b. 'Banking Supervision—Defining the Public Sector Role.' *Reserve Bank Bulletin* 55(4): 307–14.

———. 1997. 'This is the Reserve Bank.' At web site: http://www.rbnz.govt.nz/pamphlet/thisis.htm.

Rhodes, R. A. W. 1997. *Understanding Governance: Policy Networks, Governance, Reflexivity and Accountability.* Buckingham and Philidelphia: Open University Press.

Richardson, R. 1990. 'Budget Secret. Memorandum for the Cabinet Strategy Committee. Fiscal Strategy. (Released under the Official Information Act).' Office of the Minister of Finance: Wellington.

———. 1991. *Budget 1991*. Wellington: New Zealand Government.

———. 1995. *Making a Difference*. Christchurch: Shoal Bay Press.

Roberts, John. 1987. 'Ministers, the Cabinet and Public Servants.' In *The Fourth Labour Government*, eds. Jonathan Boston and Martin Holland. Auckland: Oxford University Press.

Roper, Brian. 1992. 'Business Political Activism and the Emergence of the New Right in New Zealand, 1975 to 1987.' *Political Science* 44(2): 1–23.

———. 1993. 'A Level Playing Field? Business Political Activism and State Policy Formation.' In *State and Economy in New Zealand*, eds. B. Roper and C. Rudd. Auckland: Oxford University Press.

———. 1997. 'New Zealand's Postwar Economic History.' In *The Political Economy of New Zealand*, eds. C. Rudd and B. Roper. Auckland: Oxford University Press.

Rosenberg, A. 1992. *Economics—Mathematical Politics or Science of Diminishing Returns*. Chicago: Chicago University Press.

Rudd, C. 1993. 'The New Zealand Welfare State.' In *State and Economy in New Zealand*, eds. B. Roper and C. Rudd. Auckland: Oxford University Press.

———. 1997. 'The Welfare State.' In *The Political Economy of New Zealand*, eds. C. Rudd and B. Roper. Auckland: Oxford University Press.

Russell, Marcia. 1996. *Revolution: New Zealand From Fortress to Free Market*. Auckland: Hodder Moa Beckett.

Ryan, Neal. 1994. 'Ministerial Advisers and Policy Making.' In *From Hawke to Keating*, ed. Jenny Stewart. Canberra: Centre for Research in Public Sector Management, University of Canberra & Royal Institute of Public Administration Australia.

Sabatier, Paul. 1998. 'The advocacy coalition framework: revision and relevance for Europe.' *Journal of European Public Policy* 5(1): 98–130.

Schmitter, Phillipe C., and Jurgen E. Grote.

1997. *The Corporatist Sisyphus: Past, Present and Future. EUI Working Papers SPS No 97/4.* Florence: European University Institute, Department of Political and Social Sciences.

Scobie, Grant, and Steven Lim. 1992. 'Economic Reform: A Global Revolution.' *Policy* Spring: 2–7.

Scott, Graham, Ian Ball and Tony Dale. 1997. 'New Zealand's Public Sector Management Reform: Implications for the United States.' *Journal of Policy Analysis and Management* 16(3): 357–81.

Scott, Graham, and Peter Gorringe. 1989. 'Reform of the Public Sector: The New Zealand Experience.' *Australian of Public Administration* 48(1): 81–92.

Sheppard, Simon. 1999. *Broken Circle: The Decline and Fall Of the Fourth Labour Government.* Wellington: Publishing Solutions Limited.

Shroff, M. 1993. 'The Structure and Operation of the Cabinet in Relation to the Budget.' In *Decision Making in New Zealand Government,* eds. J. Nethercote, et al. Canberra: Federalism Research Centre.

Simkin, C. 1948–9. 'Wartime Changes in the New Zealand Economy.' *Economic Record* 24/25(2): 18–31.

Singleton, Gwynneth. 1985. 'The Economic Planning Advisory Council: The Reality of Consensus.' *Politics* 20(1): 12–25.

———. 1990a. *The Accord and the Australian Labour.* Melbourne: Melbourne University Press.

———. 1990b. 'Corporatism or Labourism: The Australian Labour Movement in Accord.' *Journal of Commonwealth and Comparative Politics* 28(2): 162–82

———. 1995. 'Trial by Westminster: The Fate of Economic Advisory Councils in the United States and Australia.' *Journal of Commonwealth and Comparative Politics* 33(2): 240–56.

Skocpol, T. 1979. *States and Social Revolutions.* Cambridge: Cambridge University Press.

Skogstad, Grace. 1998. 'Ideas, Paradigms and Institutions: Agricultural Exceptionalism in the European Union and the United States.' *Governance: An International Journal of Policy and Administration* 11(4): 463–90.

Smith, James Allen. 1991. *The Idea Brokers.* New York and Toronto: The Free Press.

Snape, Richard. 1997. 'Tariffs, Then and Now.' Lecture delivered on 19 March 1997 in memory of Mr Bert Kelly. Published under the auspices of the Stan Kelly Fund. Victoria: Economic Society of Australia. Victorian Branch.

Spencer, Grant, and David Carey. 1989. 'Financial Policy Reform.' In *Rogernomics Reshaping New Zealand's Economy,* ed. Simon Walker. Wellington: New Zealand Centre for Independent Studies.

Stiglitz, Joseph. 1999. Foreword to *The New Politics: A Third Way for New Zealand,* eds. S. Chatterjee, et al. Palmerston North: Dunmore Press.

Stilwell, Frank. 1991. 'Wages Policy and the Accord.' *Journal of Australian Political Economy* 28: 27–53.

Stone, Diane. 1991. 'Old Guard Versus New Partisans.' *Australian Journal of Political Science* 26(2): 197–215.

Swank, Duane. 1998. 'Funding the Welfare State: Globalization and the Taxation of Business in Advanced Market Economies.' *Political Studies* XLVI: 671–92.

Templeton, Hugh. 1995. *All Honourable Men.* Auckland: Auckland University Press.

Thain, Colin, and Maurice Wright. 1995. *The Treasury and Whitehall.* Clarendon Press: Oxford.

Thompson, Herb. 1992. 'Enterprise Bargaining and the Accord.' *The Journal of Australian Political Economy* 30: 42–60.

Thronthwaite, Louise, and Peter Sheldon. 1996. 'The Metal Trades Industry Association, Bargaining Structures and the Accord.' *Journal of Industrial Relations* 38(2): 171–95.

Tingle, Laura. 1994. *Chasing the Future. Recession, recovery and the new politics in Australia.* Port Melbourne: William Heineman.

Treasury, The Australian. 1998. *The Treasury Annual Report.* Canberra: Australian Government Publishing Service.

Treasury, The New Zealand. 1984a. *Economic Management*. Wellington: Government Printer.

_____. 1984b. 'Budget Report No 1. Indirect Tax Change (Released under the Official Information Act).' Wellington: The Treasury.

_____. 1984c. 'Budget Report No 10. Introducing Value Added Tax (Released under the Official Information Act).' Wellington: The Treasury.

_____. 1986. 'Fiscal Strategy 1987/88 (Released under the Official Information Act).' Wellington: The Treasury.

_____. 1990a. *Briefing to the Incoming Government*. Wellington: Government Printer.

_____. 1990b. 'Social Welfare Policy— Overview. (Released under the Official Information Act).' Wellington: The Treasury.

_____. 1996. *Putting it Together: An Explanatory Guide to the New Zealand Public Sector Financial Management System*. Wellington: The Treasury.

_____. 1998. 'About Treasury.' At web site: http://www.treasury.govt.nz/abttrsy.htm.

_____. 'New Zealand Government Asset Sales as at 30 June 1999.' At web site: http://www.treasury.govt.nz/pubs/fmb/assetsal/1999/june99.htm.

Vowles, J. and P. Aimer. 1993. *Voter's Vengeance*. Auckland: Auckland University Press.

Vowles, J. and J. Roper. 1997. 'Business and Politics During the Postwar Era.' In *The Political Economy of New Zealand*, eds. B. Roper and C. Rudd. Auckland: Oxford University Press.

Wade, R. 1990. *Governing the Market: Economic Theory and the Role of Government in East Asian Industrialization*. New Jersey: Princeton University Press.

Wallis, Joe. 1997. 'Conspiracy and the Policy Process: A Case Study of the New Zealand Experience.' *Journal of Public Policy* 17(1): 1–29.

_____. 1999. 'Understanding the Role of Leadership in Economic Policy Reform.' *World Development* 27(1): 39–53.

Wallis, Joe, and Brian Dollery. 1999. *Market Failure, Government Failure, Leadership and Public Policy*. Houndmills, Basingstoke: Macmillan.

Walsh, C. 1991. 'The National Economy and Management Strategies.' In *Business and Government Under Labor*, eds. Brian Galligan and Gwynneth Singleton. Melbourne: Longman Chesire.

Walsh, Pat. 1989. 'A Family Fight? Industrial Relations Reform under the Fourth Labour Government.' In *The Making of Rogernomics*, ed. B. Easton. Auckland: Auckland University Press.

_____. 1992. 'The Employment Contracts Act.' In *The Decent Society? Essays in Response to National's Economic and Social Policies* eds. Jonathon Boston and Paul Dalziel. Auckland: Oxford University Press.

_____. 1993. 'The State and Industrial Relations in New Zealand.' In *State and Economy in New Zealand*, eds. Brian Roper and Chris Rudd. Auckland: Oxford University Press.

Walsh, Pat, and Rose Ryan. 1993. 'The Making of the Employment Contracts Act.' In *Employment Contracts: New Zealand Experiences*, ed. Raymond Harbridge. Wellington: Victoria University Press.

Walsh, Peter. 1995. *Confessions of a Failed Finance Minister*. Sydney: Random House.

Walter, James. 1986. *The Ministers' Minders: Personal Advisers in National Government*. Melbourne: Oxford University Press.

Wanna, John. 1989. 'Centralisation without corporatism: the politics of New Zealand business in the recession.' *New Zealand Journal of Industrial Relations* 14(1): 1–15.

Warhurst, John. 1994. 'The Labor Party.' In *Government, Politics, Power and Policy in Australia*, eds. Andrew Parkin, et al. Melbourne: Longman.

_____. 1996. 'Transitional Hero: Gough Whitlam and the Australian Labor Party.' *Australian Journal of Political Science* 31(2): 243–52.

Waterman, Ewen. 1993. 'Privatisation and corporatisation in the public sector.' In *Privatisation: The Financial Implications*, eds. Kevin Davis and Ian Harper. St Leonards: Allen & Unwin.

Weller, Patrick. 1989. *Malcom Fraser PM, A Study of Prime Ministerial Power in Australia*. Ringwood, Victoria:Penguin Books.

_____. 1990. 'The Cabinet.' In *Hawke and Australian Public Policy: Consensus and Restructuring*, eds. C. Jennet and R. G. Stewart. Melbourne: Macmillan.

_____, ed. 1994. *Royal Commissions and the Making of Public Policy*. Melbourne: Macmillan.

Wettenhall, Roger. 1997. 'Non-Departmental Organisation, Public Enterprise and Privatisation.' In *The Second Keating Government*, ed. Gwynneth Singleton. Canberra: Centre for Research in Public Sector Management, University of Canberra and Institute of Public Administration Australia.

White, Colin. 1992. *Mastering Risk: Environments, Markets & Politics in Australian Economic History*. Melbourne: Oxford University Press.

Whitwell, Greg. 1986. *The Treasury Line*. Sydney, London and Boston: Allen & Unwin.

_____. 1994. 'The Power of Economic Ideas? Economics Policies in Post-War Australia.' In *State, Economy and Public Policy in Australia*, eds. Stephen Bell and Brian Head. Melbourne: Oxford University Press.

Whitwell, J. 1992. 'Money and Inflation: Theories and Evidence.' In *The New Zealand Economy: Issues and Policies*. Second Edition. Eds. S. Birks and S. Chatterjee. Palmerston North: Dunmore Press.

Wilks, S., and M. Wright. 1987. 'Conclusion: comparing government-industry relations: states, sectors, and networks.' In *Comparative Government Industry Relations*, eds. S. Wilks and M. Wright. Oxford: Clarendon Press.

Williamson, John. 1994a. 'In Search of a Manual for Technopols.' In *The Political Economy of Policy Reform*, ed. John Williamson. Washington DC: Institute for International Economics.

_____, ed. 1994b. *The Political Economy of Policy Reform*. Washington DC: Institute for International Economics.

Williamson, O. 1975. *Markets and Hierarchies: Analysis and Antitrust Implications*. New York: Free Press.

_____. 1985. *The Economic Institutions of Capitalism*. New York: Free Press.

Wiltshire, Kenneth. 1990. ' The Bureaucracy.' In *Hawke and Australian Public Policy*, eds. Christine Jennet and Randal Stewart. South Melbourne: Macmillan.

Wolfson, M. 1994. 'Eligo Ergo Sum: Classical Philosophies of the Self in Neoclassical Economics.' *History of Political Economy* 26(2): 287–325.

Wooding, P. 1993. 'New Zealand in the International Community.' In *State and Economy in New Zealand*, eds. B. Roper and C. Rudd. Auckland: Oxford University Press.

World Bank. 1987. *World Development Report 1987*. New York: Oxford University Press.

Zanetti, G., et al. 1984. 'Opening the Books: A Review Article.' *New Zealand Economic Papers* 18: 13–30.

Index